COCAINE, DEATH SQUADS,
AND THE WAR ON TERROR

Cocaine, Death Squads, and the War on Terror

U.S. Imperialism and Class Struggle in Colombia

OLIVER VILLAR *and* DREW COTTLE

MONTHLY REVIEW PRESS
New York

Library of Congress Cataloging-in-Publication Data

Villar, Oliver.

  Cocaine, death squads, and the war on terror : U.S. imperialism and class
struggle in Colombia / Oliver Villar and Drew Cottle.

   p. cm.

  Includes bibliographical references and index.

  ISBN 978-1-58367-251-8 (pbk. : alk. paper) — ISBN 978-1-58367-252-5
(cloth : alk. paper) 1. Drug traffic—Prevention—Government
policy—United States. 2. Cocaine industry—Colombia. 3. Social
conflict—Colombia. 4. United States—Foreign economic relations—Colombia.
5. Colombia—Foreign economic relations—United States. I. Cottle, Drew.
II. Title.

  HV8079.N3V55 2011

  363.4509861—dc23

                            2011044284

Monthly Review Press
146 West 29th Street, Suite 6W
New York, NY 10001
www.monthlyreview.org

5 4 3 2 1

Contents

For the workers and peasants of Colombia

Acknowledgments

In a general sense, this book is indebted to the dynamic reservoir of radical and revolutionary thought and organization in Australia and the Americas (Latin America, the United States of America, and Canada). However, we would like to thank Rob O'Neill, Henry Veltmeyer, and Oktay Suleyman Kahraman. Their support made this book possible. We also thank Peter Dale Scott and Alfred W. McCoy for their generous email correspondence over the years and to all who responded to this study. The authors gratefully acknowledge the unselfish and extraordinary support from our families and friends, especially Angela Keys for her painstaking editorial assistance. Our greatest debt is to those who have paid a very high price for truth, justice, and opposition to U.S. imperialism and narco-colonialism.

—Bathurst, 2011

Foreword

by Peter Dale Scott

Colombia's history is a chronicle of violence and class warfare dating back to the Spanish era with its institutions of slavery and semifeudal land allocation. But this important book shows how in the last half-century the United States has helped to centralize and militarize the class conflict, and above all how cocaine has come to play a central role in financing this oppression.

American involvement in Colombian repression can be traced back to President Kennedy, who, faced with generals intent on ousting Fidel Castro from Cuba, authorized instead a program of anti-communist counterinsurgency in South America, and above all Colombia. In February 1962, a U.S. Special Warfare team first visited Colombia, and set in motion an era of systematic, centralized counterterror, inflicted by professionally trained paramilitary units. Fearing that Castro might soon try to export his revolution to the South American continent, the Special Warfare experts at Fort Bragg rushed to instruct the Colombian army in the same counterinsurgency techniques then being introduced into Vietnam. A trip report to the Joint Chiefs of Staff recommended development of "a civil and military structure . . . to perform counter-agent and counter-propaganda functions and as necessary execute paramilitary, sabotage, and/or terrorist activities against known communist proponents. It should be backed by the United States."[1]

In the wake of the visit, a series of training teams arrived, contributing to the Colombian army's Plan Lazo, a comprehensive counterinsurgency plan implemented between 1962 and 1965. It was in response to this systematic campaign in the reinforcement of class repression, rather than to any outside assistance from Castro, that FARC and ELN were first organized in 1964. As Michael McClintock has observed, "The banditry of the early 1960s . . . was transformed into organized revolutionary guerrilla warfare after 1965, which has continued to date."[2]

An important ingredient in the Fort Bragg approach to counterinsurgency, as reflected in its training manuals, was the organization of "self-defense units" and other paramilitary groups, including "hunter-killer teams."[3] The thinking and nomenclature of these field manuals were translated and cited in the Colombian army's counter-guerrilla manual, *Reglamento de Combate de Contraguerrillas*. It defined the self-defense group *(junta de auto-defensa)* as "an organization of a military nature made up of select civilian personnel from the combat zone who are trained and equipped to carry out actions against groups of guerrillas."[4] The *autodefensas* (as the paramilitaries are now called in Colombia) have been a scourge ever since.

The CIA and Drug-Financed Autodefensas

In the 1970s, the CIA offered further training to Colombian and other Latin American police at its so-called bomb school in Los Fresnos, Texas. There USAID, under CIA's so-called Public Safety Program, taught a curriculum including "Terrorist Concepts; Terrorist Devices; Fabrication and Functioning of Devices; Improvised Triggering Devices; Incendiaries," and "Assassination Weapons: A Discussion of Various Weapons which May Be Used by the Assassin." During congressional hearings, AID officials admitted that the so-called bomb school offered lessons not in bomb disposal but in bomb making.[5]

Trained terrorist counterrevolutionaries thus became assets of the Colombian state security apparatus. They were also employed by U.S. corporations anxious to protect their workforces from unionization, as well as in anti-union campaigns by Colombian suppliers to large U.S. corporations.[6] Oil companies in particular have been part of the state-coordinated campaign against left-wing guerrillas. In June 2001, a Colombian court heard how a U.S. security firm working for Occidental Petroleum had played a fatal role in an ill-starred army raid against FARC, "directing helicopter gunships that mistakenly killed eighteen civilians."[7]

Other accounts of the Colombian conflict have ignored this early U.S. input into paramilitary organization and date the army-paramilitary alliance from 1981. That was the year in which the country's major cocaine traffickers, collaborating with the Colombian army, established a training school for a nationwide counterterrorist network, *Muerte a Sequestradores* (Death to Kidnappers, or MAS).[8] The traffickers put up the money, and the generals contracted for Israeli and British mercenaries to come to Colombia to run the death squad school. A leading graduate was Carlos Castaño, the notorious drug trafficker and founder of the United Self-Defense Forces of Colombia (AUC).

Although the stated purpose of the network was to combat kidnapping (a preferred fund-raising technique of the FARC), MAS played an overtly political role as a criminal extension of the army. Most notably, it enabled the army to frustrate the peace agreement negotiated with the FARC by President Betancur in the 1980s, by murdering over seven hundred FARC members who entered the constitutional political process as members of a political party, the Unión Patriótica.[9] There is no sign that the Reagan administration, which disapproved of Betancur and his peace plan, exerted any pressure on the army to stop these killings.

The *autodefensas* operated with impunity until 1989, when their activities were outlawed. But Human Rights Watch, in a detailed report, has documented how in 1991 U.S. military and CIA personnel collaborated with the Colombian army to institute a new system of civilian intelligence units. Despite express prohibitions in the army's grounding document, Order 200–05/91, some of these units continued to act as paramilitaries and were armed, sometimes with U.S. equipment, by the Colombian army.[10] "In the name of fighting drugs, the CIA financed new military intelligence networks there in 1991. But the new networks did little to stop drug traffickers. Instead, they incorporated illegal paramilitary groups into their ranks and strengthened existing death squads."[11]

In a new report in 2000, Human Rights Watch continued to document the involvement of senior army commanders in the planning and execution of paramilitary massacres. According to the report, "Evidence . . . links half of Colombia's eighteen brigade-level army units to paramilitary activity." The report also describes a process, called *legalización*, whereby paramilitaries bring civilian corpses to army barracks and exchange them for weapons. The officers then claim that the corpses were guerrillas killed in battle.[12]

The intent of these U.S.-backed strategies has been to drive the FARC out of oil-bearing northern and central Colombia into the Amazon region southeast of the *cordillera*, a remote zone that for years after 1998 was virtually conceded to it by the central government. There, the former guerrilla force became in effect a governing one, administering and taxing the regions it controlled.

The Resulting Symbiosis between Militarization and the Narco-Economy

Ironically, the result of another U.S. policy, drug eradication, has been to turn this region into a major coca-producing area. This might have been predicted when the United States vigorously pursued coca eradication programs in nearby Bolivia and Peru. Despite the spectacular reductions in these countries, "there was no large decline in the total area under cultivation: coca cultivation expanded in Colombia to take up the slack."[13] Politically, however, the situation was very different. Coca production became concentrated in an area under the ongoing control of a revolutionary force, in a region where the central government could not normally operate. Thus the end result was to validate what was earlier a phantom U.S. nightmare: the "narco-guerrilla." The term "narco-guerrilla" had been mocked by experts when it was coined in the Casey-Bush years of the Reagan administration, and shown to be the deceptive rhetoric of right-wing intelligence agents in Latin America who were themselves involved with drug traffickers.[14] Even when Clinton's drug czar, General Barry McCaffrey, renewed the war cry against "narco-guerrillas" in 1997, the *New York Times* pointed out that the term had been publicly disputed by the American ambassador to Colombia, Myles R. Frechette.[15]

But after Plan Colombia in 2000, the Pentagon was finally engaged in a struggle against a drug-financed FARC, a struggle that Congress would support. Aid to the Colombian army, cut off by Congress in 1994 because of human rights violations, was restored in 2000 through Plan Colombia.

Increasing CIA Involvement in the Narcotics Traffic

In the resulting symbiosis between U.S. military assistance, the FARC, and a flourishing narco-economy, the CIA became more and more directly involved in the drug traffic.

For example, it is not disputed that in 1993, while working for the Cali cartel, AUC leader Carlos Castaño "collaborated with the CIA and the Colombian police to bring down the fugitive drug baron, Pablo Escobar."[16] Carlos Castaño and his brother were leaders of a death squad, Los Pepes, that tracked and killed members of Escobar's organization. They did so on the basis of information from the CIA, which was transmitted via a special squad of the Colombian National Police, on good terms with the Cali cartel.[17] The U.S. embassy had intelligence reports that in fact Los Pepes "had been created by the Cali Cartel," yet the Los Pepes killers fraternized with at least two DEA agents and gave one of them a gold watch.[18]

A far more dramatic involvement of the CIA was acknowledged in 1997, when General Ramon Guillén Davila, chief of a CIA-created anti-drug unit in Venezuela, was indicted in Miami for smuggling a ton of cocaine into the United States. According to the *New York Times*, "The CIA, over the objections of the Drug Enforcement Administration, approved the shipment of at least one ton of pure cocaine to Miami International Airport as a way of gathering information about the Colombian drug cartels."[19] *Time* magazine reported that a single shipment amounted to 998 pounds, following earlier ones "totaling nearly 2,000 pounds."[20] Mike Wallace on *60 Minutes* confirmed that "the CIA-national guard undercover operation quickly accumulated this cocaine, over a ton and a half that was smuggled from Colombia into Venezuela."[21] According to the *Wall Street Journal*, the total amount of drugs smuggled by General Guillén may have been more than twenty-two tons.[22]

But the United States never asked for Guillén's extradition from Venezuela to stand trial, and in 2007, when he was arrested in Venezuela for plotting to assassinate President Hugo Chávez, his indictment was still sealed in Miami.[23] Meanwhile, CIA officer Mark McFarlin, whom Drug Enforcement Administration (DEA) chief Bonner had also wished to indict, was never indicted at all; he merely resigned.[24]

According to *Time*, "The stated purpose of the scheme was to help one of the Venezuelan general's agents win the confidence of Colombia's drug lords," specifically the Medellín cartel.[25] But by facilitating multi-ton shipments, the CIA was becoming part of the Colombian drug scene. As I wrote in *Drugs, Oil, and War*:

> The CIA can (and does) point to its role in the arrest or elimination of a number of major Colombian traffickers. These arrests have not diminished the actual flow of cocaine into the United States, which on the contrary reached a new high in 2000. But they have institutionalized the relationship of law enforcement to rival cartels and visibly contributed to the increase of urban cartel violence. The true purpose of most of these campaigns, like the current Plan Colombia, has not been the hopeless ideal of eradication. It has been to alter

market share: to target specific enemies and thus ensure that the drug traffic remains under the control of those traffickers who are allies of the Colombian state security apparatus and/or the CIA. This confirms the judgment of Senate investigator Jack Blum a decade ago, that America, instead of battling a narcotics conspiracy, has "in a subtle way . . . become part of that conspiracy."[26]

Colombia as Another Example of
U.S. Narco-Imperialism

A narrow focus on Colombian history might see the excesses of the drug-financed *autodefensas* as merely a prolongation of the rural violence that preceded Plan Lazo in the 1960s. But a broader glance at how the United States has intervened in other countries would see Colombia as yet another example of how the United States works with local drug proxy forces to increase its offensive power in ungovernable areas overseas.

The best-documented instances are in Burma, Thailand, Laos, and Afghanistan. There the CIA developed, armed, and equipped proxy armies whose chief source of financing was unambiguously drugs.[27] (Americans appear to have played a similar role in Azerbaijan, Kosovo, and possibly elsewhere.) But even closer analogies to the drug-financed *autodefensas* of Colombia can be found in the Brigada Blanca of Mexico or the Gladio units established by the United States in NATO countries like Turkey and Italy, which evolved in collusion with local drug mafias into systemic forces for ongoing right-wing violence against leftist organizers, including killings.[28] The parastate described by Father Javier Giraldo in Colombia—"a structure that is illegal and clandestine, [that] increasingly takes over the dirty work, the repression"—is closely paralleled by the *gizli devet* or deep state of Turkey that performed the same function there.[29]

Moreover, as Oliver Villar and Drew Cottle note in this book, "Most of the profits from the Colombian cocaine trade are reinvested in the United States, not Colombia."[30] This too is true of profits from drug-trafficking worldwide, roughly 80 percent of which are laundered through banks of the countries of drug consumption, not the countries of origin.[31] Just one U.S. bank, Wachovia, paid federal authorities $110 million in forfeiture, for transactions later proved to be connected to drug smuggling; it incurred a $50 million fine for failing to monitor cash used to ship twenty-two tons of cocaine. More important, the bank was sanctioned for not monitoring the transfer of $378 billion—a sum equivalent to one-third of Mexico's gross national product—into dollar accounts.[32] After the 2008 economic crisis, Antonio Maria Costa, head of the UN Office on Drugs and Crime, reported that "drug money worth billions of dollars kept the financial system afloat at the height of the global crisis."[33]

It is fair to say that American narco-capitalism, committed to dominating the petroleum resources of the world, has developed a narco-dependency that will be difficult to shake off. Thus it is an urgent priority that serious students of the United States, as well as of Colombia, learn from and act on the lessons of this book.

A War of Many Wars

This is a study of the political economy of Colombia, cocaine, and the U.S. imperial state. It examines the dynamics, structure, and context of the Colombian cocaine trade and its relationship to U.S. imperialism. Such an examination is necessary because Colombia is now simply seen as synonymous with the drug cocaine, or as an American theater of war on both terrorism and drugs. Without a critical investigation of the political and economic relations of Colombia, cocaine, and imperial America, the reasons why the cocaine trade flourishes and the simultaneous war on drugs and terrorism continues will never be understood.

This study investigates the so-called Crystal Triangle, the Andean coca-growing zone, with its nodal points in Colombia, Bolivia, and Peru. The notion of the Crystal Triangle harkens back to another, different time of the American war in Vietnam, when the U.S. Central Intelligence Agency (CIA) became deeply involved in the heroin trade of Southeast Asia's Golden Triangle. In the final years of the Vietnam War, the United States was flooded with heroin from Southeast Asia. After the American defeat in Vietnam, a new drug, cocaine, in a new location, the Crystal Triangle, was found to feed the American market.

The coca leaf had replaced the poppy flower as the premier illegal drug transported to America. It wasn't long before American presidents were declaring a "war on drugs" as Andean coca leaves, processed into cocaine and crack, began to adversely affect American life in what become known as the "cocaine decade" of the 1980s.

In Colombia, the struggle to control the coca leaf sparked a different kind of war, one that transformed Colombian society. Unlike the rest of Latin America, Colombia, since the end of Spanish rule, remains deeply divided geographically and politically. Following the Wars of Independence from Spain, Colombia experienced fourteen civil wars, numerous peasant uprisings, two wars with neighboring Ecuador, and three coups d'état. These conflicts were generated by the Liberal and Conservative parties, both controlled by a bipartisan landholding oligarchy while the majority of Colombians remained rural, landless, and poor. These interminable "unfinished wars," combined with Colombia's topography, have made the country prone to instability and seemingly ungovernable by a centralized state. When in 1948 a popular Liberal candidate for president, Jorge Eliécer Gaitán, promised to end the rule of the landed oligarchy and eliminate mass poverty, he was assassinated. His murder sparked *La Violencia*, a period of civil war between 1948 and 1958 in which approximately 300,000 Colombians, primarily peasants, were killed.

From 1958 until the present, Colombia has been engulfed in another war, a "forgotten war," as Eduardo Galeano describes it.[1] This has been a war in which the oligarchic state criminalized all social resistance to oppression and exploitation. Two armed guerrilla groups, the Revolutionary Armed Forces of Colombia (Fuerzas Armadas Revolucionarias de Colombia, FARC) and the National Liberation Army (Ejército de Liberación Nacional, ELN), emerged to spearhead popular resistance to this form of state oppression. The ELN has remained an armed but small guerrilla *foco* (a strategy of establishing base areas in the countryside to lead a general insurrection) inspired by the Cuban Revolution, whereas the FARC, whose origins lay in the Colombian Communist Party, has become a mass guerrilla army rooted in the landless peasantry. Over five decades, the

FARC has waged an armed class war against the Colombian state and its ruling class. During the 1990s, the FARC held sway over nearly 60 percent of the country, primarily its poorest and undeveloped regions. Colombia seemed to be at a crossroads, as the FARC contested the ruling oligarchy's power. Never have the Colombian rulers acceded to any of the FARC's demands. Instead, as the war escalated and the FARC consolidated its territorial gains, Bogotá turned to Washington.

It was during the intensification of this Colombian struggle in the 1980s that cocaine from the Crystal Triangle became readily available within the United States. In response, the Ronald Reagan presidency and subsequent administrations declared a war on drugs in which the criminalized victims tended to be Latino and African American. Within Colombia, drug cartels organized the supply and shipment of cocaine, in its powder or rock form, to the United States. Their influence penetrated Colombian society, particularly its ruling circles. Investment of massive drug profits flowed into every sector of the Colombian economy. Pablo Escobar, drug lord and emergent political populist, was tolerated—that is, until he threatened the interests of the Colombian ruling class and its dependent relationship upon Washington. The Colombian oligarchy transformed itself into a virtual narco-bourgeoisie, ever more reliant for its wealth and power on the cocaine trade. The narco-bourgeoisie was a political outgrowth of the Colombian *comprador* class, the national business elite.

The landless poor and dispossessed were the growers of the coca leaf. The 1980s "cocaine decade" saw major landowners and the Cali and Medellín cartels organize private armies to secure control of cocaine over its producers, the *cocaleros* (coca peasant farmers). The FARC stood as the defenders of the unorganized *cocaleros*. The successes of the FARC's guerrilla war as a problem of the cocaine trade deepened the Colombian state's reliance upon U.S. military assistance and involvement. The FARC's rebellion in the cocaine borderlands allowed Washington to condemn the guerrilla army as "narco-terrorists." Through "Plan Colombia," the war on drugs and the war on terror waged by the Colombian narco-state at the behest of both the Clinton and the succeeding Bush administrations were legitimized and deepened.

Colombia's "forgotten" six-decade-long war turned the region into a "shatter zone" (an area prone to conflict due to its geography), which threatened to implode, explode, or, at best, become a country that maintained a fragile equilibrium maintained by cocaine, death squads, and terror. This form of U.S. "narco-imperialism" was a paradoxical consequence of the American war on drugs, which was transformed into a war for recolonization in a process described here as "narco-colonialism." Narco-colonialism pursued imperial objectives, as opposed to the stated objectives of the U.S. government. It aimed to foster a deeper Latin American dependency on imperial America.

Colombia's dependence upon the cocaine trade and U.S. military assistance—which is increasingly privatized—is rarely acknowledged. Instead, the state of war in Colombia is usually described as a struggle to eliminate "narco-terrorism." The FARC's protection of the *cocaleros'* coca production and the taxing of its trade continue to pose a threat to the narco-bourgeoisie and the narco-state of Colombia. The war on drugs and terror in Colombia is in fact a war for the control of the cocaine trade—in a system of imperial domination—by means of state-sponsored terror.

1. From Coca to Cocaine

According to Evo Morales, Bolivia's first indigenous president, a former coca farmer, and a longtime advocate for *cocaleros*, "Coca is not cocaine."[1] This is a view shared by many Latin Americans, including Venezuelan president Hugo Chávez, who has publicly stated that he chews coca every morning for its apparent health benefits.[2] Morales argues that it is a mistake to link the livelihood of *cocaleros* with drug trafficking. *Time* magazine has reported that "the Evo phenomenon is partly a result of what Latin American critics call Washington's antic-oca 'fundamentalism'—a heavy-handedness that seems to blame the remote *cocaleros*, or coca farmers, more than the addictive appetites of Americans."[3] Significant cultural, historical, and economic differences exist between coca and cocaine.[4] This chapter argues that Colombia's cocaine trade is largely a product of the nation's history. The legacy of Spanish colonization and the pattern of land ownership in Colombia have ensured that coca continues to be cultivated. The ongoing civil conflict in Colombia since 1964, too, has played a major role in enabling the cocaine trade to flourish.

The Legacy of Spanish Colonization

Before Colombian capitalism, the Spanish conquistadors established feudal systems to regulate labor, such as the *encomienda, concierto,* and mining *mita.*[5] Under Spanish colonialism, landowners and merchants were dominant in Colombian economic life, their power based greatly on the commercial exploitation of the coca plant, which was widely used by Europeans for medicinal purposes. The Spanish chronicler Pedro Cieza de León recorded: "There has never been in the whole world a plant or root or any growing thing that bears and yields every year as this does . . . or that is so highly valued."[6] Indians were forced from their highland villages to work in steamy lowland coca plantations. The Spaniards fed them coca leaf to nullify the need for food, water, or sleep, and to reduce resistance to their living and working conditions. To supply great quantities of coca leaves, coca plantations—*cocales*—were established. Long hours of brutal slave labor produced high death rates.[7] The coca slaves died in large numbers from poor nutrition, exhaustion, and European diseases. By 1650, the Inca population had fallen to four million, from ten million in the mid-1500s.[8] In the sixteenth century another Spaniard, Hernando de Santillán, wrote: "Down there [in the coca plantations] there is one disease worse than all the rest: the unrestrained greed of the Spaniards."[9] The colonizers' lack of concern was shown by their decision, in 1573, to tax the "sinful" commodity.

Another system of colonial exploitation, the hacienda, introduced a rural class structure consisting of Spanish landlords and landless peasants. The peasantry resisted the colonization of their land by the foreign property owners. Some of them, along with Afro-Colombians escaping slavery, rural workers escaping the haciendas, and poor settlers seeking a better life, fled to the slopes and plains of the Andes becoming *colonos* (landless workers). For the exploited classes, land meant freedom. However, the landlords had no use for freedom; when the bourgeois revolutions inspired by Simón Bolívar swept Latin America, the landlords of Colombia pledged their allegiance to Spain.[10]

The agrarian class conflict that began in the early nineteenth century has persisted into the present. The hacienda system created its own "grave diggers" as poor peasants (or campesinos in Spanish) struggled for land.[11] Complex class conflicts in the early twentieth century created *minifundias* (smallholdings) in the highlands, mixed patterns of production along the slopes, and *latifundias* (large estates) on the plains.[12] From 1875 to 1930, 450 major confrontations between the poor peasantry and landlords over land occurred in Colombia.[13]

From La Violencia *to the FARC*

A watershed in Colombian history known as *La Violencia* (1948-1958) erupted when the oligarchy split along political, ideological, and regional lines in their struggle against the landless workers and peasantry.[14] From the late 1940s, this power struggle within the Colombian ruling class determined the fate of Colombian politics. Old rivalries between the two major political parties in parliament, the Liberals and Conservatives, were consolidated. Amid the parliamentary infighting, a Liberal presidential candidate, Jorge Eliécer Gaitán, made a populist appeal against the oligarchy, pitting the "real country" against the "political country."[15] Gaitán sought the support of the shopkeepers and professionals of the petite bourgeoisie, as well as the landless workers and peasantry. For the oligarchy, populism in any form was tantamount to communist subversion and was seen as a direct threat to their class interests. This nationalist expression was demonstrated through conflict between industrialists and unions. It reached a climax when Gaitán was gunned down in Bogotá on April 9, 1948. His assassination was the first covert action by the CIA in Colombia and spurred a major uprising called the *Bogotázo*.[16]

Liberals and leftists blamed the Conservative government for Gaitán's murder. Workers and the lumpenproletariat, the middle class, and small traders stormed the city, attacking police stations and government offices, the symbols of a political system that excluded and impoverished them, instigating *La Violencia*.[17] Landowners urged the military to fire on the insurgent crowds. Communists and radicalized liberals were on death lists. The country was convulsed by the upsurge, and liberal landowners organized campesinos into guerrilla armies. Paramilitary groups of civilians and police, such as the *aplanchadores* ("flatteners" from Antioquia Department), *chulavitas* (volunteers from Chulavita in Boyaca Department), and the infamous *pajaros* ("birds" or assassins for hire from Valle and Caldas), carried out military operations against the masses.[18]

In the unremitting struggle over land, trade unions retaliated against state violence by organizing armed self-defense groups in the mountains. The Moscow-aligned Colombian Communist Party organized a broad peasant resistance, including the foundation of guerrilla base camps.[19] With the support of the United States, the Colombian military responded by attempting to systematically destroy these "Red" bases, while survivors fled and regrouped in the sparsely inhabited mountains and jungles of the interior.[20]

With U.S. guidance and aid, the counterinsurgency campaign against the rebel campesinos began on May 18, 1964, when the Colombian armed forces surrounded and attacked Marquetalia, the principal rebel agrarian community.[21] Labeling the autonomous communities "independent republics," the Colombian government sent 16,000 troops (one-third of its army), accompanied by tanks, helicopters, and warplanes, and carried out bombing campaigns against the department of Marquetalia. The Colombian Communist Party and peasant rebels retreated to the agricultural frontiers in Amazonia, where the state had a limited presence.[22] Modeled on the Phoenix Program in Vietnam, "Plan Lazo" sent "hunter-killer units" to assassinate peasants, whether armed or unarmed. Between 1963 and 1966, Colombian state forces used U.S.-supplied helicopters, vehicles, communications equipment, and weapons to destroy the rebel communities in Marquetalia, Rio Chiquito, El Pato-Guayabero, and Santa Barbara. The first military air assault on Marquetalia was in a U.S. helicopter piloted by a Colombian and accompanied by a U.S. Air Force instructor.[23]

La Violencia ensured that land ownership by the oligarchy remained unchanged in Colombia. The landless remained landless, and the power of the oligarchs continued to dominate the nation's politics. For the urban elite, particularly the industrialists, *La Violencia* was an economic success. Capital accumulation was so great that President Alberto Lleras Camargo (1958–1962) concluded that "blood and capital accumulation went together."[24] Political opposition was outlawed and repressed.

Rewarded by the United States with investment and loans, Colombia saw a huge expansion in commercial agriculture and dominant landowners became highly represented in the government. Colombia became a showcase for the Alliance for Progress, an anticommunist aid and development program begun in 1961 by the Kennedy administration to reward U.S. allies in Latin America and to offset the radicalizing effect of the Cuban Revolution. The United States moved along two Latin American tracks in the early 1960s: overthrow Cuba and neutralize revolutionary movements throughout Latin America. The Alliance for Progress was promoted as an economic solution to poverty, but its ultimate purpose was to deepen U.S. economic penetration of Latin America.[25] Colombian initiatives conformed to the Alliance emphasis on "self-help," and both U.S. secretary of state Dean Rusk and the U.S. ambassador to the United Nations, Adlai Stevenson, singled out the Colombian programs for praise in spite of growing corruption and mismanagement. Stevenson noted that Colombia continued to face problems associated with communist infiltration, bandit-like violence in the countryside, and economic dislocation, but he expressed optimism in the Colombian response to the American assistance.[26]

The political repression experienced in Colombia and other Latin American countries during the Cold War led left-wing intellectuals to seek a revolutionary alternative to capitalism. Political movements arose across Latin America, turning to the success of the Cuban Revolution for inspiration. In Colombia, these political developments culminated in the founding of the FARC in 1964 by *La Violencia* veterans Jacobo Arenas and Manuel Marulanda Vélez, then Chief Commandant of Central High Command, and other armed guerrilla groups such as the ELN, the Popular Liberation Army (EPL), and M-19 soon after.[27]

Between 1970 and 1982, the FARC expanded from the 500 who survived the earlier wave of state terror to a peasant-guerrilla army of 3,000. The campesinos stood at the forefront of the Colombian struggle. The emerging cocaine phenomenon provided Colombia's poorest campesinos with an opportunity to grow a cash crop in the form of the coca plant. In the areas pacified by the state, the campesinos faced repression and ruin. Forced off the land to make way for agricultural exports and confined mainly to the lowland regions southeast of Bogotá they helped colonize, their agricultural subsistence grew increasingly precarious. Displaced and ignored by the state, the peasant guerrillas were left with no option but to cultivate coca as a cash crop. No legal crop, like coffee, sugar, or bananas, offered the advantages of growing and selling coca, which requires neither fertilizers nor pesticides. Not only did coca find a ready market of local traffickers with a fixed price, but the constant demand made it the ideal cash crop for the peasant guerrillas. At the FARC's Seventh Conference from May 4 to 12, 1982, the guerrillas outlined the emergence of a revolutionary situation in Colombia. For the first time since the guerrilla movement in Marquetalia, this FARC conference proposed a clear strategic and operational concept for a Marxist insurgency and changed its mechanisms of leadership and command. The conference announced, "From now on, we officially call ourselves: The Revolutionary Armed Forces of Colombia—People's Army, FARC-EP."[28]

From the beginning of *La Violencia*, U.S. political and economic support to Colombia created a form of Colombian dependency. Colombia's political dependence on the United States deepened the four-decade war against the FARC and continued into the U.S. war on drugs and war on terror. These campaigns provided the United States with the pretext to condemn the FARC as "narco-terrorists" and the main threat to Colombia.

Forty-eight percent of Colombian land is owned by wealthy absentee landlords, who make up 1.3 percent of the population.[29] Poor peasants, who account for 68 percent of the population, own approximately five percent of the land. Wealth and influence are concentrated in the hands of the *compradores*, with a 1998 study estimating that 42 percent of the arable land is owned by the drug cartels, integrating drug traffickers into Colombian agribusiness, military defense, and politics.[30]

At the end of the 1990s, the FARC's power and influence extended to over 60 percent of Colombia.[31] In less than three years, over 93 percent of all regions of recent settlement in Colombia had seen guerrilla activity.[32] In the department of Cundinamarca, which surrounds the capital city of Bogotá, FARC was active in 83 of its 116 municipalities. Some areas are formally organized by the FARC, with schools, medical facilities, grassroots judicial structures, and other social projects. Field work conducted by sociologist James Brittain indicates that:

> the FARC, unlike many recent revolutionary movements and struggles in Central and South America, is a peasant-based, organized, and maintained revolutionary organization. The revolutionaries were not formed within classrooms or churches; they are not a movement led or consisting of lawyers, students, doctors, or priests. Rather, the FARC's leadership, support base, and membership comes from the very soil from which it provides its subsistence, for the insurgents largely consist of peasants from rural Colombia, who account for approximately 65 percent of its members.[33]

The current constituency of the FARC organization has grown from its base in the peasantry to include indigenous people, Afro-Colombians, landless rural laborers, intellectuals, unionists, teachers, and sectors of the urban workforce. Forty-five percent of its members and *comandantes* (leaders) are women.[34] What began as a primarily peasant-led, rural-based land struggle in the 1960s has since been transformed into a national sociopolitical movement attempting alternative development objectives through the realization of a socialist society. By constructing a substantial support base, with extensive geographical distribution, and developing a political line grounded in Marxism-Leninism, the FARC has, with the exception of Cuba, become the largest and most powerful revolutionary force politically and militarily within the Western Hemisphere.[35]

The FARC as "Narco-Terrorists"

"Narco-terrorism" was a term first used by the Reagan administration during the Cold War to condemn the left-wing Sandinista government in Nicaragua, which the administration argued had become a base of Soviet influence in Central America and a center of drug trafficking and narco-terrorism. Narco-terrorism encompassed "a variety of phenomena: guerrilla movements financed by drugs or taxes on drug traffickers, drug syndicates using terrorist methods to counter the state's law enforcement apparatus, and state-sponsored terrorism associated with drug crimes."[36] Rachel Ehrenfeld of the American Center for Democracy advanced the specter of the narco-terrorist in three books in which Latin American guerrilla movements described as narco-terrorist were linked to Cuba and the Soviet Union.[37]

U.S. government organizations—the White House, State Department, and National Security Council (NSC) —and agencies— CIA, Drug Enforcement Administration (DEA), and Federal Bureau of Investigation (FBI)—have used a narco-terrorism paradigm as a political weapon to both criminalize and wage war against the FARC.[38] This U.S. paradigm has been promoted by the Colombian government through policies and activities to combat, incarcerate, or extradite FARC members for alleged drug trafficking and terrorism.[39]

Cocaine

The simplistic labeling of the FARC as narco-terrorists is, in part, based on the peasant role in the complex process involving the manufacturing and trafficking of cocaine. Unlike other drugs, the transformation of coca into cocaine requires chemicals and specialized equipment that generally must be imported. The dynamics of the Colombian cocaine trade must be examined in the historical context of the global drug trade, which existed long before cocaine appeared on the world market, and its economic relations with great powers such as Spain, Britain, and the United States.

American missionaries documented how, in the early opium trade, "one Chinaman was both producer and consumer, and worth two Indians and four Malays, in value to the state."[40] They condemned the moral and social degeneration wrought by the British colonial opium trade.[41] Commenting on Indian finances in 1871, when the British colonial government in India amassed nine million pounds annually from opium, Sir Cecil Beadon, an English administrator in British India, pointedly observed:

Indian finances are in this position that, in a majority of years, you have very serious deficits, and you are constantly borrowing.... Shall we sacrifice the whole or any portion of the opium duty? And it seems to me that the present state of the Indian finances is such as to prevent us giving any answer but one to that question—that we cannot give up any of the opium revenue; we cannot afford to do so.[42]

Carl Trocki argues that the decline of the British Empire might have begun when Britain left the opium business.[43] Since the time of the conquistadors, the Colombian economy has been shaped by the demands of foreign markets. From coca, silver, and gold in the Spanish era to the rubber, cotton, tin, and sugar booms of the past century, the rise and fall of world demand for primary commodities has determined the fate of the Colombian people.[44] Cocaine, however, has resulted in the greatest degree of integration and incorporation of Colombia into the world market economy than any previous export commodity ever has.[45] Alfonso López Michelsen, the president of Colombia between 1974 and 1978, maintains that all Colombian presidents have achieved that office due to drug-trafficking money.[46] The former president of Peru, Alan Garcia, stated during his first term in office, 1985 to 1990, that "the only successful transnational enterprise originating in our countries is narcotics trafficking. The most successful effort to achieve Andean integration has been made by the drug traffickers."[47] In this context, cocaine can be considered a twentieth century manifestation of a historical phenomenon of Colombian dependence on the production of export commodities for foreign consumption and imperialist conquest for profit.[48]

During the final decade of the Cold War, the protection or promotion of major drug traffickers by senior CIA and NSC officials became intrinsically linked to U.S. imperial adventures in the war on drugs.[49] In South America, covert activities coexisted alongside the debt crisis of the 1970s and 1980s which incurred drastic balance of payments and external crises, a sharp increase in unemployment, and a decline in national incomes. Within the Andean coca-growing zone Crystal Triangle, Colombia succeeded in developing sophisticated drug cartels and international marketing networks.[50]

The manufacture of cocaine fundamentally relies upon chemicals and equipment imported by American and Western European companies. The coca leaf must undergo chemical processing before it can be transformed into cocaine hydrochloride (HCL).[51] First, the narcotic must be extracted from the coca leaves. The leaves are dried to remove as much moisture as possible, and then soaked in a solution of sulphuric acid and water. The liquid is drained off from the large soaking vats and mixed with an alkaline solution of calcium oxide or sodium carbonate, leaving a thick, alkaloid, whitish fluid. This fluid is mixed with kerosene to remove impurities, and, as it settles, the kerosene separates from the top of the mixture. In the next stage of processing, the mixture is placed into another solution of water and sulphuric acid, producing a clear liquid. Sodium carbonate is again added to the liquid and the dirty white substance that forms from this process is called coca paste.[52] The coca paste is placed on a fine-mesh cloth to allow the liquid to drain off.

Coca leaves are run through this process two or three times to ensure that the maximum amount of coca paste is produced. This is the raw material from which cocaine is subsequently distilled. The processing labs in guerrilla-controlled areas are no more than tin sheds, described as "kitchens" by the media. They are located in the rainforest, equipped with portable diesel power generators protected by plastic sheeting. In contrast, the massive secret state laboratories described as "plants" and "complexes" are protected as private property and are off limits to the general public.

The second step in the production of cocaine is dominated by the Colombian state. In areas under state control, particularly in northern Colombia, private paramilitaries operate freely to protect cocaine operations. They collect the coca paste and deliver it to state facilities, under high-level protection from the Colombian military or the United Self-Defense Forces of Colombia (*Autodefensas Unidas de Colombia;* AUC), a right-wing paramilitary umbrella organization renamed the Black Eagles. In what is known as a "shell game strategy," business elites from the chemical industry provide the essential chemicals for processing cocaine through "third- or fourth-level distributors" in order to conceal the identities of all parties involved including the chemical manufacturing companies.[53] In areas under guerrilla control, the paramilitaries, the army, and their U.S. advisers are military targets. The trafficker must approach the campesino directly and pay the price demanded. The guerrillas provide the security and enforce a drug tax, as they do with all products under their control. By protecting its campesino base, the FARC accepts the cash crop as a supplementary income for the campesinos' subsistence. According to U.S. intelligence estimates, the FARC tax on agricultural production, which includes coca, is worth between $30 million and $100 million a year.[54] A major study in 1999 by Colombia's National Planning Department and the Colombian army estimated that both the FARC and ELN earned twice as much from kidnapping and robbery than from alleged drug-trafficking activities to finance the popular resistance.[55]

When chemists turn the coca paste into cocaine hydrochloride (HCL) in the secret state facilities sophisticated laboratory techniques and industrial volumes of ether, acetone, and hydrochloric acid are required. According to DEA intelligence, the essential chemicals required for cocaine processing have become available in vast quantities throughout South America. In Colombia alone, there are about 4,500 companies registered to import and distribute these essential chemicals. However, many Colombian chemical companies have lost their permits for trafficking controlled substances for their involvement in the purchase and distribution of potassium permanganate and n-propyl acetate, diverted for use in cocaine processing.[56] Most of these chemicals must enter Colombia by sea from the United

States, Europe (Germany and the Netherlands), or China. Most chemicals destined for drug laboratories enter legally through the seaports at Barranquilla, Cartagena, and Buenaventura, brought into Colombia from Ecuador, Venezuela, and Brazil. The highway between San Antonio (Venezuela) and Cúcuta (Colombia) is a major chemical transportation route into Colombia. They also enter Colombia from Venezuela via the Orinoco River and from Brazil along Amazon River tributaries.[57]

This final process of refining is extremely corrosive. High-quality containers and expensive processing equipment are needed. Glass or porcelain containers have hitherto been the common equipment to process the coca paste, but high-tech equipment for the sheer volume of cocaine produced must be anticipated. The paste is dissolved in acetone, and then heated to evaporate the acetone and hydrochloric acid. From this process a whitish sludge appears, which is then heated by placing light bulbs above the mixture.[58] When dried, the semi-processed material becomes the crystalline white salt—cocaine hydrochloride—ready for packaging and transport to the international market, destined primarily for consumption in the United States. Available evidence shows that the price of a gram of cocaine (depending on its quality) has remained in a band between $20 and $150 since the late 1990s, with a spike in 2008 in the lead-up to the global financial crisis between $40 and $197.06 then down to $164.91 in 2010.[59] The amount of land under coca cultivation in South America has also remained on average between 150,000 and 200,000 hectares with dynamic trends concentrated in Colombia, Bolivia, and Peru.[60]

Cocaine is exported to the United States by air from remote airstrips or by sea from Colombia's northern and western coasts. Paramilitary helicopters fly to army garrisons to collect the cocaine to be transported to Antioquia and then exported. In the areas to the south of Bolívar and Catatumbo, the helicopters that come to collect the cocaine are reported to come from Colombian army bases.[61] Transport routes change depending on the policy issues. According to former head of the DEA in Colombia, Jeff Brunner, "Over the years, [the AUC] have worked to control the coast, knowing that's where all the dope's got to leave from. They have their hand in every bit of dope. It has to, at a minimum, be authorized and taxed by them and, at a maximum, controlled by them."[62] The *Tampa Tribune* reports that U.S government court filings indicate the AUC controls the manufacture, as well as the transportation, of tons of cocaine from the Pacific coast of southwest Colombia to Mexico for distribution in the United States.[63] Leaders may change, but traffickers described as "pro-American" by U.S. authorities are rarely extradited despite "a credible body of information" in the possession of the DEA.[64]

The next chapter explores how U.S. counterinsurgency policies in the Cold War intersected with drug-trafficking activities. It argues that the cocaine trade in Colombia has echoes of U.S. involvement in Asia's opium trade during the Cold War.

2. From the Golden Triangle to the Crystal Triangle

The Allied victory that ended the Second World War (1939–1945) saw the United States and the Soviet Union emerge as the world's two leading superpowers. The Cold War that followed split the world into two ideological camps, one capitalist the other socialist. For successive U.S. presidents and policymakers, the Cold War necessitated the militarized containment and ideological defeat of communism, especially in areas of the third world where the threat of revolution was imminent. The role of U.S. imperialism in the drug trade can be traced to the height of America's efforts to fight communism, particularly in Southeast Asia's Golden Triangle, when covert operations and drug-trafficking activities became entwined with the U.S. imperial state and its foreign policy objectives. The U.S. defeat in Vietnam shifted U.S. imperial efforts to other areas of the third world, the "Golden Crescent" and "Crystal Triangle."

Roots of the Global Drug Trade

In 1949, 85 percent of the world's heroin came from Shanghai and Tientsin in China.[1] Chiang Kai-shek, the leader of the Nationalist Chinese Kuomintang (KMT), used the profits of criminal drug syndicates to finance his campaign against the Chinese Communists in a long civil war.[2] Before the Chinese Revolution, the Office of Strategic Services (OSS), the CIA's predecessor, had forged a strategic alliance with the Sicilian and Corsican mafias to prevent possible communist uprisings in postwar Italy and other parts of Western Europe. These mafiosi along with European fascists applied the "strategy of tension," which meant terrorizing workers and breaking up left-wing labor unions, then blaming the revolutionary left through widespread propaganda campaigns.[3] In prerevolutionary China, the ruling class relied upon the KMT and secretive yet powerful criminal and drug organizations to prevent social revolution. As Mao Tse-tung pointed out, these organizations possessed arms and, because of their backwardness, could be easily turned into reactionary forces by the local landlords.[4] From the middle of the nineteenth century, opium farms in Southeast Asia were always connected to the secret societies that flourished within Chinese communities.

During the Chinese civil war, the United States formulated and maintained a counterrevolutionary strategy of integrating their intelligence operations with local criminal networks and corrupt high-ranking military officers like Chiang Kai-shek. In Yunnan and Sichuan, the Chinese Communists denounced opium use as a reactionary activity and a destroyer of people. By destroying the opium crops, the communists removed the chief source of the world's opium supply and eliminated a major source of income for the Chinese Nationalists.[5] In response to the Chinese civil war, the Truman administration planned ways to stem "the southward flow of communism" into Southeast Asia. Dean Rusk, an influential hawk in the U.S. State Department, argued that America "should employ whatever means were indicated . . . arms here, opium there, bribery and propaganda in the third place."[6] Rusk's advice was thus implemented through strategies of propaganda and covert action in major drug-producing regions of the world: the Golden Triangle of Burma, Laos, Thailand; the Golden Crescent of Afghanistan, Pakistan, Iran, and eventually the Crystal Triangle.

The China Lobby

After the Chinese Revolution, Chinese drug lords collaborated with the American-sponsored KMT exiled in Taiwan to coordinate the Asian heroin trade. Drawing upon the support of the China lobby in the United States, the KMT army, the Thai police, and the French military in Indochina, the CIA made tactical decisions that led to covert operations with known drug-trafficking organizations.[7] Chiang Kai-shek's dominance of the KMT had been achieved through an alliance with opium trafficking organizations at a time when China produced seven-eighths of the world's opium.[8] The KMT's drug connection in China was the Green Gang of Tu Yueh-sheng, and shipments of opium arrived in the United States through this Chinese Tong (organized crime group) and their contacts.[9] Support for CIA activities in the Golden Triangle was based upon the preservation and restoration of the traffic in opium.[10] Profits from narcotics smuggling were channeled into the United States by the China lobby, while bribery ensured opium supply lines through Laos and Thailand.[11] A banned book on the China lobby concluded: "The evidence indicates that several prominent Americans participated in and profited from these transactions."[12] The identities of these Americans with links to the CIA were never revealed.

In the early 1970s, global drug trafficking originating from the Golden Triangle increased rapidly. President Richard Nixon responded by making drugs an international issue and initiating the "War on Drugs." Journalists Alexander Cockburn and Jeffrey St. Clair argue that the DEA suggested to Nixon that if he wanted to halt the heroin trade his government could buy Burma's entire opium crop for $12 million.[13] The State Department and the CIA maintained, however, that any "buy-out" would fund communist insurgencies against the "friendly" governments of Burma and Thailand. CIA director Allen Dulles described this kind of drug diplomacy as "propaganda," in its simplest form—"accusing the other guy of doing what you are doing."[14] According to a number of DEA agents who served in Southeast Asia at the time, the heroin smugglers moving the drugs were all on the CIA's payroll.[15]

The CIA's airline, Civil Air Transport (later known as Air America), flew weapons and supplies from its base in Bangkok to Vietnam, Laos, and Cambodia and the mountain camps of Burma. Ten thousand Chinese troops loyal to Chiang Kai-shek in Taiwan were stationed in Burma. Under the direction of the CIA, plans to invade China across Burma's northern border were prepared. The deployment of KMT troops was important for the transportation of opium. Civil Air Transport supplied the KMT with weapons and transported opium on return flights to other bases, where it was delivered to contacts such as Thailand's secret police for sale.[16] The CIA provided remote airstrips and planes, and the KMT exported opium from Burma and Laos to international wholesalers.[17] A CIA-backed military coup in Thailand in 1948 had ensured that Thailand's left would be destroyed and opium would be supplied on behalf of the CIA.[18] Despite U.S. influence in Thailand, KMT attempts to invade China failed, nonetheless incurring nine hundred casualties, including CIA advisers.[19]

These early U.S.-sponsored covert actions in Asia coincided with the beginning of private financing on behalf of the CIA. The World Anti-Communist League (WACL) was set up by remnants of the Nazi Anti-Komintern and Eastern European Ostpolitik with the assistance of the CIA.[20] It served as an organization for right-wing political and financial interests, as illicit funds from all over the world, including Iran, Greece, and Romania, were deposited into Richard Nixon's election campaign chest and the chests of other prominent politicians in the United States.[21] Backed by leading capitalists such as Nelson Rockefeller, the World Finance Corporation and Castle Bank of the Bahamas were established. They had links to Financial General Bankshares, a bank-holding company headquartered in Washington, DC, which was taken over by the Bank of Credit and Commerce International (BCCI).[22] Capital investments were encouraged from South Vietnamese, Chinese, and Thai sources, as well as other underworld connections in the United States. Drug profits flowed to the United States through land deals in real estate and other CIA-linked businesses, such as the National Bank of Miami and General Development Corporation, contributing to the postwar boom in America and the Bahamas.[23] The 1959 U.S. Congress Senate Select Committee on Improper Activities in the Labor or Management Field helped to discover that Miami had become the base where banks, companies, and drug traffickers linked to the CIA congregated.[24] The committee did not reveal the CIA connection or make it public, instead focusing on organized crime contacts.

The Golden Triangle

Alfred W. McCoy documented in *The Politics of Heroin* that the failure to invade China in the fight against communism forced the CIA to move its covert drug-trafficking operations westward.[25] The CIA's new focus was on the fight against Vietnamese Communists. As opium production in Burma, Thailand, and Laos increased tenfold, heroin distribution in Western Europe was facilitated by the CIA's intelligence connections in Palermo and Marseilles, the Sicilian and Corsican mafia. The United States inherited the drug-smuggling contacts of the French in Laos and Vietnam, which had been used during the First Indochina War (1945–1954).[26] Laos, and in particular South Vietnam, where the U.S. military presence was concentrated, became the organizational base for the heroin trade from Asia to North America via Latin America. Narcotics agents were expected to fabricate evidence about communist drug trafficking and to suppress evidence about CIA covert operations.[27]

With the support of the CIA, the government of South Vietnam established a network of drug contacts across the Golden Triangle.[28] A U.S. congressional investigation found that American soldiers in Vietnam ran a greater risk of becoming heroin addicts than combat casualties. In the early 1970s, allegations surfaced concerning heroin being smuggled back to the United States in body bags containing the corpses of U.S. servicemen. Michael Levine, a former DEA agent stationed in Southeast Asia, claims he was warned by his superiors not to interfere when he attempted to reveal this operation.[29] Harry Anslinger, Commissioner of the Federal Bureau of Narcotics (FBN, later the DEA) from 1930 to 1962, had earlier blamed "invading drug-trafficking Communists" for the drug problem in the United States, often depicting China as a vast, communist-state heroin complex.[30] However, an internal CIA survey revealed that 60 percent of the world's opium came from the Golden Triangle, with the four largest heroin laboratories located in villages in Laos, Burma, and Thailand, all next to CIA stations and financed by the CIA.[31] Rodney Stich, a former CIA operative involved in Southeast Asian and Latin American drug operations, subsequently asserted that the Vietnam War provided a cover for a massive CIA drug operation.[32]

The Golden Crescent

After its military failure in Indochina, the United States turned its attention to securing global military victories in other regions of conflict. Central America and Afghanistan became the last major battlegrounds of the Cold War. Following the Soviet campaign in Afghanistan in 1979, U.S. president Jimmy Carter authorized the secret backing of the chief smugglers of Afghan opium, the anti-communist Mujahedin rebels in Afghanistan, who worked together with Pakistan's military intelligence service.[33] The "Golden

Crescent" of Afghanistan, Iran, and Pakistan was not a major heroin supplier to the U.S. market, and heroin was virtually unknown in most of Pakistan. With the support of the CIA and Saudi intelligence, Osama Bin Laden has been identified as the financier and logistics expert for the Saudi-financed Makhtab al-Khidamat, a terrorist organization believed to be the precursor organization of al Qaeda that recruited foreign fighters from all over the world including the United States.[34]

The United States financed and trained the Mujahedin in CIA terrorist camps in Egypt and in at least one of the Gulf States to wage war against the Soviet Union and the pro-Soviet government of the Marxist People's Democratic Party of Afghanistan (PDPA).[35] Drugs were shipped out in Pakistani army trucks that brought in covert U.S. aid to Afghan guerrillas.[36] Afghanistan became the supplier of 50 percent of the heroin consumed in the United States and 70 percent of the world's high-grade heroin. Before the war was over, the CIA-linked BCCI was deeply enmeshed in the drug trade.[37] Zbigniew Brzezinski, Jimmy Carter's National Security Adviser, has suggested that propaganda about the Soviet invasion of Afghanistan and claims that Islamic fundamentalists entering Afghanistan from all over the world were "dissidents" defending "self-determination" provided the United States with a justification to support the Mujahedin in Kabul.[38]

The United States was drawn into Latin America in the same way that it had been drawn into the Golden Crescent, as its attention turned to revolutionary movements and leftist governments in the region. The Cuban Revolution in 1959 was described by President John F. Kennedy as "the spread of the Castro idea of taking matters into one's own hands."[39] In many ways, Kennedy's response was similar to President Truman's toward stemming the southward flow of communism from China to Southeast Asia.[40] The Kennedy administration planned to stem the spread of communism into Latin America by depicting the Cuban Revolution as a "virus" that could infect other Latin American peoples into believing that they too might have a decent life.[41] CIA support for anti-Castro Cubans who were eager to overthrow the communist government extended beyond Cuban interests in Miami and led to a reestablishment of pre-Castro Cuba's connections in the drug trade, which had grown to rival the CIA's other organized crime contacts.[42] Coupled with the arms race between the United States and the Soviet Union, Kennedy also made a major commitment to fight communism throughout the third world. This had political significance for Latin America, which became the region that experienced the greatest number of U.S. interventions under the American government's policy of anticommunist containment.[43] As in Indochina, the anticommunist crusade was characterized by counterinsurgency, subversion, intervention, and public propaganda about defending Western civilization from the communist threat.

U.S. Counterinsurgency Policy in Latin America

The U.S. counterinsurgency policy implemented throughout the Latin American continent failed to eliminate the peasant guerrillas in Colombia. By the late 1970s the FARC's numbers had grown sixfold in two decades, from five hundred guerrillas concentrated in rebel-held agrarian communities to some three thousand. Ongoing counterinsurgency failures in Colombia, however, were balanced with "success stories" elsewhere. From the Mexican-American border to the southern tip of Argentina, anticommunist forces fought Marxist insurgencies and left-wing governments, often with financial backing from the United States.[44] The Latin American Anti-Communist Confederation (CAL), the regional section of the WACL, embraced the CIA strategy of using covert drug-trafficking operations to fight communism.[45] Military dictatorships, right-wing groups, and criminal organizations moved into closer associations, meeting annually at CAL conferences led by Argentina's military junta.[46]

The WACL, which maintained overt contact with right-wing political and financial interests in the West, as well as with overseas Asian communities during America's imperial adventures in the Far East and Indochina, became a political organization, and its Latin American branch, the CAL, was prepared to coordinate its own drug-trafficking operations. The Southern Cone—Argentina, Uruguay, Chile, Paraguay, and Brazil—was known as the "Triangle of Death," a product of the so-called French Connection, which traded cocaine to Europe in exchange for heroin. It became the drug network favored by an international network within CAL called the Argentine Anticommunist Alliance (AAA), which aimed to make Buenos Aires its neo-fascist center.[47] Both the United States and its anticommunist allies feared that Bolivia, with its first female president in 1979, Lidia Gueiler Tejada of the Revolutionary Nationalist Movement Party (MNR), along with politicized indigenous peasants and radical labor unions, was ripe terrain for revolt.[48] In Nicaragua that same year, the U.S.-backed Somoza dictatorship was overthrown by the Sandinista National Liberation Front (FSLN), which launched agrarian reform, a mass literacy campaign, a popular health system, and the nationalization of Somoza's nonproductive assets.[49]

According to DEA figures in 1980, 80 percent of the world's cocaine came from *La Corporacion* in Bolivia, known then as South America's "General Motors of Cocaine."[50] The Argentineans deployed over two hundred military personnel to help coordinate the seizure of power in Bolivia, including an international band of neo-fascist mercenaries as well as a wanted Nazi war criminal working with the CIA.[51] Michael Levine offered an insider's account of a cocaine coup that unfolded on July 17, 1980, after he became the DEA's country attaché to Argentina and Uruguay:

> Explosions and gunfire began to echo through the surrounding hills. More men in combat fatigues and ski masks roared into Trinidad, fir- ing at everything that moved. They broke into stores and homes, loot-

ing and shooting. The masked thugs were not Bolivians; they spoke Spanish with German, French, and Italian accents. Some, like [Alfredo Mario Mingolla] and his men, had Argentine accents. Their uniforms bore neither their national identification nor any markings, although many of them wore Nazi swastika armbands and insignias. The foreigners were soon joined in the frenzy by mutinying Bolivian soldiers calling for a Bolivian army colonel named Luis Arce-Gomez to lead a national revolution.[52]

The following day, the Bolivian generals were in power, and international support and diplomatic recognition for the regime was secured through the WACL, Argentina, Chile, El Salvador, and South Africa.[53] A victory party was held in Buenos Aires in which the United States was represented by Nat Hamrick, a former business partner of the Somoza family, and John Carbaugh. They were both WACL-linked aides of Republican senator Jesse Helms who arranged for Argentinean delegates to visit the Reagan White House and attend the Republican Convention.[54]

The cocaine coup crushed the Bolivian left and installed narco-militarists in government. The U.S. State Department eerily portrayed the coup as a "cocaine revolution" for the left-wing threat was neutralized. Jake Sales, a CIA pilot based in Bolivia, described what he saw as an extensive, jungle-based cocaine-manufacturing complex containing laboratories, heavy armaments, radio communications, and landing fields that could accommodate a modern jumbo jet. Sales stated, "The Bolivians had a military-industrial setup that was right out of a West Point textbook. It's unbelievable."[55] The Bolivian dictatorship became the primary source of coca for the Colombian drug cartels that formed during this period, and the cartels, in turn, became the main distributors of cocaine into the United States. It was the beginning of the cocaine decade between 1980 and 1989.[56]

Toward Cocaine Production

The debt crisis of the 1970s and 1980s devastated the balance of payments in many Latin American countries, creating a sharp increase in unemployment and a decline in national incomes. Colombia remained immune to these calamities because of its prosperity throughout the cocaine decade. Funding for the U.S. war on drugs increased and was directed to the arrest of drug traffickers and the seizure of drugs, arms, and equipment. In addition, programs of crop eradication and drug law enforcement were instituted to assist Colombian police and judicial authorities. However, this expensive intervention was paralleled by expansion in Colombian drug production, which meant that by 1983 79 percent of marijuana and 75 percent of cocaine consumed in the United States was processed or originated in Colombia, representing a paradoxical consequence of the U.S. war on drugs.[57]

During the cocaine decade, tensions also arose in relation to attempts to extradite Colombian drug cartel leaders, such as the infamous Pablo Escobar, to the United States for prosecution. Funding from the U.S. war on drugs gave Colombia's military substantial aid, training, and assistance, as well as more advanced weaponry and technology. However, drug war critics and human rights groups in the United States argued that the Colombian military was using its U.S.-funded arms against political opponents, and not the emerging drug lords and networks of traffickers.

The growing economic power of the cocaine trade did not merely influence the Colombian political system, but also allowed it to become virtually institutionalized within the system. At the beginning of the cocaine decade, the nation was embroiled in its seemingly paradoxical war on drugs. The Colombian state continued to target its political opponents under the aegis of its authority in waging the war on drugs in conjunction with the United States. Colombia's right wing was empowered by President Reagan's condemnation of narco-terrorism, which Colonel John Waghelstein, a U.S. Army counterinsurgency expert, used to capitalize on a popular fear of terrorists and drug traffickers and thus mobilize support for foreign interventions against leftist regimes in Latin America.[58] Colombia's FARC insurgency was viewed by the Reagan-Bush White House as Cuban-Soviet inspired, in the style of Marxist groups such as the ELN, EPL, and M-19 guerrilla movements. CIA director William Casey and U.S. ambassador to Colombia Lewis Tambs sought to capitalize politically on the FARC's alleged links to the cocaine trade in Colombia. Their arguments about the FARC as narco-terrorists were drawn from studies by Rachel Ehrenfeld, which criticized the FARC's links with the Medellín drug cartel led by Pablo Escobar.[59] However, Colombia's cocaine industry and the circumstances of the FARC's insurgency have a complexity far greater than Ehrenfeld's notion of a dependency between the two would suggest.

The CIA Inside the Crystal Triangle

As a result of cocaine's growing importance to Colombia, Pablo Escobar Gaviria, a former petty thief from the outskirts of Medellín, became the most successful of the narcotics entrepreneurs. Prior to venturing into the commercialization of cocaine, Escobar was a tombstone thief and dealer in stolen vehicles.[60] Coming from Medellín, he was uniquely positioned to instigate the substitution of cocaine for marijuana as Colombia's growing premier illicit export commodity. While other traffickers remained immersed in the coastal marijuana trade, Escobar and his associates established contacts with coca producers in Bolivia and Peru.

The Colombian cocaine trade expanded rapidly. The *capos,* heads of large drug-trafficking clans, organized meetings to centralize production, distribution, and commercialization of the drug, as well as to establish large-scale transportation systems and export routes. Those who secured control of trade routes to the United States became cocaine's monopolists.[61] Escobar not only perfected the cocaine-refining technology but developed ingenious schemes for cocaine distribution.

According to Trenton Parker, a former CIA operative, the CIA set up two preliminary meetings attended by various Colombian drug dealers for the purpose of organizing a drug-trafficking cartel.[62] The first meeting occurred in early 1981 with twenty of the biggest cocaine dealers in Colombia present.[63] The second meeting, held at the Hotel International Medellín in December 1981 and attended by two hundred drug dealers, established the Medellín cartel. Each member of the cartel paid an initial $35,000 fee to fund a security force that would protect its drug operations.[64] A paramilitary organization called Muerte a los Secuestradores (Death to Kidnappers; MAS) was also established at this meeting. MAS assassinated leftists, trade unionists, civil rights activists, and peasants collaborating with left-wing guerrillas and members of the Union Patriotica (UP), the civilian arm of the FARC.[65] In addition, Israeli and British mercenaries, paid with drug money, organized a death-squad paramilitary school where Carlos Castaño, the future leader of the AUC–MAS's successor organization was an early trainee. Colombia's state security apparatus was incorporated into the AAA international network as the "Andean Brigade."[66]

Gunther Russbacher, another CIA operative, confirmed the CIA's role in establishing the Medellín cartel. He attended the two meetings in December 1981, and reported that there had been a preliminary meeting in September 1981 in Buenaventura, Colombia, that established the format for the subsequent meetings.[67] According to Russbacher, the meetings were initiated by the CIA to deal with a group rather than many independent drug dealers: "At least half a dozen former CIA, OSS, and DEA personnel gave me many hours of statements over a three-year period concerning Central and South America drug operations in which U.S. intelligence agencies and the [Israeli] Mossad participated."[68]

Testimonies by former CIA operatives Kenneth C. Bucchi, and Al Martin detail covert drug-trafficking operations in Latin America involving the CIA. Bucchi tells of a third meeting in

Zurich, Switzerland, in August 1984, which was linked to a major covert operation named "Pseudo Miranda."[69] According to Bucchi, Vice President George Bush and CIA director William Casey were behind the operation. The aim was to centralize the cocaine trade in Colombia and neutralize Bolivia and Peru as rivals.[70] As tactical commander of Pseudo Miranda, Bucchi attended the Zurich meeting. His mission was to fund the Colombian drug lords and provide cover for their distribution routes; for instance, one operation flew drugs from Colombia to a CIA airstrip in Texas where it would be unloaded for normal distribution. In an interview on CNN, he stated:

> We could save a lot of money if the government just went to Colombia and asked, "How much for all the cocaine?" It's not that farcical. The cost would be tremendous, but it would still be less than what we are spending now for the Drug War. But then we would not be able to justify giving weapons to governments. If we bought it all, the drug dealers would have the same amount of money as the people in power. The CIA doesn't want leftist guerrillas or Pablo Escobars to have the same power as the people they help put in power.[71]

The Medellín cartel systematically outmaneuvered its competitors, particularly the Florida-based Cuban mafia and others involved in the trade. By eliminating these middlemen and installing their own, the Colombians not only improved profit margins but also disposed of many Cuban-American informants working with the CIA and other U.S. law enforcement agencies, thereby lowering their risks.[72]

Medellín cocaine traders gained a reputation as violent thugs, whose leader, Pablo Escobar, would stop at nothing to maintain control of the market, eventually mounting a military campaign against the Colombian state. By the urban poor, Escobar was viewed as a modern Robin Hood, an image born in the slums surrounding Medellín.[73] In a place known as Barrio Pablo Escobar, local residents have gathered to pray for his soul in a church he built, where over two hundred homes he also built can be seen from the steeple.[74] The poor in Barrio Pablo Escobar prefer to forget Escobar's violent reputation. Escobar's brother, Roberto, says they called him "El Patron" (The Boss) out of respect. People began to call him that because he would supply truckloads of food to the poor.[75] Although Escobar enjoyed popular appeal with his defiant Robin Hood image, rival narcotics traffickers from the Cali cartel were often viewed by the poor as being corrupt and greedy. The Cali cartel, which consolidated its interests in cocaine production and trafficking through a management and marketing strategy, was seen as being too close to the Colombian state.[76]

Despite the spectacular growth of the cartels in Colombia, which the U.S. government had played an instrumental role in organizing, the primary source of raw coca and cocaine paste was Bolivia. This Andean nation held a near monopoly in coca production—80 percent of the world's processed cocaine came from Bolivia in the early 1980s.[77] Stephen Crittenden, a CIA veteran of Southeast Asia and Latin America, has reported that the Bolivian Air Force flew numerous flights for the CIA, distributing cocaine to the United States. Two CIA proprietary airlines, Southern Air Transport and Evergreen International Aviation, distributed cocaine in covert operations involving the DEA as well.[78] Colombian and Bolivian drug cartel figures landed their Cessna Citations and Lear jets at Marana Airport in Arizona, sanctioned by the CIA.[79] CIA money was flown from headquarters in McLean, Virginia, to pay their South American contacts in the heavily guarded Marana Airport, sometimes using a Boeing 707 aircraft with NASA markings. Crittenden, who flew the planes with other CIA pilots, explained that part of this money paid for drug shipments arriving from South and Central America which would be distributed by Bolivians or Colombians.[80] The cocaine flights came from a network of private airstrips in Bolivia via Colombia. After the January 1973 ceasefire in Vietnam, the United States engaged in what has been described as the "biggest rummage sale of spy equipment in history."[81] By February 1975, the CIA's proprietary airline, Air America, held meetings over ten days in Hong Kong with officials and senior representatives of South American republics. Top-secret deals were made involving the sale of a large number of transport and semi-military aircraft to these countries.

Salomon Kalmanovitz, an economist from Colombia's Central Bank, has observed that in Colombia's changing political economy of the 1980s, "cocaine stopped the balance of payments from collapsing, which would have pushed us into the spiral of hyper-devaluation and hyper-inflation that shook most of the rest of the continent, for which the 1980s were a lost decade."[82] The establishment of the cocaine trade in Colombia had social, economic, and political repercussions that reached beyond Colombia, to other parts of the Crystal Triangle and Latin America and extended to the primary cocaine market in the United States.[83]

The Role of U.S. Imperialism in the Cocaine Trade

The role of U.S. imperialism in the global drug trade was a consequence of efforts by the United States to enhance its political and economic position in the global economic system. Doug Stokes in *America's Other War* explains:

> The imperial state acted to protect the interests of capital through the maintenance of an international system open to capital penetration while destroying social forces that threatened the process of global capital accumulation.[84]

Drugs provided useful funding for right-wing groups where geostrategic interests were concerned. U.S. imperial adventures globally have generally occurred close to significant oil-producing nations or regions.[85] Colombia became the eighth-largest supplier of oil to the United States in 2000.

At the height of the cocaine decade, the Iran-Contra scandal revealed U.S. involvement in the drug trade during the Reagan and Bush presidencies. Evidence emerged about CIA involvement in covert drug-trafficking operations. Lt. Colonel Oliver North of the U.S. Marines was selected by the Reagan administration to coordinate the covert war against the Sandinista government in Nicaragua.[86] Reagan authorized covert operations through CIA director William Casey, and North carried them out through the principal CIA airline in Latin America, Southern Air Transport, and the use of private contractors linked to organized crime and money-laundering activities.[87] One contractor was SETCO Air, owned by a Honduran drug trafficker named Juan Ramón Matta Ballesteros. General Richard Secord, a CIA veteran in Vietnam, directed both SETCO and Southern Air Transport. The second contractor was DIACSA, owned by a Bay of Pigs veteran, Alfredo Caballero. The third was Vortex, whose vice president, Michael Palmer, was an American drug trafficker. The fourth contractor was a company named Frigorificos de Puntarenas that was owned by another anti-Castro Cuban, Luis Rodriguez.[88]

In Oliver North's personal diary, five hundred pages were devoted to detailing drug-trafficking activities, which are now in the possession of the National Security Archives in Washington.[89] A small, select team of State Department, Defense, CIA, and NSC officials—referred to as the "208 Committee" or "Policy Development Group"—met frequently throughout the cocaine decade.[90] This group organized secret Contra supply missions and arms deals with Iran, including logistics such as which weapons would be shipped, which secret warehouses would be used, and which middlemen would deliver goods to clandestine airstrips.[91] For many of these sensitive operations, only a few members knew of their actual existence.[92] According to Caspar Weinberger, then U.S. secretary of defense, "People with their own agenda were doing everything they could to put this agenda into effect."[93]

The growth of cocaine production in Colombia and trade involved the ascendancy of military and civilian regimes committed

to extending market relations with the United States. These included Argentina's military junta of 1976, Bolivia's narco-militarists of
1980, the Nicaraguan Contras (rebel groups opposing the FSLN),
Manuel Noriega in Panama, the Honduran military, the Costa
Rican government, the ARENA party of Colonel Roberto
d'Aubuisson in El Salvador, and later Alberto Fujimori in Peru.[94]

The CIA did not establish the Colombian drug cartels, but the
CIA's role in assisting the organization of Colombian traffickers
into cocaine producers, distributors, and marketing networks was
vital to the cocaine trade's takeoff. The traffickers acted on the U.S.
government's behalf in a de facto relationship when it financially
benefited them. Pablo Escobar's Medellín cartel demonstrated that
some of the traffickers had their own interests in participating in
the drug trade. Escobar himself appeared quite opposed to U.S.
involvement. The Reagan administration linked the FARC insurgency to cocaine production and distribution networks. This was
demonstrated in an account of a joint raid by Colombian police
and the DEA on Tranquilandia, a large complex of cocaine-processing laboratories in the Colombian jungle:

> The Colombian police reported that they believed the snipers who
> fired at them [at the lab] were members of the FARC, the armed wing
> of the Colombian Communist Party. In the next weeks, Colombian
> forces . . . found . . . a camp that appeared to have been used by FARC
> guerrillas. [In] another large lab complex . . . they found three hun-
> dred empty ether barrels, an arsenal of weapons, and a FARC uni-
> form. . . . For the Reagan Right, all this was proof that the narco-ter-
> rorism marriage had been consummated. Lewis Tambs, the US
> Ambassador to Colombia, went so far as to suggest that the labs were
> somehow linked to Cuba. After the raid on Tranquilandia, Tambs
> flew to Washington and offered a background briefing to a few
> American reporters. He emphasized the presence of guerrillas.[95]

The *New York Times* echoed Tamb's story that the Colombian
police had seized a cocaine-processing plant guarded by commu-

nist FARC guerrillas. Another article repeated the claim made by the Colombian military that smugglers hauled cocaine out of the country and returned with Cuban arms for leftist insurgents.[96] Analyses of various journalists' accounts and statements made by U.S. State Department officials have since revealed that the claim of the FARC's involvement in Tranquilandia was baseless.[97]

Senator John Kerry's Senate Subcommittee on Narcotics and International Terrorism began its investigation in early 1986, but it barely exposed the role of the United States in drug trafficking in Latin America.[98] Its work was overshadowed by the media-feeding frenzy surrounding Iran-Contra and Oliver North, which began in late 1986. The subcommittee took testimony from forty-seven witnesses. Many witnesses, some who were convicted drug traffickers, testified in great detail about the drug links to the Contra operations. Some were eyewitnesses or direct participants in guns-for-drugs shipments to Contra bases in Central America.[99] The final report, issued in 1993, contains information about the central role of George H. W. Bush and the Office of the Vice President in the Contra supply operations.[100] The most important material is in the chapter on Donald Gregg, a thirty-year CIA veteran who became Bush's National Security Adviser in 1982. Gregg had a decades-long friendship and association with Felix Rodriguez, a Cuban-born CIA operative credited with tracking down Che Guevara in Bolivia. It was Bush's office that deployed Rodriguez to Central America and made arrangements for him to operate out of Ilopango military air base in El Salvador. The Gregg chapter documents numerous meetings and communications among Bush, Gregg, and Rodriguez, and also among them and Oliver North and Contra leaders.

The BCCI's link with the CIA strengthened under President Ronald Reagan and Vice President George Bush.[101] Bush and CIA director William Casey, with the assistance of British intelligence, set up BCCI's Cayman Island affiliate bank called the International Credit and Investment Company Ltd. (ICIC). The law firm involved was Bruce Campbell & Company, which acted as a registered agent for the CIA-linked Nugan Hand Bank in Australia. Both BCCI and Nugan Hand used Price Waterhouse as auditors. Nugan Hand's president, Admiral Earl Yates, also headed the Great American Bank of Miami, which was indicted in 1982 for money-laundering. When Nugan Hand collapsed, Yates became president of the City National Bank, whose owner was Alberto Duque, a member of the Colombian narco-bourgeoisie involved with George Bush's son Jeb in the construction of a downtown Miami high-rise.[102] The Reagan-Bush White House took an "off-the-books" approach toward money-laundering throughout the cocaine decade.[103] The DEA estimated that overall profits from cocaine imported into the United States amounted to $30 billion. The Medellín cartel received $10 billion of that sum a year in sales, prompting *Forbes* magazine to place the Medellín leaders, Pablo Escobar and Jorge Ochoa, on its list of the world's richest men in 1988.[104]

The cocaine decade saw the consolidation of the Colombian drug trade as a source of profit for U.S. capital via banks that were established to launder and invest drug money in legitimate U.S. corporations.[105] The United States contended it was at war with drugs and terrorists in Colombia, but, in reality, the economic relations between U.S. imperialism and the Colombian narco-bourgeoisie permitted cocaine production to flourish in Colombia, and the cocaine market to expand within the United States and Western Europe.

3. A Narco-State and a Narco-Economy

The cocaine decade of the 1980s, also known as the "lost decade," was historically significant for the construction of a stable economic and political Colombian state based on the cocaine trade. Colombia took extraordinary measures to mobilize army and paramilitary forces in its war against the FARC as it implemented extraordinary measures in coca cultivation and cocaine production, marketing, transportation, and distribution networks to ensure profit-making opportunities. In the new "narco-state," major drug traffickers and paramilitary militias of the AUC were integrated into Colombian legal, political, and financial institutions.

A narco-bourgeoisie emerged with the assistance of drug traffickers from the lowest social levels such as Pablo Escobar and the state created modes of production and distribution to form a new narco-economy. Money-laundering was the financial basis of the narco-connection between Colombia and the United States. The U.S. Financial Crimes Enforcement Network (FINCEN) defines money-laundering as the process by which criminals or criminal organizations seek to disguise the illicit nature of their proceeds by introducing them into the stream of legitimate commerce and finance.[1] It is a process associated with globalization, market integration, and technological innovations that have reshaped both the formal and informal economies—or illegal, underground economies—of developed and developing countries.[2] Further, investigative journalists have drawn attention to the global rise of organized crime and their organizations.[3] However, the links between the Colombian economy and the cocaine trade indicate that the political economy of cocaine extends further and deeper than simply money-laundering.

Although Colombia became a major supplier for the global drug trade during the cocaine decade, a number of myths, aimed at downplaying this or explaining it in a self-serving manner, have been concocted and presented by both Colombian and U.S. officials. They argue that 1) cocaine is not important to Colombia; 2) the importance of cocaine to Colombia is often exaggerated; 3) the killing or imprisonment of cartel leaders makes a difference; 4) the cocaine trade exists because of corruption and criminal organizations that outsmart resource-superior authorities and the law; 5) the CIA has never (or hardly ever) trafficked in drugs; 6) drugs are not important to the U.S. economy. To unravel these myths, it is necessary to make a class analysis of both Colombian society and the relationship between Colombia and the United States.

The formation of Colombian drug cartels helped to coordinate coca production, but it also intensified existing class antagonisms within the country. Colombia was the only country in the Andean coca-growing zone that succeeded in developing sophisticated drug cartels and international marketing networks.[4] A new class, the narco-bourgeoisie, exploited the economic opportunities in cocaine.

In Colombian history, state institutions have always protected the political and economic interests of Colombia's ruling classes.[5] The cocaine trade in Colombia created a narco-bourgeoisie whose development from the Colombian *comprador* class was linked to the cartels' operations. Right-wing paramilitary militias were set up by the *compradores* to target their traditional enemies, the FARC and other guerrilla organizations, but also any other obstacle to economic operations and foreign investment.[6] Those who opposed the militias—trade unionists, human rights workers, investigative journalists, progressive teachers, and academics— were considered enemies of the state. The continuing class conflict between *compradores* backed by U.S. imperialism against urban workers and campesinos appears to have been inevitable.

Among the *compradores*, short-term agreements were made on coca production that paved the road for longer-term agreements of all kinds, one of which supported the emergence of the narco-bourgeoisie, whose business operations had remained relatively independent. They agreed amongst themselves not to increase the amount of cocaine sold on American streets beyond certain limits policed by the CIA, in order not to adversely affect rival enterprises. The resulting drug cartels gave rise to coca production of a monopolistic nature. The emerging narco-capitalism permeated Colombia's financial system, creating financial connections throughout the Colombian economy. The active participation of banks in the cocaine industry greatly strengthened financial connections among the narco-bourgeoisie. The Cali cartel metamorphosed into numerous legitimate business enterprises such as pharmaceutical companies and real estate firms to operate the cocaine trade, whereas the Medellín cartel focused on money-laundering.

The cartels' monopoly presented opportunities for the enrichment of all Colombian capital, regardless of whether enterprises were directly or indirectly involved in the cocaine trade. This situation created fierce competition among traffickers with connections to the Colombian ruling class. The Medellín cartel waged a desperate battle against enterprises that refused to enter into an alliance with them. All manner of underhanded methods, from blackmail to murder, were employed in this battle. The violent liquidation of rival enterprises, many who collaborated with the CIA, provoked retaliation from the United States which declared a war on drugs that targeted Pablo Escobar. An Amnesty International report described the Colombian state's struggle for control of Colombia's cocaine trade:

The Prosecutor-General's Public Ministry and civilian security agencies have initiated investigations into the composition of paramilitary groups and the source of their financial support. Through such investigations, evidence has emerged that many paramilitary "death squads" are financed by landowners, industrialists, and alleged drug traffickers and operate in coordination with, or under the authority of, sectors of the Colombian armed forces. Armed forces units which have persistently been implicated in paramilitary death squad activities include the intelligence unit of the National Police, F-2, the army's intelligence division, B-2, and the army's intelligence and counter-intelligence unit, BINCI.[7]

As the Colombian state became embroiled in the cocaine trade, the problem for the narco-bourgeoisie soon became the prominence of the Medellín cartel, which acted independently of the national business elite.

Of all the state's institutions, the military is the best-equipped to defend the state's interests. As army officers recruited from the urban middle class or bourgeoisie were conceivably open to politicization by leftist ideologies and thus posed a security risk, they were predominantly drawn from the peasantry.[8] As in other Latin American countries, the role of the military in Colombia was crucial. According to the United Nations Drug Control Program, the biggest heroin and cocaine trading institutions in the world are the militaries of Burma, Pakistan, Mexico, Peru, and Colombia—"all armed and trained by U.S. military intelligence in the name of anti-drug efforts."[9] The CIA justifies these antidrug efforts through its operational guidelines which claims its interest in the drug trade is confined only to the effects the drug business has on geopolitical power.[10]

The war on drugs and the war on terror have forged strong connections between the military forces of the United States and Colombia. Since contributing to the creation of the paramilitary network MAS, the Colombian military and U.S. intelligence services continued to work in tandem in fomenting alliances to fight the guerrillas as an integral part of their counterinsurgency doctrine.[11] With the inauguration of President Julio Cesar Turbay Ayala (1978–1982), the military and police assumed a prominent role as defenders of a Colombian state enmeshed in the cocaine trade. High-ranking military officers and paramilitary leaders began to buy land close to areas controlled by the FARC in an effort to drive them off the land and liquidate their support base, a counterinsurgency strategy that later developed into campaigns of extensive crop fumigation and military enforced relocation.

Active and reserve army officers played a leading role in the emerging narco-state. One paramilitary group was formed in Segovia, Antioquia Department, by Fidel and Carlos Castaño, the leaders of the AUC. The Castaños, from an upper-middle-class landowning family, offered their services, particularly in the area of intelligence, to the military Batallion Bombona that operated in Segovia.[12] Another paramilitary group known as the Frente Calima in Valle del Cauca Department was founded with the participation of active, retired, and reserve military officers attached to the military's Third Brigade, along with paramilitaries from the Self-Defense Groups of Cordoba and Uraba (Las Autodefensas Campesinas de Cordoba y Uraba, ACCU) which operated mainly in Antioquia and Cordoba Departments.[13] Colombia's paramilitary militias are not independent entities of the state but rather a component of Colombia's intelligence network. U.S. military advisers, with British and Israeli assistance, helped reshape the military intelligence network.[14] According to a Human Rights Watch report in 2000, half of the commanders of the Colombian army have been investigated for their links to paramilitary groups.[15]

In Antioquia, Cordoba, and Valle de Cauca, the Castaños played a central role in Colombia's national counterinsurgency strategy against FARC. Carlos Castaño's control of Uraba and other areas close to the border with Panama, a major transshipment route, placed him in a favorable position to shape and ultimately inherit a drug-trafficking network with contacts in the interior of the country and international markets. While the military and police remained as the official army of the Colombian state, the paramilitaries became the clandestine army of the narco-state.

As late as 1998, further restructuring of the Colombian state was occurring. Two widely publicized foiled drug-trafficking attempts by Colombian air force officers, one that used the presidential plane and the other an air force plane on a "training mission" to the United States, revealed the air force command system's involvement in drug trafficking. The officers were referred to as the "Blue Cartel," an allusion to their blue uniforms.[16] In another example, 1,600 pounds of cocaine were found in a Colombian air force plane that landed at Fort Lauderdale-Hollywood International Airport in 1998.[17] In 2000, Colombia's director of intelligence in the Department of Administrative Security (DAS), which coordinates the security functions of the military and police, along with the head of Colombia's counterintelligence unit and the coordinator for security operations were implicated in trafficking arms and the embezzling of public funds, among other charges.[18]

The influence of the cocaine trade is further reflected in the influx of newcomers to the Colombian political system.[19] The political career of Alvaro Uribe Velez, the country's former president and a leading exponent of Washington's war on drugs and terror, began by granting pilot licenses to drug traffickers as head of the aviation company Aerocivil.[20] With the support of his father, Alberto Uribe Sierra, he made his most important contacts with the emerging narco-state as head of Aerocivil. Uribe Sierra became a household name when he was indicted for his involvement in the widely reported raid on the Tranquilandia cocaine-processing laboratory.[21] According to Colombian investigative journalist Ignacio Gomez,[22] "The police had tried to pin the laboratory on FARC guerrillas when in fact [the laboratory] had enjoyed high-level protection from the Colombian military."[23] CIA director William Casey contended at the time that the laboratory was guarded by communist guerrillas and planned by the Medellín cartel, but it was later revealed that the laboratory was planned in Cali and protected by the army.[24] The charge that FARC protected the cocaine laboratory arose from the discovery of a FARC uniform, which was allegedly planted by the CIA.[25]

Uribe Sierra, who owned extensive cattle ranches in Antioquia and Cordoba and became a real estate intermediary for the traffickers, was connected by marriage to the Ochoas, an elite family that joined the narco-bourgeoisie to help form the Medellín cartel. When Pablo Escobar launched his Medellín Sin Tugurios (Medellín without Slums) campaign in 1982, Uribe Sierra organized an exclusive horse race to raise funds. When he was killed in 1983, his son Alvaro Uribe flew to his ranch in Escobar's helicopter.[26] Alvaro Uribe's wealth and connections to the underworld through his father practically assured him a place in the new establishment.[27]

During Alvaro Uribe's four-month tenure as mayor of Medellín in 1982, the city was known as "the sanctuary" for its controversial untouchable status. Medellín, under Escobar's control, linked the central and western highlands to the eastern lowlands and Pacific and Atlantic coasts through new cities—Florencia, Villavicencio, Leticia—with roads, airports, and motorboats. For frontier settlers in Caquetá, Putumayo, Guaviare, Vichada, Guainía, Vaupés, Sucre, Córdoba, the Chocó, Bolívar, the Santanders, and to a lesser extent, in Antioquia, Huila, Tolima, Cauca, and Meta, coca became a profitable cash crop providing known traffickers such as Escobar, the Ochoas, the Galeanos, the Castaños, Kiko Moncada, and others with local distributors. When Alvaro Uribe's attendance at a Medellín cartel meeting at Escobar's ranch, Napoles, was made public, he was removed from his post as mayor.[28] The political implications, however, were far from negative, as the fallout permitted him to become associated with the narco-bourgeoisie. Such an event would have destroyed most political careers, but between 1995 and 1997, Alvaro Uribe was governor of Antioquía and in 2002 he became president of Colombia. As governor of Antioquía, he helped set up a paramilitary force called Convivir, later controlled by the AUC. His right-hand man, Pedro Juan Moreno Villa, was Colombia's leading importer of potassium permanganate, the main chemical in the manufacture of cocaine.[29] According to a

DEA report released in 2000, potassium permanganate importation was linked to Moreno's company—GMP Productos Quimicos, S. A. (GMP Chemical Products).[30]

The most distinguishing feature of the Colombian narco-economy is that all goods and services, both legal—for example, oil, coal, coffee—and illegal—arms, human trafficking, contraband—are dependent on cocaine for the economic stability of the nation. Cocaine generates jobs not only directly in the production of cocaine but indirectly, in areas such as transportation, security, banking, and communications. It is because of Colombia's narco-economy and its economic relation with the United States that the Crystal Triangle supplies 100 percent of the cocaine (and 60 percent of the heroin) consumed on American streets.[31] Drug trafficking and drug money deposited into U.S. and Colombian banks is common, yet virtually ignored by authorities.

A major DEA report in 1999 cited heavy involvement in pervasive "drug-related corruption" in "all branches of the [Colombian] government" including the military.[32] For example, Reuters reported that Colonel James Hiett, the head of the U.S. Army antidrug program in Colombia, was arrested, along with his wife, for smuggling cocaine into the United States in 2000.[33] The cocaine was found in a diplomatic pouch.[34] The brother of General Luis Camacho Leiva of the Colombian army was found with cocaine on a Ministry of Defense plane and Fernando Botero, a former Colombian defense minister, was forced to resign for accepting drug money.[35] In 1983, an elite army squadron transported an entire cocaine-processing laboratory from Colombia to Brazil using Colombian air force planes. When the elite antinarcotics force was established in 1989, it was created within the police force because military involvement in the drug trade was no secret. The commander of this force, Colonel Hugo Martinez, and the head of the national police force, General Vargas, were accused but not convicted of accepting money from the Cali cartel. In 1996, Colombian air force officers were caught smuggling heroin into the United States aboard the plane used by President Samper.

However, such cases are increasingly sealed off from investigations and only documented during random inspection checks by U.S. Customs or DEA personnel, indicating that substantially more drug shipments are carried out using government or armed forces aircraft. With a narco-economy other forms of transportation with private airplanes or speedboats would be assured by the narco-state.

4. The Narco-Cartel System
(1980–1993)

The Colombian narco-economy's driving market force is consumption, which is at the heart of the United States' political and economic interest in cocaine. Many critics maintain that it is impossible to eliminate the drug trade by targeting drug production and that by ignoring the demand side that fuels market growth, the United States is only aggravating the problem.[1] Narcotics are produced, trafficked, and laundered in the United States (e.g. amphetamines, marijuana), and they are consumed there as well.

Coca has been cultivated for thousands of years in the Andean region, and no doubt it will be cultivated for thousands of years in the future. However, if there is no demand for cocaine, the drug trade will dry up. The United States imposes repressive measures that punish drug offenders, but this does not prevent drug crimes from occurring—the money is too seductive. The United States has been involved in counterinsurgency measures in the name of fighting drugs and terrorism in producer countries, yet neither drugs nor drug "terrorism" has disappeared.

The so-called war on drugs and the war on terror rhetoric mask the links between the narco-bourgeoisie, the drug cartels, and the

Colombian economy. The cocaine trade exploits the *cocaleros* in Colombia and marginalized consumers in the United States, predominantly Latinos and African Americans addicted to hard drugs, which include cocaine or crack, who subsequently are incarcerated for drug-related crimes.

Throughout the cocaine decade, U.S. demand for cocaine surged to unprecedented levels and Colombia became a cartel-run narco-economy. Between 1970 and 1987, Peruvian coca production rose from 15,000 to 191,000 tons, while Bolivia's production rate kept pace.[2] Both fed the narco-economy of Colombia. The number of seized laboratories recorded by the U.S. government almost tripled from 275 in 1984 to 725 the following year. By the late 1980s, cocaine had become a major export commodity that was financially and legally institutionalized in legitimate Colombian-U.S. economic relations with banks, corporations, and major investments in property, real estate and other business ventures. The cartel system was made up of regionally based trafficking organizations that coalesced to rationalize the system of production, smuggling, and marketing of cocaine.[3] Management decisions concerning the cocaine economy were left to contacts in the national military intelligence network or, in some cases, to the CIA, depending on the importance of issues such as transportation, exchange, and distribution to the United States. The aim was to maximize export volumes and profits while reducing risk to each participant. This involved various co-financing and co-insurance schemes, as well as the pooling of services—such as financial advisers, lawyers, counterintelligence, and security operatives. The larger participating organizations either owned trafficking assets such as planes, cocaine laboratories, shipping companies, and submarines, or had exclusive access to them through their connections in the narco-state.[4]

The principal cartels based in Medellín and Cali controlled 80 percent or more of the cocaine exported from Colombia. Other quasi-independent groups centered in Bogotá or on the Atlantic coast maintained loose associations with the Medellín and Cali drug cartels and tended to follow their lead on issues about the

quantity of drugs that could be exported from Colombia; the transshipment routes that could be used, including how (via land, sea,
or air) and when the product could be exported; and the wholesale
price of cocaine per kilogram sold in the United States. The price
had to be approved by representatives of either the Medellín or Cali
cartels; after distribution, the retail price of cocaine per gram was
left to the discretion of local dealers.[5] At their most powerful, in the
late 1980s, the cartels earned combined annual revenues of at least
$6 billion, of which three to four billion was profit, and coordinat-
ed a trafficking workforce of eight thousand to ten thousand skilled
workers and professionals.[6]

The profits of cocaine placed an enormous concentration of
economic power in the hands of the narco-bourgeoisie. To a certain extent, this was centralized power, with a leadership structure
composed of the heads of the dominant trafficking organizations in
each coalition within Colombia's cartel system. Cartel leaders,
such as Pablo Escobar Gaviria in Medellín and the Rodriguez-
Orejuela brothers in Cali, played a vital role in the national coordination of Colombia's narco-economy and the cartels' representa-
tion in parliamentary politics. The cartel system was not simply a
group of gangsters who ran around shooting people. It was a system crucial for the economic stability of a nation dependent on the
export of cocaine.

A clear-headed picture of what a narco-economy entails is often
blurred with numbers and statistics presented by official sources.
Peter Reuter, a RAND Corporation economist, notes: "Officials
often use the drug issue to build public support for their own agen-
das. Every statistic on drugs—prices, volume, earnings, arrests,
numbers of users and addicts—must be interpreted in this light.
But although drug statistics are imprecise, they can point toward
reasonable generalizations."[7]

The private ownership of cocaine production and the dangerous nature of the drug trade make it difficult to calculate accurate-
ly the size of the narco-economy. Much of the available data provide
approximations but no exact figures, though conclusive evidence

regarding large quantities of illegal drugs exported to the United States, Canada, and Europe provides a general framework for analysis.[8] Cocaine production increased so much that it became the most important economic activity in the Andean region.[9] The huge sums of money rapidly accumulated under the cartel system, which led the cartels to invest their profits outside of Colombia in banks and corporations within the United States.

The profits generated by cocaine had an impact on land ownership in Colombia. The narco-bourgeoisie forcibly acquired an estimated one million hectares of farmland from a total of thirteen million hectares of land in 1989.[10] The effect of this direct investment of capital from the increasingly influential narco-bourgeoisie and international sources capital was apparent in escalating prices for farmland.[11] Between 1982 and 1984, and in 1989, the prices of land captured by paramilitary forces skyrocketed. The price per hectare in some areas increased from $100,000 to $1,000,000.[12]

The narco-bourgeoisie capitalized on Colombia's long tradition of smuggling and trading in contraband goods that dated back to Spanish colonial rule. The Colombian narco-state undertook extraordinary measures to industrialize coca cultivation and cocaine production, and the trafficking process included large-scale smuggling by boats, planes, and containers.

Colombian Society and the Rise of Pablo Escobar

The narco-bourgeoisie included some of Colombia's oldest families with lineages dating back to the Spanish conquest. The Davilas and Diaz Granados, two of the better-known families, are from departments on the northern Atlantic coast, notably Cesar, Buajira, Magdalena, and Bolivar. Many regional and local political systems in Colombia became intertwined with the drug trade, especially when individuals from these well-established families served as mayors, senators, and governors and could provide political protection to the drug-trafficking networks that enriched them.[13]

In stark contrast to these well-established individuals, Pablo Escobar Gaviria came from a low socioeconomic background like most traffickers from Medellín, Antioquia. Although investigative journalism tends to dwell on his personality,[14] his political rise illuminates many aspects of the Colombian state's relationship with cocaine. A child of *La Violencia* (1948–1958) and a teenage delinquent, Pablo Escobar's nationalist and vehemently anti-American political views were shaped by the class struggle in Colombia.[15] A study of twenty middle and top ranking drug traffickers from Medellín and other areas from the Antioquia Department in 1988 revealed their class origins: 70 percent were from the countryside (40 percent from the middle and lower peasantry); 30 percent from the urban lower class; 55 percent had only primary education, 35 percent secondary; 10 percent had been to university.[16] On the other hand, traffickers from the rival Cali cartel came from more privileged backgrounds. They were nicknamed *los caballeros* (the gentlemen) of Cali, as opposed to *los hampones* (the hoodlums) of Medellín. Large portions of the Medellín cartel's drug profits were invested, somewhat conspicuously, into social development projects such as building housing for the poor, water wells, sports facilities, and even installing satellite TV dishes in outskirt communities.[17] Defying the Colombian status quo, these cocaine-funded development projects were said to extend across the border into Peru, providing "monies to repair local roads, docking facilities, the school, and the medical clinic."[18] Escobar established the political movement *Civismo en Marcha* (Good Citizenship on the March), which sponsored various civic programs. These social endeavors were belittled by U.S. government spokespersons and scholars, but, according to Escobar, they frightened Colombian politicians and bureaucrats.[19]

One of Escobar's first contacts with Colombia's elite was a property dealer and politician from a leading Antioquia family, Diego Londono White. Through him, Escobar sought to invest his profits in land. White was already a friend of the Ochoa brothers, high-ranking members of the Medellín cartel, and was the

Antioquia coordinator for Conservative Party candidate Belisario Betancur's presidential campaign. Neither of Colombia's two major parties, the Conservatives and the Liberals, was discriminating when it came to drug money. "Political campaigns need a lot of finance and politicians look for money wherever they can get it," White said in an interview in the 1990s. A colleague of White contended, "Belisario himself attended campaign auctions of art, horses, and cattle, knowing that drug traffickers were the main vendors."[20] The traffickers financed the presidential campaign of Liberal candidate Julio Cesar Turbay Ayala, who won the election in 1978.[21]

Exchange houses, real estate agencies, and "various financial corporations" came into existence, offering high returns and tailor-made services to cocaine traffickers.[22] The Federal Reserve Bank of Miami reported a cash surplus of $5.5 billion, greater than the total surplus of all other Federal Reserve Bank branches in the United States in 1979.[23] Remarkably, a connection between the drug cartels and this cash surplus has not been established. Central Bank of Colombia figures indicated that construction in Medellín quadrupled between 1975 and 1981, accounting for 28 percent of the national total. At least half the finance was estimated to come from the drug cartels—Escobar invested his money in land and buildings. The cartels had joined Colombia's elite business and landowning narco-bourgeoisie, and they, too, became military targets for kidnapping and extortion by the FARC.[24]

Escobar made his first trip to Bolivia sometime in the early 1980s, where he met Roberto Suarez of *La Corporacion*, then the major single supplier of coca paste. They agreed that Escobar would buy the coca paste from Bolivia and process it into powdered cocaine in Colombian laboratories. Anxious to see his cartel members legitimized as businessmen, Escobar forged an alliance with Colombia's business elite, the army, and politicians. Cocaine money funded areas where the state had failed, particularly in housing and urban development, sports and recreation, and public works.[25] Indeed, Mario Arango, a Colombian historian, observed:

"The moral rejection of so-called hot money is not so much that it comes from illicit activities but that it has enabled the rise of a new economic sector coming mainly from the lowest social levels."[26] Escobar's politics and market share in the cocaine trade came into conflict with the Miami-based Cuban mafia, whose political links with anti-Castro Cubans and the Bush family in Florida played a significant role in the events leading up to Escobar's conflict with the Colombian state and his assassination.[27] In 1984, Jeb Bush (son of George H. W. Bush) began a close association with Camilo Padreda, a former intelligence officer with the Batista dictatorship overthrown by Fidel Castro, but the association dates back to the recruitment of Cuban exiles into CIA political activity in Latin America from the early 1960s onward.[28]

In 1978 and 1979, South Florida experienced what became known as the cocaine wars, where rival Colombian traffickers and the Cuban mafia fought for control of the state's lucrative drug market.[29] The conflict peaked in 1981 and was not resolved until 1993 with Escobar's death. Bruce Bagley writes:

> In the process, [the Medellín Cartel] systematically exterminated the Cuban-Americans and others who were involved in the trade on the U.S. side. By eliminating these middlemen and installing their own, the Colombians not only improved their profit margins, but also disposed of many Cuban informants who had ties with the CIA and other U.S. law enforcement agencies, thereby lowering their risks.[30]

The Medellín cartel enforced their political power by liquidating rival competitors in Miami, New York, and all along the East Coast of the United States, as they assassinated opponents and police officers, judges, and journalists who could not be bought in Colombia.[31]

A 1979 extradition treaty between Colombia and the United States was negotiated not to address the drug problem and the violence it brought to the two countries, but in relation to Pablo Escobar's political activities and, in particular, his social development projects.[32] The Medellín cartel assassinated Minister of Justice Rodrigo Lara Bonilla, a leading campaigner against Escobar and a vocal advocate for Escobar's extradition. A cofounder of the Medellín cartel denounced the extradition treaty as a plot instigated by the DEA or CIA to target the Medellín cartel for political reasons rather than drug-trafficking charges.[33] In a newspaper founded by Escobar's uncle and financed by Escobar himself, the *Medellín Cívico,* the editor argued, "The nation's face has been disfigured by the imperialist boot of the treaty."[34] The *Medellín Cívico* directed its attack toward Washington.

The treaty became highly controversial in Colombian politics, as the question of Colombian sovereignty was raised in parliamentary debates and media commentary. Escobar campaigned publicly against the treaty. In 1982 he was elected to Congress as an alternative representative from Antioquia, which ensured his immunity from arrest and extradition. As a prominent member of parliament, Escobar rallied considerable support against the extradition treaty at a time when the narco-bourgeoisie were undecided in their support for the treaty.[35] The *Medellín Cívico's* editorials portrayed Escobar as a public-spirited man who contrasted sharply with the selfish and hypocritical Colombian political establishment. Conversely, the Cali cartel meanwhile showed no interest in social issues, backing instead so-called *grupos de limpieza social* (social cleansing groups) in the cities along with members of the local bourgeoisie.[36] The Cali cartel "cleaners" killed urban vagrants, thieves, prostitutes, drug addicts, and even beggars. The bodies of these *desechables* (disposable people) were usually found wearing signs reading, *"Cali limpia, Cali linda"* (Cali clean, Cali beautiful). In many cases, the bodies were dumped into the Cauca River, which locals called the "River of Death."[37]

Meanwhile, Medellín cartel cofounder Carlos Lehder established a political party, the Movimiento Latino Nacional (National Latin Movement; MLN). The party's ideology opposed imperialism, communism, neocolonialism, and Zionism. Its aims included the nationalization of banks, transport, and the assets of multinationals, and called for an end to foreign intervention in Colombia, abrogation of the extradition treaty, and the creation of a united Latin American army to safeguard Latin sovereignty, culture, and frontiers.[38]

Escobar donated five thousand toys every Christmas to children of needy families in the Middle Magdalena Valley, where his family estate, Napoles, was located.[39] In Quindio department, Carlos Lehder distributed cash and medical supplies to the inhabitants of Popayan after a 1983 earthquake.[40] More politically significant than acts of charity was the Medellín cartel's contributions to development of poor communities and regions, for example, a housing project built in San Julian, outside Armenia, the capital city of Quindio. Literacy campaigns were sponsored in some of the rural areas of the department. Gonzalo Rodriguez Gacha, a high-ranking member of the Medellín cartel, restored the facade of the town hall in his native town of Pacho in Cundinamarca, eighty kilometers from Bogotá, and built a large outdoor basketball court for the residents of the town.

Escobar's image as a modern "Robin Hood" by Medellín's residents was greatly enhanced through his "Medellín without Slums" campaign, launched in 1982 to build two thousand new housing units for poor families in that city. However, only five hundred dwellings were completed because of Escobar's conflict with the state.[41] He also built eighty illuminated sports arenas in Medellín and Antioquia.[42] In another major project, Escobar and some of his relatives linked to the Medellín cartel built an immense zoological park on his estate. The zoo was open to the public and entry to the park was free of charge. Escobar said, "The fact is that the Napoles Zoo belongs not to us but to the Colombian people—and the people cannot pay to visit that which it owns."[43] At the zoo's front entrance is an old Piper Cub airplane mounted on a concrete arch. The plane was reportedly used to fly some of the first shipments of Colombian cocaine to the United States. Escobar's newspaper praised his social programs and his engaged populism:

Fifty thousand trees planted in fifty barrios of Medellín . . . schools built with plenty of space, with an eye to beauty and pedagogical function. Broken sewers repaired to protect residents from contaminated water and from epidemics, [sewers that were] a health hazard that the government has ignored for years. Basketball courts, skating rinks, multi-sport arenas . . . thousands of bricks to expand the houses of poor families, to finish buildings, churches, and wings of schools. Illumination of barrios trapped in darkness because of indifferent bureaucrats or politicians who do not keep their promises.[44]

The narco-bourgeoisie was unable to control Escobar, and the *compradores* could no longer afford to publicly associate themselves with him. Medellín authorities accused Escobar of taking matters into his own hands. The secretary of education, recreation, and culture wrote that Escobar's efforts to refit a sports arena in the Santander section of Medellín reflected a "scorn for order and procedure" and told him to desist from further activity.[45] Escobar wrote back, stating that the project and others like it "filled a vacuum created by the indifference, the apathy, the negligence, and the irresponsibility of the municipal administration."[46] Escobar's self-promoting populism created tensions within the Colombian establishment. As a supporter wrote in Escobar's newspaper:

There exist in Colombia two classes of bourgeoisie. That of the Lleras, Sampers, Ospinas, and Laras who earned their capital at the expense of the labor of millions and millions of Colombians, only to invest it in North America or Europe . . . and the other bourgeois class which invests in Colombia out of concern for the misery of the masses and their desperate struggle for survival. To this second class belongs Pablo Escobar.[47]

Escobar ran on the Liberal Party ticket for the House of Representatives in 1982 for a seat in Antioquia; his campaign centered largely on civic and social programs.[48] Escobar was elected as assistant parliamentarian to Jairo Ortega, despite the increasing tensions within the Colombian ruling class. In mid-1987, a Conservative Party leader issued a public statement denouncing "the strange political movements that seem to be in vogue," and called for an investigation into its aims and sources of funding.[49] Copies of the declaration were sent to President Belisario Betancur, the ministers of government and defense, the attorney general, the governor of Quindio, and the mayor of Armenia.[50] Escobar was accused of complicity in the assassination of the minister of justice and was denounced as a major drug lord. Old trafficking charges were reactivated. This was when the U.S. government requested Escobar's extradition for "conspiring to introduce cocaine into the United States via Nicaragua." The Colombian government issued a warrant for Escobar's arrest, not for drug trafficking or murder, but for contraband: "one rhinoceros and eighty-five exotic birds," which he had imported to stock his zoo. The Colombian Congress lifted Escobar's parliamentary immunity, thus marking the end of his political career.[51]

The End of Escobar

A long and bloody bombing campaign directed by Escobar began. The highly esteemed Colombian author Gabriel Garcia Marquez criticized Escobar but wrote explaining that Escobar had not forgotten past insults, which fuelled his all-out war against the state.[52] Escobar was blamed by Colombian authorities for assassinating three of the five candidates running for the Colombian presidency in 1989. The campaign spread to the United States, where Escobar's hit men were suspected of killing Barry Seal, an American drug trafficker and CIA asset who had become a key government witness against Escobar in 1986.[53] When forces allied to Escobar blew up an Avianca airliner in Colombia, his war with the Colombian narco-state and Washington intensified.

The CIA and the Bush family had their own reasons for targeting the Medellín cartel. The Florida distribution of cocaine and money-laundering had been largely in the hands of ex-CIA Cuban Americans, not Colombians,[54] and Escobar's rise to power had cost the lives of many of them. The CIA's Cuban-American connections in Miami included a network of agents and informants who ran the South Florida Task Force or were members of the Cuban mafia. This network was traceable to then-CIA director George H. W. Bush. Republicans in Washington were bound to respond to the powerful Cuban lobby in Florida, which Bush's son Jeb strongly supported with his own connections to anti-Castro politics including ex-CIA Cubans residing in Miami.[55] Jeb Bush had numerous dealings with the Miami BCCI concerning his investments in real estate, including one with a company controlled by a BCCI customer who was later sent to prison for defrauding BCCI and other U.S. banks.[56]

Since support for Escobar was widespread in Colombia, sectors of the state's armed forces, namely the narco-military, were reluctant to move against him, which created a greater problem for the United States and other enemies of Escobar in Colombia.[57] The military's reluctance to move against Escobar had social, political, ideological, and pragmatic foundations: many of the rank-and-file soldiers were drawn from the same social base as the drug traffickers, from the peasantry or lower urban classes.[58] According to Betancourt and Garcia in *Contrabandistas, Marimberos y Mafiosos*, Pablo Escobar and some other traffickers in the Medellín cartel were seen by the poor as "generous, good men, simple, and were persecuted because they ascended from humble class origins" and simply because they helped them.[59] The military's reluctance to move against Escobar can also be attributed to the political culture that arose during the cocaine decade, which accepted contraband and money-laundering as a normal state of affairs.[60]

In 1989, President George Bush authorized a covert operation to track down leaders of the Medellín cartel.[61] In the same year, another important relationship with the United States was terminated. The U.S. invaded Panama and Manuel Noriega's government, which had close financial ties to Escobar, was overthrown.

Noriega was detained as a prisoner of war and taken to the United States, where he was convicted under federal charges of cocaine trafficking, racketeering, and money-laundering. Noriega claimed that his real crime was refusing requests by Colonel Roberto d'Aubuisson of El Salvador to restrict the movements of leaders of the Farabundo Martí National Liberation Front (FMLN) in Panama, and more important, failing to comply with the demands of Lieutenant Colonel Oliver North to provide military assistance to the Nicaraguan Contras.[62] Noriega insists that his refusal to meet North's demands was the basis for the invasion and his removal as a CIA asset.[63]

The code name for the U.S. manhunt for Escobar was "Heavy Shadow." Centra Spike, a top-secret U.S. Army unit that specialized in tracking, monitored Escobar's telephone and radio calls, which were covertly sent to Colombian intelligence. The sophistication involved in Escobar's surveillance forced him into hiding and a life on the run. He surrendered to Colombian authorities in 1991 after negotiating a deal that allowed him to live with his closest associates in a comfortable prison, built for him in his hometown of Envigado near Medellín.[64]

Escobar soon fled the prison, which compelled Colombian president Cesar Gaviria to ask the United States to expand the mission. Bush authorized the clandestine deployment of Delta Force and other U.S. armed forces personnel, which continued as a multimillion-dollar operation under President Bill Clinton.[65] Delta Force, along with an army electronic surveillance team, tracked the movements of Escobar and his associates and helped plan raids for a special Colombian police unit called the "Search Bloc." Morris Busby, the U.S. ambassador to Colombia, directed the U.S. effort with assistance from the CIA, DEA, FBI, and NSA (National Security Agency).[66]

An investigation conducted by Amnesty International in 2001 led to a lawsuit to obtain CIA records of Los Pepes (People Persecuted by Pablo Escobar), a vigilante group set up by Carlos Castaño and backed by the Cali cartel. Its findings pointed to: "an extremely suspect relationship between the U.S. government and the Castaño family—at a time when the U.S. government was well aware of that family's involvement in paramilitary violence and narcotics trafficking."[67]

Carlos Castaño was instrumental in bringing down Escobar by collaborating with the CIA while working for the Cali cartel. By 1989 the Cali cartel had become the principal source of information to the Colombian security agencies.[68] The Castaños did the dirty work for their backers in Bogotá and Washington based on CIA information, which, according to Mark Bowden, a reporter for the *Philadelphia Inquirer*, was transmitted via a special squad of the Colombian National Police who were on good terms with the Cali cartel.[69] Intelligence reports later confirmed that Los Pepes had in fact been created by the Cali cartel; Los Pepes fraternized with at least two DEA agents and gave one of them a gold watch.[70]

Escobar's last stand was on December 3, 1993, on a rooftop in his home city of Medellín. Guns blazing, Escobar was easily outnumbered. He was shot by a rain of bullets and plummeted from the rooftop of the building and onto the ground. Who fired the fatal shot that killed him during the confrontation has been a source of debate, but as an unnamed senior Pentagon official described it, Pablo Escobar stood on top of a powerful mountain and the only way to get at him was to take down the mountain, one person at a time, until there was no place left to hide.[71] President Gaviria was given worldwide credit for Escobar's downfall. He contended that "the battle against Pablo Escobar was never primarily about stopping drug smuggling. He was a very serious problem because he was so violent."[72] Moreover, "he was a threat to the state. The level of terrorism we had to live with was something awful."[73]

Miguel Antonio Gomez Padilla, the longtime Colombian National Police director, resigned over increasing levels of corruption after Escobar's demise. According to a declassified cable between the U.S. State Department and the U.S. embassy in Bogotá, Padilla was "especially disturbed over the influence of the Cali cartel in numerous levels of government" and, as a result, "had simply had enough of the situation."[74] The Cali cartel simply took over Escobar's market share and a new era of trafficking was established that linked the narco-bourgeoisie, the Colombian state, and the United States.[75] This became ever more apparent under President Alvaro Uribe Velez, who released the Cali cartel's founders, Gilberto and Miguel Rodriguez Orejuela, almost immediately after his inauguration as president in November of 2002. The Orejuela brothers, their services no longer required, were later extradited to the United States. Business assets worth $2.1 billion were given up to U.S. authorities and twenty-eight family members of the Cali cartel were given immunity from prosecution.[76] Alvaro Uribe relied heavily on this new version of the narco-military network, which was consolidated under Clinton's Plan Colombia.[77]

Pablo Escobar, as a force in Colombian politics and a cartel kingpin, strained relations between the United States and Colombia. In the desperate battle waged by Escobar and the Medellín cartel, the narco-bourgeoisie was effectively split over his place in high society. The involvement of the United States in the downfall of Pablo Escobar did not end cocaine production in Colombia or its export to America. The prominence that cocaine had achieved in Colombia's political economy only deepened its relationship with the United States and strengthened the Colombian narco-state. Joe Toft, then the DEA chief in Colombia, stated:

> I don't know what the lesson of the story is, I hope it's not that the end justifies the means. Colombians need functioning institutions capable of protecting them, a police and judiciary that aren't cowed by rapacious criminals who buy political protection. The United States does its allies no service by looking the other way while they pursue expedient but counterproductive policies. It could contribute more by blowing the whistle early on, and above all by curbing its own insatiable appetite for drugs.[78]

With the elimination of Escobar and his brand of populism, the cartels were able to permeate all sections of the Colombian economy. With the assistance of Castaño's paramilitary militias, the narco-military network was groomed to perform its task of defending the class interests of the narco-bourgeoisie without compromise, which would eventually turn the Colombian narco-state into something far beyond anything Escobar could have imagined.

5. The Post-Cartel System

In the late 1970s and early 1980s, the Colombian narco-bourgeoisie relied heavily on the drug cartels' money-laundering specialists to deposit their profits in banks. The introduction of the U.S. money-laundering Control Act in 1986 changed that, forcing a major restructuring of the Colombian narco-economy. The narco-bourgeoisie switched to contracting out money-laundering services,[1] which offered financial options beyond those offered by the usual banks that laundered drug money. They were now able to accumulate capital through ownership of various legitimate enterprises as well as attract foreign investors in legal business operations—for example, potassium permanganate companies, transport companies, and private security firms.

In contrast to the conventional framework—an organized crime model with a centralized hierarchy—the post-cartel system after the death of Pablo Escobar provided an unusual degree of order and control. Sophisticated modes of production and distribution and technological developments increased efficiency. When the Medellín cartel was destroyed in the early 1990s, it had little impact upon the narco-bourgeoisie. Decentralization and privatization would prove to be key to the success of the narco-economy in Colombia in the post-cartel period.

The destruction of the Medellín cartel did not affect the collaboration among the narco-bourgeoisie, sectors of the ruling class, and the military, particularly in regions where the FARC contested Medellín's control: Middle Magdalena, Uraba, North Santander, Bolivar, Putumayo, Antioquia, Cauca, and Caqueta. The cartel system had relied too heavily on drug lords like Pablo Escobar. Now the Colombian government, with the support of the United States, took firm measures that resulted in structural changes in the organization of cocaine production and distribution.

In the transition from the cartel system, the Colombian cocaine industry was decentralized into as many as eighty to three hundred distinct private enterprises, according to widely varying official estimates.[2] The restructuring did not affect cocaine exports but made it easier for corporations and other businesses in Colombia to prosper without taking too many risks.[3] Colombian traffickers adopted a management strategy and moved into legal business activities, even negotiating with Mexican drug cartels to hand over parts of their distribution networks in the United States. One such Mexican cartel that emerged from this arrangement is the Henao-Montoya organization (also known as the Norte de Valle Cartel), with which the AUC was affiliated.[4]

By the end of the twentieth century, Colombia became the most advanced cocaine-producing country in the Crystal Triangle. Two factors made this possible: 1) the institutionalization of the cocaine trade in Colombia; and 2) Colombia's proximity to neighboring Crystal Triangle countries Peru and Bolivia, service country Panama, transit countries Mexico, Jamaica, and the Dominican Republic, and consumer and distribution countries the United States and Spain (the gateway country for smuggling operations in Europe).

The Medellín cartel had attempted to establish monopoly control over the trade without negotiating its market share with other enterprises. The Cali cartel, on the other hand, assisted state efforts to eliminate the Medellín cartel from the cocaine trade, and it was left to the Cali group to link together the various components of the industry in a broader drug-trafficking organization, with opportunities to branch out into other markets such as heroin and amphetamines.[5] According to a United Nations report in 1994, a year after Pablo Escobar's death and the final year of the cartel system of cocaine production:

> In spite of the rise of licit transnational corporations in developing countries, the Cali Cartel remains, in effect, the developing countries' most successful transnational corporation. That is not only a comment about the importance of the drug-trafficking industry, but is also a reflection of the continued economic problems that face developing countries. In that connection, some researchers credit the Colombian cartels and their huge monetary base with providing much of the economic stability and even prosperity that Colombia enjoyed throughout the 1980s and early 1990s.[6]

The post-Medellín cartel narco-economy system involves a complex network of banks, corporations, and professionals, with offices in New York, Miami, the Caribbean, and throughout Latin America.[7] The rise of "legitimate" transnational drug corporations coincided with the rise of a new kind of drug trafficker, the "white collar" trafficker, to suit the era of globalization, market integration, and technological innovation.

The United States and Colombia appeared to develop a "mutual dependency" on the export of cocaine and an interest in preserving existing economic conditions and the political status quo. The narco-bourgeoisie acquired continuously greater capital and assumed greater economic power through these arrangements. Nevertheless, most of the profits went to the United States as illegal money to be laundered in CIA-linked banks. Banks that have been involved in money-laundering include the BCCI, Nugan Hand Bank, J. P. Morgan, Chase Manhattan, World Finance Corporation, Castle Bank of the Bahamas, Citibank, Citicorp, and the Bank of America.[8]

A narco-economy is not a product of capital flight, in which capital leaves the country, because the profits accumulated from the drug trade are too high and ongoing. The black-market peso exchange in Colombia's narco-economy assists in the elimination of the nation's trade deficit.[9] Raymond W. Kelly, a former U.S. Customs Commissioner and currently New York City Police Commissioner, suggests this underground money market "is the ultimate nexus between crime and commerce, using global trade to mask global money-laundering."[10] Leading Fortune 500 companies benefit directly and indirectly, and some dealings of American corporations have been exposed through the U.S. government's anti-laundering probes.[11] One case involved Philip Morris, which was found to have laundered $40 million in Colombian black-market pesos in 1995. That case was closed without prosecution. Three years later, and again in 2000, Philip Morris was accused of smuggling Marlboro cigarettes into Colombia that had been purchased with black-market pesos. Another company involved in dubious dealings in Colombia was Bell Helicopter Textron, which had been a contractor for Plan Colombia. In August 2000, Panamanian officials impounded a helicopter belonging to Victor Carranza, a Colombian property owner and paramilitary leader.[12] The helicopter was purchased from Bell Helicopter Textron with the proceeds from a major cocaine and heroin operation. Only $335,800 was seized from Bell's accounts in the Chase Manhattan Bank. The narco-bourgeoisie can exchange U.S. dollars for Colombian pesos, buy American goods for sale back home that, according to U.S. federal officials, are worth approximately $5 billion a year, and can direct billions of dollars in narco-capital into legitimate commerce and trade.[13] According to Mike Wald, who runs a consortium of law enforcement agencies in Florida, "This is positive for U.S. business, there is no doubt about it. The Colombian *comprador*, if he pays less for his dollars, can buy more goods. That's a pretty obvious economic fact."[14] This demonstrates how the Colombian cocaine trade is linked to the U.S. economy in more diverse ways, and not simply limited to money-laundering activities involving American banks. The U.S.-Colombian mutual dependency on the cocaine market and its profits is intrinsic to the continuous operation of the cocaine trade.

The post-cartel system amalgamated Colombia's narco-economy and the cocaine trade with the corporate world in Colombia and the United States. The narco-bourgeoisie's access to the global market ensured that the Colombian narco-economy now intersected with global drug production and trade. The global drug trade is a "self-generating engine" of economic growth shaping the international economy, despite drug seizures and interdiction measures, according to a United Nations report, which also states: "Drug traffickers introduce new products into an untapped market, buyers are found, and once users become addicted, a minimum level of demand is virtually guaranteed."[15] The drug trade "has been characterized by a trend toward globalization and proliferation of trafficking routes."[16]

A Cocaine Mode of Production, Exchange, and Distribution

The decentralization of the cocaine trade brought a division of labor in production and distribution, from poor peasants selling coca leaves and paste to skilled professionals working as chemists, financial advisers, lawyers, managers, security and intelligence personnel, transporters and distributors, entrepreneurs and investors—in Colombia and the United States who specialized in only one aspect of the cocaine industry—for example, chemical diversion, communications, sales, marketing, finance, shipping, aviation, information technology, and distribution. In this way, no one individual enterprise could dominate the drug trade as the cartel had in the past. These new methods of organization and operation concealed the economic relations between the narco-bourgeoisie, the Colombian state, and U.S. corporations.

Economic operations for cocaine today are in many ways similar to other modes of commodity production, such as the manufacture of electronics components in Asia that are then shipped off to the United States for the assembly line, or the way in which General Motors manufactures parts overseas then transports them back to the United States for assembly into automobiles. Whether manufacturing cars, computers, or narcotics, these enterprises comprise a complex organization with many departments and occupations.

In Colombia, the narco-bourgeoisie established their domination over the coca production process when they had first emerged, by consolidating their political base in areas where drug production was concentrated. They built a working relationship with the military in the regions of coca production to fight the increasing influence of the FARC. This opened the door for private clandestine armies that became an integral part of their security. This narco-military intelligence network defended the interests of the *compradores* and their organized crime contacts, and ensured the ongoing production of cocaine.[17]

Many drug traffickers like Carlos Castaño and Victor Carranza (of the Bell Helicopter case) became wealthy by imitating the narco-bourgeoisie, with vast land holdings in Middle Magdalena, Cesar, and surrounding areas. By the late 1990s, this institutionalizing process continued in the areas of Cordoba, Uraba, Middle Magdalena, Cesar, and Putumayo. In all cases of drug-trafficking activity, military personnel, police officers, and local officials worked in tandem with the narco-military network and were even listed on the payrolls of the *compradores'* businesses.[18] A Human Rights Watch report in 2001 revealed the payroll was based on rank: a captain received between $2,000 and $3,000 per month, a major $2,500 per month, and a lieutenant $1,500 per month.[19] The AUC alone had approximately eight thousand soldiers in the 1990s soaring to at least 30,000 in the mid 2000s with thirty aircraft (eleven of which are Cessnas), four shipping planes, fourteen military helicopters (including Black Hawks), one state-of-the-art military helicopter with emergency operations, and speedboats for water transportation.[20]

The AUC consists largely of mercenaries with military backgrounds or experience, with the remainder trained by the United States, Britain, or Israel. One of the largest cocaine-processing laboratory complexes is near Puerto Boyaca in the Boyaca department, an AUC base and special handling zone by the Magdalena River with the capacity to produce eight tons of cocaine per month. In 1999, the Colombian newspaper *El Tiempo* estimated that the cost of constructing this plant was approximately $5 million with the potential to employ well over one hundred workers.[21] The AUC controls the strategic drug-trafficking route from Santander, passing by Middle Magdalena, and reaching the Panama border on the Gulf of Uraba. It is estimated that the AUC's annual net income (as cocaine is not taxed) from protecting economic operations is $75 million, which is approximately 80 percent of the group's total income.[22] The narco-military network operates cocaine-processing plants in Aguachica, Rio Negro, Cimitarra, and Puerto Parra, which are all in Middle Magdalena, and is aided by the narco-bourgeoisie's investments in properties, ranches, and resorts in rural areas.[23] Real estate has become an effective method of circulating drug money within the narco-economy: 4.4 million hectares, with an estimated value of $2.4 billion, have been purchased by the narco-bourgeoisie, which throughout the narco-cartel system period up until the new millennium earned approximately $23 billion in cocaine profits.[24] In 2003 the narco-bourgeoisie had acquired approximately 18 million hectares for coca cultivation.[25]

The AUC, instrumental to the trafficking of cocaine, controls the coastal region from which cocaine is exported. Jeff Brunner, a DEA supervisor in Colombia in 2004, claimed traditional drug lords still existed but they had to work with the AUC if they wanted to ship their drugs to the United States, Europe, or Africa.[26] The DEA estimated that Colombia's net coca cultivation more than tripled from 50,000 hectares in 1995 to 169,800 hectares in 2001. At the same time, cultivation in Peru and Bolivia was believed to have declined. Colombia's coca cultivation increase marked the eighth consecutive year of net growth for that premier cash crop.[27]

In 1995, Colombia produced only about 25 percent of the world's cocaine base product. Colombian traffickers were dependent on Peruvian and Bolivian sources for two-thirds of their base product, which amounted to hundreds of tons imported each year by aircraft from Peru and Bolivia. In 2001, Colombia's total land area under coca cultivation was three times the size of that used to grow the combined Peru-Bolivia crop. In terms of potential cocaine base product export, Colombia's production had increased 217 percent, from 230 metric tons in 1995 to 730 metric tons in 2001. Colombia accounted for 76 percent of the world's cocaine base production in 2001, marking a turning point for Colombian cocaine production as traffickers switched to relying more on Colombian rather than Peruvian or Bolivian sources for their cocaine base supply (see Figure 1).[28] Almost a decade later total Colombian cocaine output remained steady, producing 600 metric tons a year despite dramatic "success stories" in coca eradication.[29]

Technology, Globalization and the Colombian Cocaine Trade

Technological developments in communications, finance, transportation, and distribution have meant that the ramifications of Colombia's cocaine industry extend well beyond the borders of Colombia. The lucrative and dynamic cocaine industry has not merely provided the United States with a constant supply of cocaine, but it has presented profit-making opportunities for American banks, corporations, and investors through money-laundering, currency exchange, and more legitimate activities.

The 1994 discovery of a computer owned by members of the Cali cartel offered clues on the complexities of the system and illustrated the technological sophistication of Colombia's narco-economy. The computer was a $1.5 million IBM AS400 mainframe, networked with half a dozen terminals and monitors and six technicians overseeing its operations. The cartel had assembled a database that contained both the office and residential telephone numbers of U.S. diplomats and agents based in Colombia, along with the entire call log for the phone company in Cali. Custom-written data-mining software cross-referenced the Cali phone exchange's traffic with the phone numbers of American personnel and Colombian intelligence and law enforcement officials. The computer was seized and taken back to the United States for a forensic examination by the DEA,[30] which never released the results of that examination. Officials at the U.S. embassy in Colombia have not commented, and the DEA in Washington does

Figure 1: Andean Cocaine Production (figures are in metric tons)

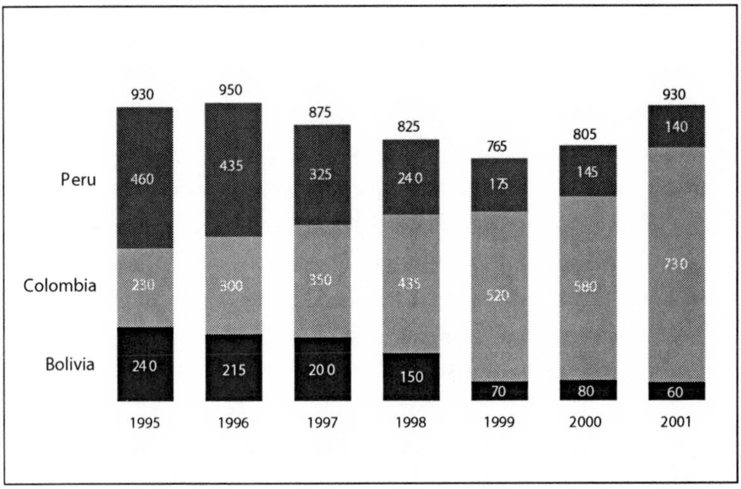

	1995	1996	1997	1998	1999	2000	2001
Total	930	950	875	825	765	805	930
Peru	460	435	325	240	175	145	140
Colombia	230	300	350	435	520	580	730
Bolivia	240	215	200	150	70	80	60

Source: "Changing Dynamics of Cocaine Production in the Andean Region," DEA, Drug Intelligence Brief, June 2002.

not confirm or deny the incident. The Colombian government denies any knowledge of the computer,[31] which was set up by a retired Colombian army intelligence officer.[32] The Colombian government had established a toll-free hotline for information about the Cali cartel leaders, but a former high-ranking DEA official said: "All of these anonymous callers were immediately identified, and they were killed," including informants within the Cali cartel. Another high-level DEA official stated: "It is very reasonable to assume that people were killed as a result of this capability. Potential sources of information were compromised by the system."[33]

Advanced communications encryption technologies are used in drug-related economic operations. The Internet is used to camouflage the movement of illegal money through international financial markets. Traffickers track radar sweeps of drug-surveillance planes and map out gaps in coverage to avoid detection. Fleets of submarines, mini-subs, and semi-submersibles are also used to transport drugs, often to cargo ships that haul hazardous waste, within which insulated bales of cocaine can be concealed. Much of the high-technology equipment used in finance, communications, transportation, and distribution is American-made and many of the technicians have been trained in the United States.[34]

In 2003, a former Colombian army general, Gabriel Ramon Diaz, reported that DEA and Colombian police agents were involved in the murders of two informants in a case involving two tons of cocaine. A U.S. embassy spokesperson immediately issued a statement: "The DEA is in no way involved in any illegal activities." Diaz, who had been blamed but not charged for the disappearance of the cocaine shipment, was removed from his post by President Alvaro Uribe. The *Miami Herald* reported that:

> [Diaz] has claimed that he delivered to the DEA office at the U.S. Embassy in Bogotá three informants who had approached him with information about a local drug trafficking cartel in Barranquilla. Based on the informants' tips, Colombian police intercepted a truck in Barranquilla in August 2002 containing the two tons of cocaine. But the shipment, with a U.S. street value of $40 million, was later returned to the smugglers. Two of the informants were later murdered.[35]

Seven police officers were arrested in relation to the case, and eighteen were fired in the wake of the ensuing scandal. However, the case was finally dismissed.

The shared use of intelligence system technology may be seen as evidence of the broader narco-military network comprising police, military, intelligence, and high-profile traffickers.[36] According to a top special operations commander in 2001, a Bell helicopter used for the government's coca fumigation programs was also used by members of the Henao-Montoya cocaine trafficking organization for an attempted assassination. They sought to target an imprisoned rival trafficker, using the helicopter to drop a bomb on the jail where the trafficker was held, but the bomb failed to explode.

The profitability of the $80 billion per year cocaine trade poses some challenges. The Internet has concealed the source of such vast sums of illegal money, as well as presented opportunities for the laundering of drug profits through online investments in legitimate corporations. According to an unnamed veteran Treasury Department investigator, password-protected websites are used to update the daily inventory of U.S. currency available from drug distributors across America.[37] In business-to-business exchanges, the websites allow stockbrokers to bid on the black-market funds for traffickers who want to convert the dollars to Colombian pesos to use for their operations at home. A trafficker can bid on different rates; for instance, what he can sell for $1 million in cash in Miami is the equivalent of approximately $800,000 in Colombian pesos. The annual turnover from this online finance was estimated to be worth $3 billion in 2003.[38]

Information technology specialists from legitimate local businesses are also involved in providing technological support to Colombia's traffickers and cocaine profiteers. A number of retired electronic experts with experience in military technology or special operations units in the United States, Israel, and elsewhere have been given contracts in Colombia. At the same time, the narco-bourgeoisie has members of their own families attending top U.S. engineering and aeronautical schools.[39] Most of the technology used directly or indirectly in the cocaine trade comes from famous American multinational companies such as IBM, Motorola, and Cisco Systems and front companies owned by traffickers are used to purchase equipment from sales offices in Colombia or through a series of intermediaries operating in the United States.[40]

The network command center of the AUC-linked Henao-Montoya organization was hidden in a Bogotá warehouse with up to twenty computers networked with servers and a relatively small mainframe. The command center of that particular enterprise was outfitted with a retractable German-made Rhode & Schwarz transmission antenna approximately forty feet high. Seized invoices and letters show that the organization had bought $100,000 of Motorola (MOT) gear, twelve base stations, sixteen mobile stations installed in trucks and cars, fifty radio phones, and eight repeaters that boost radio signals over long distances. The range of Colombia's network extends across the Caribbean and into the upper half of South America. According to one intelligence official, Henao-Montoya transmitted one thousand messages per day and not one of them was intercepted by U.S. spy planes. When messages are typed into computers, they create a digital bitstream that is encrypted and fed through a converter that parcels the data out at high frequencies. Digital communications over a radio network can be put into a code much more easily than voice transmissions and are far more difficult to intercept and decipher.[41] Colombian intelligence officials say that communications have never been intercepted.[42]

By sea or air, fleets and vessels today still need to dodge surveillance such as the P3 Orion aircraft used by the U.S. Customs and Border Protection (CBP) service. Bribing officials and drawing on an elaborate counterintelligence database seem to be outdated. According to an anonymous retired narcotics operative in the U.S. Army's Southern Command, Colombian pilots routinely map the radar coverage of U.S. spy planes by putting "Fuzz Buster" radar detectors in their airplane cockpits and logging the hits. The traffickers use every piece of data to build a picture of the radar signature, much like a jigsaw puzzle, to avoid detection. They continually upgrade their technology based on the latest advances in communications and encryption gear.[43]

In addition to surveillance and encryption technology, submarines have been used by drug-trafficking organizations for at least two decades. The Cali cartel purchased a Soviet Tango-class diesel submarine in the early 1990s.[44] Italian engineers, after overseeing the construction of the Colombian navy's fleet of commando submarines, helped to build submarines for use in the trafficking of cocaine.[45]

The FARC and the Production of Coca and Cocaine Today

Colombia has been experiencing a civil war for more than half a century. What had begun as a mission of the Colombian army, backed by the United States, to attack and destroy peasant-based subsistence communities in the southern mountains of Colombia, evolved into a high-intensity conflict. The principal forces in this conflict are the FARC and the Colombian state backed by the United States. Many analysts from a variety of disciplines contend that the FARC deserves serious examination as a powerful political and military force in Colombia.[46] The FARC, Latin America's largest and longest-running insurgency since the Mexican revolution, aims to overthrow the Colombian government.

Colombia's central role in the cocaine trade has elevated a decades-old civil conflict into a possible regional conflict that challenges United States control of the hemisphere.[47] Throughout Colombia's civil war, more than half of Colombian territory has been contested by the FARC. Apart from the common source of funds collected by this insurgent group, which includes membership fees, donations, and the sale of music, art, literature, and films produced by the organization, the FARC funds its military wing through extortion of the Colombian ruling class, kidnapping members of the Colombian government for ransom or prisoner exchanges, bank robberies (especially the Agrarian Bank, Caja Agraria, defunct since 1999), and cattle rustling on *comprador* land. The FARC is allegedly also involved in drug-trafficking activities.[48]

Given the sophistication and secrecy involved in the political economy of cocaine, the FARC's alleged involvement in drug trafficking is an intensely political issue. The claim of extensive FARC involvement has been rejected by a number of authoritative sources. For example, a report produced by the Council on Hemispheric Affairs found no evidence of FARC involvement in drug trafficking, but its main finding pointed to extensive drug smuggling to the United States by "right-wing paramilitary groups in collaboration with wealthy drug barons, the armed forces, key financial figures and senior government bureaucrats."[49] According to the DEA, which played at least a compliant if not complicit role with the CIA in drug trafficking during the cocaine decade, FARC involvement in the drug trade mainly involves the taxation of coca, which does not involve cocaine manufacturing, trafficking, and transshipment. Congressional testimony by James

Milford, a former deputy administrator of the DEA, indicates that there is little to support the drug-trafficking claim: "The FARC controls certain areas of Colombia and the FARC in those regions generate revenue by taxing local drug related activities."[50] This position is confirmed by Klaus Nyholm, the director of the United Nations Drug Control Program (UNDCP), which has agents throughout the drug-producing regions. He argues that local FARC fronts are "quite autonomous," and in some areas "they are not involved at all" in coca production (which is not cocaine production), and in others "they actually tell the farmers not to grow coca."[51] Ricardo Vargas of the Transnational Institute (TNI), an independent research center that specializes in drug issues in Colombia, describes the role of the FARC as "primarily focused on the taxation of illicit crops," and says that the guerrillas have long called for a development plan for the peasants that would "allow eradication of coca on the basis of alternative crops."[52]

The punitive approach of the United States to the problem of the drug industry in Latin America has fostered a new form of cultural imperialism on the continent.[53] Despite recognition of the significant cultural, historical, and economic differences between the production of coca as opposed to cocaine, much of the literature and popular commentary on the FARC continues to focus upon the group's alleged drug trafficking and terrorism.[54] Those allegations underpin the U.S. role in contemporary Colombia, and in the context of the war on drugs and war on terror, the United States has backed the Colombian state in its war on the FARC. The Colombian narco-bourgeoisie, at the profit end of the cocaine commodity chain, is also determined to defend its political and economic interests through a counterinsurgency strategy, that involves the use of paramilitary organizations.[55]

The existence of the FARC has complicated and, in some cases, constrained the production of coca in rural areas of Colombia. For the FARC campesino, their *raison d'être* is not to get rich from coca. The narco-bourgeoisie view the FARC as an obstacle to their source of wealth and, more critically, a threat to their existence as a class. In contrast to the Central American Peace Accords of the 1980s that demobilized guerrilla movements, the FARC continues to wage its long strug-

gle with the support of the poor peasantry, which relies on coca cultivation for their subsistence. If the FARC did not exist, the potential for
coca's exploitation for cocaine production would be unbounded.
The FARC maintains that only armed struggle can overthrow
Colombian capitalism and defeat U.S. imperialism. While the end of
the Cold War and the demise of the Soviet Union were widely interpreted as the death of communism, these events did not weaken the
resolve of the FARC-led insurgency in Colombia.[56] The chief commandant of the FARC, Manuel Marulanda Velez, criticized the Soviet
leadership for its inefficient bureaucracy and its isolation from the
people: "Many revolutionaries with weak ideological foundations
and convictions came to believe the socialist ideal of building a more
just and humane society was truly a utopia with no historical standing, as the imperialist propaganda claimed."[57] According to the
FARC, "What finally happened was the surrender of the achievements of socialism that gave human life more dignity by guaranteeing
employment, housing, health care, education, etc., to the unlimited
voracity of savage capitalism."[58] At the end of the Cold War in 1989,
Marulanda issued a statement surrounding the dramatic events in
the former eastern bloc:

> The music about the collapse of socialism has been used to demand
> the Colombian guerrilla movement to surrender its arms and become
> part of civilian life. This is what M-19, the EPL, the Quintin Lame
> and the PRT did, agreeing with the government to unconditionally
> demobilize, thinking that the armed struggle had lost its validity.
> They forgot the extremely grave problems which affect the country
> and which were not solved by their demobilization. On the contrary,
> the situation in which we are living, far from having improved, has
> been deteriorating and at the rate we are going, things will get much
> worse due to the political, economic, social and cultural crisis. The
> validity of the armed struggle is not determined by whether the Berlin
> Wall fell or not; it is determined by the reality of our country and
> here, the political, economic and social disequilibrium and the state
> violence that impelled the rebellion, continue in place.[59]

Although both conservatives and liberals in the United States seemed to agree in 1989 that communism was dead, this was not the case.[60] Michael Radu, co-chairman of the U.S. Foreign Policy Research Institute's (FPRI) Center on Terrorism, Counter-Terrorism, and Homeland Security, argued that "Marxism-Leninism is far from dead in Latin America, regardless of its fate elsewhere." Radu concluded it is politically inaccurate to think otherwise, because the politics of the Latin American left have not always mirrored their Western European and American counterparts.[61]

The FARC understood that adjustments were needed to wage their armed struggle against the Colombian state. Their socialist program, Movimiento Bolivariano por la Nueva Colombia (Bolivarian Movement for the New Colombia), was inspired by Simon Bolivar, the leader of the struggle for South American independence from Spanish rule.[62] The FARC adapted tactics of the popular guerrilla warfare waged in Central America and neighboring Peru.[63] By constructing solid bases of support in rural and urban areas and tapping into revenues obtained by exploiting primary commodities, the FARC resisted absorption into the Colombian economic system, a phenomenon identified by a World Bank study on the growth of rebel movements in the third world.[64] The FARC forged an alliance between the Colombian campesinos, or poor peasantry, and the urban working class, as well as incorporating indigenous peoples into the organization's rank and file. The FARC opened diplomatic channels with the international community, the European Union, NGOs, and other participants to raise awareness of the social and political realities of Colombia. In response to the worsening poverty among agrarian communities in Colombia, the FARC established a frontier survival program of agricultural production. Coca began to play a significant role as a means of subsistence for the peasantry, and this has had consequences for all sides of the Colombian conflict.

The Role of Coca in the Conflict

In spite of the narco-bourgeoisie's sophisticated cocaine production and distribution systems, the growing of the fundamental ingredient, the coca leaf, has been complicated by the presence of the FARC in the Colombian countryside. Indeed, the FARC is considered an intractable problem for a Colombian state and economy fortified by the cocaine industry and its profits.

The FARC's struggle is waged in an unwelcoming terrain of mountains and jungle that overlooks Colombia in its entirety favoring guerrilla war. Figures that indicate the size of FARC controlled territory are increasingly outdated or unreliable; however in the late 1990s the insurgency was the dominant political force in 1,050 municipalities across Colombia, which included rural areas without coca cultivation.[65] The export of cocaine is worth from $4 to $25 billion a year, according to widely varying estimates.[66] A Putumayo mayor downplayed the role of coca in the insurgency: "The guerrillas will be just as strong without coca. They can increase kidnapping and extortion to support themselves [and] they're powerful in many parts of the country that don't have any coca."[67] Evidence shows that the FARC taxes only six-tenths of a percent from peasants who have no choice but to grow coca for their subsistence.[68] Another source estimates that no more than 2.5 percent of all coca cultivation in the country is indirectly connected to the insurgents by such means as taxation.[69] The taxation system introduced by the FARC not only reduces the profits of the narco-bourgeoisie, but has made coca cultivation a focal point in the conflict between the FARC rebels and a Colombian state benefiting from the cocaine trade.

Throughout the cocaine decade, members of the narco-bourgeoisie—the cartels, high-ranking military officers, and paramilitary leaders—bought land close to areas controlled by the FARC to drive them off and kill their support base. This counterinsurgency strategy has been contested both militarily and economically, with taxes on coca and traffickers, by the FARC rebels. When territory is captured by the FARC insurgents the narco-bourgeoisie is driven out, and Colombian land and resources are exploited for the insurgent cause.

By depicting the FARC as a major drug-trafficking organization, the United States and Colombia capitalize on the conflicting forces involved in cocaine production, between rebel-held zones and the rest of Colombia where coca is also cultivated in the hope it will corrupt the insurgency. Yet, if the FARC dominated the multibillion-dollar cocaine trade in any way, it could not be in conflict with needed contacts within the Colombian establishment and the United States. Donnie Marshall, the head of the DEA under President George W. Bush, presented the agency's view on the role of cocaine in the conflict:

> The most recent DEA reporting indicates that some FARC units in southern Colombia are indeed involved in drug trafficking activities, such as controlling local cocaine base markets. Some insurgent units have assisted drug trafficking groups in transporting and storing cocaine and marijuana within Colombia. In particular, some insurgent units protect clandestine airstrips in southern Colombia. However, despite the fact that uncorroborated information from other law enforcement agencies does indicate a nexus between certain traffickers and the FARC, there is no evidence that any FARC or ELN units have established international transportation, wholesale distribution, or drug money-laundering networks in the United States or Europe.[70]

The eventual domination of coca in much of rural Colombia is part of the FARC's resistance to U.S. imperialism. Colombia's cocaine decade coincided with a period of intensified political activity on behalf of the United States via MAS, the first paramilitary wing of the narcostate, and the CIA. This political activity involved the assassination of five thousand activists and leaders, including two presidential candidates, when the Union Patriotica (UP) and sectors of the Colombian left signed a peace pact with the government to engage in electoral politics.[71] The FARC contends that only the legalization of drug consumption and a plan of eradication and development of alternative crops can eliminate the drug trade, and only armed struggle can overthrow Colombian capitalism, which the United States aims to prevent.[72]

In response to a deepening civil war, the FARC expanded and reorganized its guerrilla forces. A military academy was established to prepare guerrilla fighters, with a chain of command comparable to that of a regular army.[73] The FARC army, complete with an armament, command, control, and communications system, moved its zone of operations closer to middle-sized cities and areas of natural resources like oil, gold, coal, and emeralds.[74] By the new millennium, the FARC had eighteen thousand fighters on sixty fronts and had built support bases in the *barrios* across the country that brought the total to at least thirty thousand fighters. The numbers of militant supporters in Bogotá alone were estimated to be between two thousand and two thousand five hundred and between four thousand and six thousand nationwide.[75] At its peak from the late 1990s to the mid-2000s the FARC numbered between 40,000 and 50,000 fighters.[76] The stated objective of the FARC was to create a strong economic infrastructure to wage war against the Colombian state. The coca plantations in rebel-held territories became the sole source of economic survival for more than a million peasants and landless workers.[77] Support for the FARC grew as the guerrillas protected the peasants who earned a living from the coca cash crop, which campesinos also use to make tea called coca *maté* and has been chewed for centuries by Indians. Coca sold at an average of $1.50 per kilogram, far more than coffee, Colombia's traditional agricultural export, or any other crop.[78] The FARC forced drug merchants and drug traffickers to pay the peasants and rural laborers the estimated market price for coca leaves and coca paste. Law 002 was created by the FARC to force any Colombians with more than one million dollars to hand over 10 percent of their income.[79] Targeting the cocaine trade assisted the FARC to finance its guerrilla war against U.S. narco-colonialism.

Toward Dual Power?

Since the turn of the millennium, the struggle within Colombia framed by the cocaine drug trade has created the possibility of a revolutionary situation of dual power; the incumbent government has been weakened in its claim to rule and another government refuses to disappear.[80] Certainly, the FARC represents a powerful political, economic, and military force in the country; however, dual power has not emerged thus far. Historically, Colombia has been a country reliant on its rich natural resources. Since the time of Spanish colonialism, Colombia's land has been concentrated in the hands of the country's oligarchy. The emergence of the FARC insurgency is linked to the fact that the ownership and control of land in Colombia remains in their hands.

According to Thomas Marks, active Maoist-oriented insurgent groups exist in Colombia, the Philippines, Nepal, and Turkey, among other places.[81] He maintains it is a mistake to overlook their political and military significance, as it confuses strategic Cold War victory with local operational circumstances. The FARC, he says, will remain largely "out there, out of sight, out of mind, patiently building an alternative society."[82] However, the FARC's potential to create a situation of dual power has been undermined and contradicted by the U.S. counterinsurgency aimed against them.

In the post–Cold War era, the United States has faced a world of increasing uncertainty and regional disorder.[83] In the contemporary political context, the FARC is free from the Cold War politics that dominated debate among revolutionary groups decades earlier, but is forced to be a resourceful and modern, self-reliant guerrilla army.[84] The "war on terror" pronounced by President George W. Bush has only intensified the Colombian conflict.

Colombia's oligarchy remains composed primarily of the *comprador* class in the cities and the landlord class in the countryside, and it has been unable to defeat the FARC. Many years of counterproductive politics by the Colombian ruling class has achieved a backward economy dependent on the export of cocaine, subjecting the working class and peasantry to greater economic exploitation and political repression. The paramilitary armies that once protected the *compradores* and their cocaine industry have been transformed into counterinsurgents, dependent on aid from the United States to wage their war against the FARC. War among the paramilitary forces and splits among the narco-bourgeoisie along political, ideological, and regional lines have weakened the power of the Colombian government. The FARC and the labor movement have capitalized on this weakness, despite U.S. capital injected into the country and the occasional encirclement of guerrillas by state forces. One such example was the Colombian military offensive in February 2002 on San Vicente Del Caguan in southern Colombia, which was controlled by the FARC. San Vicente Del Caguan was named the *zona de despeje*, or the demilitarized zone (DMZ), by the Colombian government of Andres Pastrana. The DMZ consisted of five municipalities where tens of thousands of workers and peasants lived and participated in its daily management.[85] The zone's capital, San Vicente Del Caguan, lay approximately 175 miles south of Bogotá at the headwaters of the Amazon River. Social progress was evident, with residents forming their own police force, which they named Policía Cívica (Civic Police). A new 250-kilometer highway was constructed, and another 250 kilometers of roads was repaired for the population; twenty bridges were constructed, connecting the rural population with the markets in town, which allowed trucks to deliver agricultural produce. San Vicente was paved free of mud and mire and the work was carried out with the participation of its population. Villages were given electricity, virtually unknown prior to the FARC's involvement; schools and medical clinics were established and improved; massive vaccination campaigns were carried out with the participation of hospitals and pharmacies; cultural and sports activities were developed with local and foreign artists invited to present theater, dance, and music at the central square of San Vicente and in other communities of the zone.[86]

London's *Telegraph* described San Vicente Del Caguan as "FARClandia, the world's newest country," and the Western media rallied behind the U.S. government's portrayal of the zone as a safe haven for drug trafficking and terrorism.[87] On February 21, 2002, President Pastrana accused the FARC of running a lucrative drug-trafficking business from San Vicente and hiding kidnapping victims within the DMZ.[88] Under pressure by the United States, Pastrana ordered the Colombian military to invade the zone and the air force to bomb its communities. A-37 and A-47 aircraft supplied by the United States dropped bombs of up to 500 pounds followed by an incursion of 13,000 U.S.-trained Colombian troops.[89] According to the Colombian air force, several FARC camps, cocaine laboratories, stores, and airstrips were destroyed.[90] Anticipating bloodshed for the zone's population, the FARC ordered residents to evacuate and retreat to nearby mountain jungles where most of the guerrillas were located.[91]

The Colombian military offensive on San Vicente Del Caguan is comparable to the attack on Marquetalia, the principal rebel agrarian community, in 1964 for its attempts to build an alternative society. The decision by the Colombian government to carry out a military assault on San Vicente Del Caguan was based upon its growing frustration and dissatisfaction over the FARC's apparent popularity and territorial gains. Journalist and historian Forrest Hylton notes: "That the FARC's 'independent republic' in the south, human rights violations and all, was the safest region in Colombia by far, is a fact beyond dispute. The army and the paramilitaries, not the FARC, will displace most of the 100,000 people that live in the area."[92]

The *compradores'* paramilitary militias, stationed in northern Colombia, swiftly moved in to capture San Vicente Del Caguan for *limpieza* (social cleansing by killing). Colombia's southern plains were sparsely populated by mostly indigenous groups until the 1960s and 1970s, but conflict and unequal landholdings pushed a wave of settlers to this agricultural frontier.[93] For the narco-bourgeoisie, it was important to regain control of this zone because small-scale coca cultivation hindered expansion of large-scale coca estates in the style of those in northern Colombia.[94] Therefore, this invasion was a continuation of the counterinsurgency strategy of driving landless peasants away with force for the *compradores'* vast landholdings.

The Colombian state's invasion of San Vicente Del Caguan in 2002 forced the FARC to melt into the jungles and towns across the country. The guerrillas' insurgency strategy grew more clandestine. Some moved into the urban areas, while others maintained the FARC's traditional stronghold in the rural areas. Although the guerrillas continued to construct solid bases of support, the counterinsurgency strategy of the *compradores* was undermined by labeling the FARC as narco-terrorists and seeking a military solution to what is essentially a social crisis created by a civil war. In Colombia in 2001, 80.5 percent of people in the countryside lived below the poverty line (up from 65 percent in 1993) and more than 33 percent of the rural population was living in extreme poverty.[95] In 2003, 67 percent of the entire Colombian population lived below the poverty line with an unemployment rate of 22 percent.[96] In a country whose perception of the United States was the least anti-American in Latin America, according to a BBC World Survey, an increasing number of Colombians have come to question whether the policy of "peace with social justice" as proposed by the FARC is a better solution to the nation's unresolved land dispute than the United States' influence in the Colombian government, which is driving the country further into war.[97]

Colombia is divided geographically, in effect making two Colombias. One is west of the Cordillera Oriental, which is the high country. It is there that the country's productive forces are concentrated. The other, east of the Andes, the Ilanos, is savannah, vast plains, and the Amazon jungle. More than 95 percent of the populace live in the high country. The other 5 percent and key insurgent formations are in the second zone. The FARC has searched for a mass base, and after many years of resistance, has found one, sustaining their *foco* (center) by exploiting Colombia's resources and managing them for political ends. The FARC stands out from all other insurgencies in the world for endurance and pragmatism in waging its struggle with sophisticated methods of guerrilla warfare. The FARC is a Marxist-Leninist movement modeled on third-world liberation struggles in Southeast Asia, Africa, and Latin America. The FARC has learned from past guerrilla achievements and failures due to its critical, practical, yet technical praxis. Not only has the number of FARC combatants increased a hundred-fold since its founding in the early 1960s, but the administrative and physical infrastructures built and lost for its constituents have enabled the FARC to fight for dual power. In areas of guerrilla control, the Colombian state can no longer destroy communities with impunity, as it did in Marquetalia in 1964 or San

Vicente Del Caguan in 2002, unless it is prepared for a long and costly fight. Instead, the state has relied upon selective assassinations to attack the FARC. Yet despite their advances in an insurgent war, the FARC have not brought an end to the power of the Colombian state.

Class Struggle

Unlike Pablo Escobar, who, as a member of the narco-bourgeoisie, sought to control the Colombian narco-economy and thus was liquidated, the FARC has become a target of the state not for its role in the drug trade but for waging a class struggle. The issue is not whether the FARC should be benefitting from the drug trade but how would it affect the Colombian conflict if they simply abandoned their political demands once and for all. The issue for the *compradores* is to ensure that coca production will serve their cocaine profiteering and not the FARC's insurgency. The price of cocaine is determined by its supply and production. The retail price for cocaine (as well as heroin) in the United States was at a record low at the beginning of the twenty-first century.[98] According to the Washington Office on Latin America, the price fell every year since 2000, settling at an all-time low in the first half of 2003: $37.96 per gram before the 2008 spike in the wake of the global financial crisis.[99]

Throughout the 2000s, the FARC expanded its base in the llanos, Putumayo, Guaviare, Meta, and Caqueta. Collecting taxes is the job of the guerrillas in their zones of control, which now consist of villages, municipalities, and regions in ephemeral clandestine form. The FARC channels funds to its fighting forces, as well as to vocational schools, public health and environmental protection resources, and to road paving in the midst of war. Political scientist Nazih Richani notes:

> The guerrillas play another important role in areas where they exercise influence or can project its influence: they cite public officials for corruption and force them to reinvest in public work. Governors, local council members, *alcaldes* (mayors), and even senators have

been subject to guerrilla justice, which might include assassination (revolutionary execution) of the person implicated. Citing public officials for corruption by *los muchachos* ("the guys," as the guerrillas are amicably called) is generally well received in communities.[100]

The guerrillas have been known to force employers to provide work and better pay for the townspeople, even threatening to burn down their premises or kidnap the owners.[101] In many municipalities in these areas, the only authority beyond the symbolic police station is that of the FARC, which makes them sole providers of essential public services.[102]

The FARC has been able to recruit members and maintain numerous bases, some which may still virtually encircle Bogotá and other key cities, as well as consolidate its power base in the Cordillera Oriental, the eastern mountain range of the Andes which has been held since the mid 1990s. In the Alto Naya, nearly all of the guerrilla fighters have been Indians from the mountains that run north-south, on the eastern side of the Cordillera Central, which is farther west of the Cordillera Oriental.[103] In the mountains, the narco-bourgeoisie have waged a war against the indigenous groups, while pursuing a continual war against the peasantry. In response, the FARC has fought for its military presence in nine municipalities in Cundinamarca, primarily those adjacent to the department of Meta, a traditional FARC stronghold in central Colombia, as well as in the department of Boyaca within the Cordillera Oriental. This has created small or temporary situations of dual power at the local level, where the Colombian state is weakest. The Colombian government has been destabilized by the FARC's extraction of money from landlords, cattle ranchers, drug traffickers, and multinational corporations, which include Westinghouse, Occidental Oil, British Petroleum, Merielectric, and TPL.[104] According to Richani's field study, these corporations have been involved with the guerrillas for local projects and social investment.[105] The narco-bourgeoisie have responded by contracting private security firms to work alongside their paramilitary militias for *"limpieza"* killings.[106] In the urban areas, this polarization of the conflict between rich and poor has drawn socially marginalized groups—the homeless, street vendors, prostitutes, homosexuals, drug addicts, street children, and garbage pickers—into supporting or joining the guerrillas.[107] Remaining marginalized groups have been coerced into the state's network of spies, collaborators, and killers set up under Alvaro Uribe Velez.[108] Since 2005, 173,183 political assassinations targeting leftists have been carried out.[109]

The FARC's insurgency strategy demonstrates a political commitment to its constituency in rebel-held areas. The FARC has coerced taxes from private and public enterprises of the elite and it actively supports the labor movement in Colombia.[110] Evidence of "greater involvement" in the drug trade meant an intensification of the class war as coca spread to all areas of the country not just in Southern Colombia. The FARC's strategic war plans were designed to achieve two main objectives: 1) to move the war closer to urban centers and intermediate cities, and 2) to exert political pressure on the state and the ruling class to fund their cause.[111] To reverse the FARC's achievements, the Colombian ruling class and agents of U.S. imperialism sought a plan that, paradoxically, would intensify the counterinsurgency against the FARC and exponentially increase the supply of cocaine from Colombia.

6. The United States and "Plan Colombia"

In 2000, President Bill Clinton authorized "Plan Colombia," a $1.3 billion U.S. package for the war on drugs with military assistance that included helicopters, planes, and training, a massive chemical and biological warfare effort, and electronic surveillance technology.[1] The total budget for Plan Colombia was $7.5 billion, of which the Colombian government originally pledged $4 billion, the United States $1.3 billion, and the European Union and other countries $2.2 billion.[2]

The original version of Plan Colombia was initiated by then-president Andres Pastrana, who argued that drug crops are "a social problem whose solution must pass through the solution to the armed conflict.... Developed countries should help us to implement some sort of 'Marshall Plan' for Colombia, which will allow us to develop great investments in the social field, in order to offer our peasants different alternatives to the illicit crops."[3] Pastrana's Plan Colombia did not focus on drug trafficking, military aid, or fumigation, but instead advocated the manual eradication of drug crops.[4] Under pressure by the Clinton administration, Pastrana saw that it was necessary to create an official document that specifically "served to convene important U.S. aid, as well as that of other countries and international organizations" by adequately addressing U.S. concerns, which were principally focused on the FARC insurgency.[5] As a result, the first formal draft of Plan Colombia was written in English; the Spanish version became available only months later, when a revised English version was already in place.[6] Clinton's version of Plan Colombia focused on drug trafficking and the strengthening of the Colombian military.[7] Former U.S. ambassador to Colombia Robert White stated:

> If you read the original Plan Colombia, not the one that was written in Washington but the original Plan Colombia, there's no mention of military drives against the FARC rebels. Quite the contrary. [President Pastrana] says the FARC is part of the history of Colombia and a historical phenomenon, he says, and they must be treated as Colombians. . . . [Colombia] comes and asks for bread and you [America] give them stones.[8]

Under the legal banner and drug policies of the Colombian plan, Clinton militarized the nation and financed the counterinsurgency with the political support of George Soros's organization, Human Rights Watch.[9] In 2001, President George W. Bush added $550 million, renaming it the "Andean Initiative."[10] Between 1996 and 2001, U.S. military aid to Colombia increased fifteen-fold, from $67 million to $1 billion.[11] During this same period, raw coca cultivation grew 150 percent, from 67,200 to 169,800 hectares (1 hectare = 2.471 acres).[12] A leaked Colombian government document of 2001 estimated that Colombia produced eight hundred to nine hundred tons of cocaine annually, not the 580 tons announced by the U.S. State Department and the DEA.[13] In 2004, President Alvaro Uribe Velez and the Bush administration negotiated an extension to Plan Colombia named Plan Colombia II, which was to last until 2009. During the negotiations, President Uribe extolled the advances achieved through the war on drugs and the war on terror, and asserted that U.S. capital injected into Colombia had succeeded in making Colombia a safer country.[14]

Plan Colombia has been maintained as an ongoing military program by successive White House administrations that aim to assist the

Colombian state to end the cocaine trade in Colombia and combat the influence of the FARC. Since 2000, U.S. military aid and training to Colombia has totaled just over $6.8 billion.[15] Initially there had been an organized resistance mounted against President Clinton's Plan Colombia by international activists, which resulted in limiting the number of U.S. troops and privately contracted forces to eight hundred (four hundred U.S. personnel and four hundred contracted personnel).[16] Despite this, Colombian cocaine remains a major illicit export, and the FARC insurgency has not been brought to an end.

After the terrorist attacks on the United States on September 11, 2001, George W. Bush and Colombian president Andrés Pastrana Arango intensified the armed campaign against the FARC insurgency's support base within the context of the global war on terror. In 2003, Bush and Colombian president Alvaro Uribe Velez launched an all-out offensive named "Plan Patriota," which imposed Uribe's "democratic security" measures, viewed by some as a legitimized campaign of state terror. In October 2002, reports were leaked indicating that U.S. special operations teams were on orders "to eliminate all high officers of the FARC" and "scattering those who escape to the remote corners of the Amazon," but the operation failed to force the FARC into strategic retreat or limit its military operations.[17]

During Uribe's presidency, coca production increased in Colombia and throughout the whole Crystal Triangle, with a rise in rates of return from U.S. capital investment.[18] Plan Colombia ushered in an era of mega-projects, massive U.S. and international investment in capital-intensive infrastructure such as pipelines, highways, and dams to exploit the country's natural resources, including oil and coal. In the countryside, land was cleared, and oil, wood, water, and cash crops extracted. Communities that had neighborhood beaches lost them to large hotels. In major cities, a desperate, repressed, and impoverished working class and peasantry were forced to live on starvation wages, without protections or services.[19] Neoliberal legislation enacted by President Uribe included Law 71 of 1988, which privatized pension funds; Law 50 of 1990, which dismantled labor laws and protections of workers' rights; and Law 100 of 1993, which privatized health care and social security. Consequently, in centers of coca crop production in Guaviare, Putumayo, and Caqueta, as much as 50 percent of Colombia's workforce was employed in the cocaine industry by 2002.[20] As described by *Fortune* magazine in 1988, the cocaine industry was "probably the fastest growing and unquestionably the most profitable" industry in the world.[21]

As Plan Colombia targeted the FARC, the narco-bourgeoisie concentrated within the cities of Bogotá, Medellín, Cali, and Barranquilla were protected by the Colombian state.[22] President Uribe supported the introduction of International Monetary Fund (IMF) structural adjustment programs, privatization, and Colombia's membership in the Free Trade Area of the Americas (FTAA) thereby strengthening the narco-economy.[23] Colombia's narco-economy has affected the nation in terms of savings, inflation, and employment. In 2002, public debt was close to 54 percent of the Gross National Product (GNP), but the threat of an Argentinean-style collapse was warded off by the strength and competitiveness of cocaine exports.[24] A 2002 UN report estimated the average wholesale price of cocaine for the new millennium per kilogram: United States $20,500 / Europe $38,000. At retail, per gram: United States $80 / Europe $70. These are average prices; prices vary in major cities and the quality of cocaine will also affect the price.[25]

The United States invests money in oil-rich countries for the purpose of exporting uninterrupted supplies of oil. The investment covers the costs of drilling, refining, distributing, servicing, and securing oilfields and pipelines. In areas of anti-imperialist resistance such as Afghanistan and Iraq, estimates for the total U.S. cost of protecting and securing oil reserves have reached a staggering $3.7 trillion.[26] However, the United States does not invest money in drug-rich countries for the purpose of exporting drugs. The cocaine business is for the shadows of the underworld, not daily market reports alongside legal stocks and commodities. The United States benefits from it nonetheless because most of the profits from the cocaine trade are invested in the United States, not Colombia. It is difficult to precisely calculate the value of Colombian cocaine revenues, which according to one study "differing methodologies of older studies and a lack of more recent scholarship" makes the task of estimating its real value to the Colombian economic system almost impossible.[27] Further, as an illegal business, the apparent secrecy of cocaine profits generated by Colombia's narco-economy remains its real strength. Conservatively, the total revenue for the commercial export of cocaine for Colombia in 2002 was $3.5 billion (close to the $3.75 billion made from oil and more than two and a half times the earnings made from coffee, whereas North America's gross revenue from sales to consumers was $11 billion.[28] Colombia's National Association of Financial Institutions (ANIF) estimated the nation's total 1999 income from the illegal drug trade to be $3.5 billion.[29] The ANIF estimate was based on an assumption that somewhat less than 10 percent of total earnings from illicit drug sales are repatriated to Colombia each year, and on reported total world retail sales of Colombian cocaine, heroin, and marijuana of $46 billion. Although the figures are based on a 1999 study, on these estimates it is possible to assume that Colombian drug earnings would be considerably higher today if current productive forces and relations of production are considered. One source estimates that U.S. gross revenue from cocaine sales reached up to $52.8 billion in 2003.[30]

U.S. investment in Colombia and its economic growth depends on the narco-bourgeoisie's access to and involvement in the global market that ties them to international capital flows and principally U.S. capital.[31] It is the *comprador* who organizes cocaine production locally and is financially linked to U.S. capital. However, the *comprador*'s relationship with the imperialists is not merely economic but also political.

The historical events in Latin America that facilitated the growth of the cocaine trade involved the ascendancy of military and civilian regimes committed to free-market policies, which made the institutionalization of the cocaine trade in Colombia all the more likely. Neoliberal policies had a profound impact on the Colombian economy and social structure, creating a powerful transnational class of businessmen and investors.[32] As Alfredo Rangel Suarez noted, "The

notorious frequency with which the [paramilitaries] situate themselves where drug dealers are active, or where there are mega-projects
such as hydroelectric dams or new highways pushing up land values,
indicates that behind paramilitarism there is something other than an
altruistic interest in counterinsurgency."[33]

To protect and secure its capital in Colombia, the United States
must promote and protect its agents of economic operations inside
Colombia, paramilitaries and state security forces who are connected to the counterinsurgency campaign. Further, to secure cocaine
for American markets, the narco-bourgeoisie must rely on large
sums of U.S. capital for a counterinsurgency effort dedicated to a
war on "drugs," "terrorism," or any other pretext to justify U.S. rul-
ing-class interests. Legitimizing spending on arms, equipment, and
training to fight the insurgency thus becomes a necessary function of
U.S. imperialism.

Behind the official discourse of fighting drugs and terrorism
there remains an agenda in Colombia that is no longer hidden: to
secure military victory over the FARC and eliminate obstacles to
U.S. and international investment in mega-projects for the efficient
exploitation of Colombia's rich natural resources.[34] Automated fac-
tories with no need for unskilled labor, many of them multinational,
have relocated to state-declared tax-free zones called "industrial
parks." These developments plunder natural and genetic resources:
gold, platinum, silver, bauxite, manganese, radioactive cobalt, zinc,
chrome, nickel, copper, exotic wood, and large fishing
resources.[35] Oil resources in Colombia are as enormous as cocaine.
Colombian *compradores* have pronounced, "We want to turn this
region into a giant enterprise!"[36]

To secure Colombia's resources for American markets, the police,
military, and paramilitary forces of the narco-military network have carried out U.S.-led counterinsurgency operations. As Figure 2 illustrates,
a re-colonization process to penetrate Colombia for cocaine exports was
cemented through Clinton's "Plan Colombia." It promoted the war on
FARC while it militarily secured coca production for the narco-bourgeoisie. Before the lead up to the global financial crisis in 2007, more

Figure 2: Colombian Coca: Eradicating plus Remaining

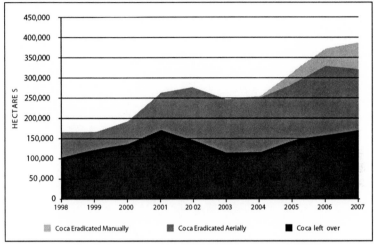

Source: U.S. government coca estimates; UNODC reporting on eradication levels.

coca had been grown in Colombia than at any other time in the nation's history. Since then, both the United Nations and the United States reported dramatic "declines" in coca cultivation of 18% in 2008 and 16% in 2009 halting in 2010 with increases in Bolivia and Peru.[37] The 2000s demonstrated the dynamics of cocaine production and "success stories" within the Crystal Triangle with Colombia at center stage.

A strategy to take control of territory strategically valuable to economic interests of the imperial-*comprador* partnership has been imperative since the cocaine decade in the face of the FARC's resistance.[37] Rebel strongholds of the FARC and Colombia's second-largest Marxist insurgency, the ELN, contest the counterinsurgency.[38] One displaced activist from the department of Choco explained in 2001, "It's simply a war about land and resources, and the people living in these lands happen to be in the way."[39] Paramilitary militias target not only guerrillas but also social, labor, popular, or peasant movements that dare to question the development of mega-projects and the consolidation of economic interests.[40] Resistance from the FARC would spell further retaliatory action from the narco-state.

7. Narco-State Terror

The AUC paramilitary death squads in Colombia are directly linked to the counterinsurgency strategy devised by Washington and Bogotá to combat the FARC rebels. However, the AUC is also an important component of Colombia's narco-military network. The FARC campaign has seen the Colombian state, backed by Washington, adopt a variety of measures to engage the guerrillas in direct and indirect warfare, and the civilian population is caught in the crossfire. In Colombia, the most significant decisions made by Bogotá in conjunction with Washington have been about what kind of war will be fought, a decision dictated by long-range goals, and about what kind of weapons will be used. This chapter examines the tactics and the weapons used by the Colombian state in its war against the FARC.

State Terror as a Political Instrument

Before Vietnam, counterinsurgency was a type of warfare devised under the Kennedy administration during the Cold War to neutralize insurgencies in the third world. A principal aspect of counterinsurgency strategy involved the physical separation of the local population from the guerrilla forces through political, military, and economic means. Counterinsurgency doctrine recognized that political, economic, and social reforms could be the foundation of an effective military strategy.[1] Theodore Shackley, a CIA veteran of covert operations in Southeast Asia and Latin America, described counterinsurgency strategy the "third option." It required not only cross-agency support and networking, but also recruiting anyone who might prove useful to a military campaign, such as corrupt military officers, right-wing groups, professional criminals, or drug traffickers.[2] According to Douglas Valentine, the tracking down of Che Guevara by the CIA in 1967 was a classic case of a covert intelligence operation utilizing drug trafficking, a Bolivian counter-narcotics unit, and the FBN, which later became the DEA.[3] In the twenty-first century, American counterinsurgency strategies have become more sophisticated due to advancements and innovations in military technology, particularly in relation to communications, surveillance, and other systems.[4]

A Secret Narco-Military Network

In 2004, President Alvaro Uribe Velez met with President George W. Bush in Washington to ask that the United States remove its limit on the number of U.S. service members and contractors in Colombia. Bush agreed to increase their numbers from four hundred U.S. military personnel, mostly Special Operations Forces, and another four hundred U.S. private military contractors to eight hundred and six hundred, respectively. This presidential decision changed the way covert operations had been conducted in the past, during the Cold War.[5]

Rather than working closely with the national military network, U.S. covert operation service members and contractors in the post–Cold War period are decentralized and carry out operations as privatized armies, which the U.S. military calls "special operations teams." Special units of land, sea, or air maintain a presence in Colombia and engage in various covert activities. Their covert operations are categorized as 1) direct action, 2) strategic reconnaissance, 3) unconventional warfare, 4) foreign internal defense, 5) civil affairs, 6) psychological operations, 7) counterterrorism, 8) humanitarian assistance, 9) theater search and rescue, and 10) activities "specified by the President or Secretary of Defense."[6]

The principal advisory and assistance unit in Colombia has been the 7th Special Forces Group, subordinate to the control of the U.S. Southern Command, SOUTHCOM, and the United States Army Special Operations Command (USASOC) at Fort Bragg.[7] MilGroup (in-country military group) is an advisory unit nominally under the control of the U.S. embassy in Bogotá. SOUTHCOM coordinates the deployments and missions of U.S.-based units in Latin America. MilGroup supervises and supports, USASOC provides the forces, SOUTHCOM coordinates, and MilGroup links these operations, maintaining a constant liaison with the Colombian military. Former AAA members within Colombian military command such as General Mario Montoya Uribe have worked closely with special operations personnel.[8] The CIA contingent in Colombia is based in the U.S. embassy in Bogotá and is in close contact with the U.S. ambassador, the U.S. Department of Defense (DOD), and the National Command Authority (NCA).[9] The latter consists of the U.S. president, vice president, secretary of defense, and national security advisor.

American special operations personnel assisting Colombian covert operations is top secret; however, the following incident carried the hallmarks of the narco-military network in action. On May 4, 2001, a bomb exploded outside the Cali hotel El Torre. Twenty people were wounded in the incident but no group claimed responsibility. This was followed by a month of other bombings in Medellín, Barancabermega, and Bogotá, close to the Universidad Nacional de Colombia, all following the same method. First, a small bomb explodes and a crowd gathers. Local police, explosives experts, and dog squads arrive. Then, a much larger bomb explodes, killing them.[10] The Colombian media adopted the official version of these events from military sources, which blamed FARC guerrillas for the attacks. Some variations of the story of these bombings were circulated, but there were only limited investigations of these incidents.[11] FARC members were blamed and presumed to be the killers.

Special operations teams have also targeted FARC sympathizers and supporters with bombings, kidnappings, and assassinations. These activities have created and maintained a climate of fear among the civilian population of Colombia. Those on the political left and trade union members are seen as rebels who are in opposition to the Colombian government. Trade unionists have been murdered, along with community activists, human rights campaigners, and church leaders. This form of secret state terror has become almost normalized in a Colombia that is geared for a situation of permanent civil war. The counterinsurgency methods deployed in Colombia have been taught since the 1960s at the notorious School of the Americas, now called the Western Hemisphere Institute for Security Cooperation (WHISC) in Fort Benning, Georgia.[12] Special operations agents, including former Green Berets, veterans from covert operations in Central America and the first Gulf War, mercenaries, private contractors, and active-duty Colombian military personnel, have all engaged Colombian guerrillas in direct combat.[13]

According to Stan Goff, a former U.S. Special Forces adviser to Colombian anti-narcotics batallions in the 1990s, the involvement of the United States in the Colombian conflict is not subject to official oversight. The U.S. role in Colombia is described as "private security," and is supported by the active, energetic, and highly sophisticated collaboration of the corporate media.[14] Roger Pardo-Maurer, former U.S. deputy assistant defense secretary for Western Hemisphere affairs contends that the teams were designed to increase the ability of Colombian units to turn intelligence into operations and to help the Colombian military bring the FARC to the negotiating table.[15]

Psychological Warfare

As has been done by governments in other regions of conflict, or "shatter zones," in the third world—Afghanistan, Iraq, Pakistan, and more recently across the Middle East—the Colombian government has enforced a "law of silence," aimed at neutralizing not only resistance or opposition to its repressive regime but to counter negative perceptions from the public with fear and compliance as a form of low-intensity conflict. The CIA terms psychological warfare (PSYWAR) and psychological operations (PSYOPS) are defined by the DOD as "the planned use of propaganda and other psychological actions having the primary purpose of influencing the opinions, emotions, attitudes, and behavior of hostile foreign groups in such a way as to support the achievement of national objectives."[16]

During the cocaine decade, U.S. counterinsurgency strategy took a new direction to low-intensity conflict.[17] Its planners had learned crucial lessons from mistakes committed in Indochina, one of which was the recognition of "Vietnam syndrome." The American public had been told that the war was winnable, and it was not. The consequence was that heavy U.S. casualties would not be tolerated by the people in any future conflict. Thus, in subsequent conflicts a greater focus was placed on the political delegitimization of the enemy, through the management of public opinion, both nationally and internationally. U.S. planners recognized that low-intensity conflict and PSYWAR could be crucial to the management of consent and central to overall victory.[18] Put simply, if popular support for the enemy was destroyed, victory could be achieved through constant "perception management," combined with military operations and state repression. The preface of a CIA manual prepared for the Nicaraguan Contras reflects this emphasis on the crucial importance of psychology in a conflict:

> Guerrilla warfare is essentially a political war. Therefore, its area of operations exceeds the territorial limits of conventional warfare, to penetrate the political entity itself: the "political animal" that Aristotle defined. In effect, the human should be considered the priority objective in a political war. And conceived as the military target of guerrilla war, the human being has his most critical point in his mind. Once his mind has been reached, the "political animal"

has been defeated, without necessarily receiving bullets. Guerrilla warfare is born and grows in the political environment; in the constant combat to dominate that area of political mentality that is inherent to all human beings and which collectively constitutes the "environment" in which guerrilla warfare moves, and which is where precisely its victory or failure is defined. This conception of guerrilla warfare as political war turns Psychological Operations into the decisive factor of the results. The target, then, is the minds of the population, all the populations: our troops, the enemy troops and the civilian population.[19]

From the late 1980s the Colombian state commenced efforts to manufacture its image as a defender of democracy at war with narco-terrorists. The state employed the services of the Sawyer/Miller Group, a leading public relations company in the United States to wage PSYWAR on Colombia's narco-terrorists, the FARC. In the first six months of 1991 alone, Sawyer/Miller earned almost a million dollars in manufacturing the left-wing narco-terrorist conspiracy against FARC.[20] David Meszaros, the director of Sawyer/Miller's Colombia account, then explained that "the main mission is to educate the American media about Colombia, get good coverage, and nurture contacts with journalists, columnists, and think tanks. The message is that there are 'bad' and 'good' people in Colombia and that the government is the good guy."[21] By the early 1990s the Sawyer/Miller Group had regularly used the American press to disseminate Colombian government propaganda, with the routine production of pamphlets, letters to editors signed by Colombian officials, and advertisements placed in the *New York Times* and *Washington Post*.[22]

Despite the propaganda about the FARC as narco-terrorists, in 2001 Colombian intelligence estimated that FARC controlled less than 2.5 percent of Colombia's cocaine exports, while the AUC controlled 40 percent, not counting the narco-bourgeoisie as a whole.[23] The ideological engineering through the media is consistent with the U.S. crusade in the Cold War against international communism. Sociologist James Brittain has argued:

Movements like the FARC-EP have embarrassed and de-legitimized the postmodernist argument of the end of ideology and the demise of Marxism by having subjectively proven that Marxism has not only continued throughout the past half-century, but has continued to thrive. Such ideological movements materially demonstrate that they are in struggle with ideological purpose and meaning. . . . The disturbing reality in this, however, is that by doing so [postmodernists] legitimize the current geopolitical construct of power, thus having one believe that they are unable to effect change.[24]

The U.S. war on drugs and terror have drawn Washington and the repressive Colombian regime closer in their campaign to combat the FARC insurgents ideologically and militarily. The consensus created by CIA propaganda views the FARC as narco-terrorists, which has accorded the Colombian government a significant degree of freedom to carry out attacks, and to detain and neutralize anyone within the civilian population it believes is an enemy. The state's task is made easier in this respect by the involvement of death squads and paramilitary forces and the assistance of professional criminals in carrying out selective operations against the Colombian population.[25]

In the struggle for state power, hegemony is contested in different ways in Colombia. At Puerto Boyaca, a paramilitary stronghold on the Magdalena River, a huge billboard reads "WELCOME TO THE ANTI-COMMUNIST CAPITAL OF COLOMBIA," reminding all visitors of the political significance of ideology in the conflict.[26] Members of the Colombian revolutionary left must remain anonymous or risk being arrested for subversion. Nevertheless, antigovernment political graffiti is visible, and criticism of the Colombian state is evident in anonymous Internet blogs and websites. In Colombian news broadcasts, Marxist guerrillas and trade unionists are blamed for every disorder, and the Colombian army is always victorious.[27] Colombian media expert Silvio Waisbord stresses that the role of the Colombian media is to serve "political and economic interests" rather than support for "freedom of expression and the right of citizens to information."[28]

In Colombia's 2002 presidential elections, Alvaro Uribe's running mate Francisco Santos Calderon was from Colombia's most prominent media family and a former editor of the leading *El Tiempo*. Contrary to media headlines about Uribe's "landslide victory," it was the lowest voter turnout ever in Colombian history, and in southern Colombia voter abstention rates were over 70 percent after calls by FARC to boycott the election. Nine percent who voted returned a blank or spoiled voting card or marked the "no candidate" box. Only 41.3 percent of all registered voters cast a ballot.[29] In Cordoba, a paramilitary stronghold, Uribe's ranch shared a boundary with the property of former AUC commander Salvatore Mancuso. According to Rafael Garcia, a former high-level official in Colombia's intelligence agency currently serving 11 years in Colombia for money-laundering, among other charges, Uribe's election win was "massive electoral fraud" as paramilitary groups personally selected the candidates for Congress.[30] With a compliant Colombian media, the Uribe administration and the narco-military network won approval in the urban areas, where a frightened urban middle class were subjected to an atmosphere of anxiety, fear, and repression.[31]

Michael Taussig argues that creating a political atmosphere of fear and terror sustains the war machine in Colombia. An anonymous Bogotá journalist Taussig interviewed said, "When I write anything I ask myself how Castaño is going to react. . . . most journalists in Colombia are killed for exposing corruption."[32] Human rights experts pay little attention to a prevailing culture of paramilitary terror. Some non-governmental organizations in Colombia have offered virtual endorsement of the interventions by the United States.[33] Human Rights Watch, for example, has effectively legitimized U.S. military aid to Colombia in the war on terror.[34] Billionaire George Soros's organization, Human Rights Watch (HRW), is relatively silent on the routine killings of labor leaders in Colombia.[35] In April 2002, HRW's spokesman, Jose Vivanco, testified before the U.S. Senate in favor of Plan Colombia: "Colombians remain committed to human rights and democracy. They need help. Human Rights Watch has no fundamental problem with the United States providing that help."[36]

In the repressive situation in Colombia, a coerced population is expected to oppose the FARC insurgency and support the Colombian government. On February 7, 2003, Colombia and the United States blamed the FARC for the bombing of Club El Nogal in Bogotá, which made world news headlines.[37] The event exemplified essential features of PSYWAR in the way that it targeted people's opinions, emotions, attitudes and behavior to achieve national objectives. The bombing took place at an exclusive venue, a high-society club; there was tight security at the club; guards with bomb-sniffing dogs searched for explosives prior to the event; and not even the bodyguards of club members could enter the premises.[38] The Colombian government charged that three alleged members of the Irish Republican Army (IRA) assisted the FARC, a charge that was later proven false.[39] Accusations and denunciations overrode and replaced evidence regarding the perpetrators of the El Nogal bombing. Colombia's vice president, Francisco Santos, asserted, "There is absolutely no doubt it was the FARC."[40] President George W. Bush stated, "We stand with the Colombian people in their fight against narco-terrorists who threaten their democratic way of life."[41] Colombian President Alvaro Uribe declared, "We don't want any more indulgence, any more complicity, any more soft treatment for terrorists. What we want is to defeat them."[42]

Draining the Sea to Kill the Fish

As part of its PSYWAR against the FARC insurgency, the Colombian military adopted a method used in America's war in Vietnam, which became known as "draining the sea to kill the fish."[43] The aim was to defeat the Vietnamese communists by killing the local population in which they operated, similarly in Colombia, this method has been applied to drive the rural FARC supporters out of their homes in the countryside in order to separate and isolate the FARC guerrillas from their largest support base. In 2002, Alvaro Uribe declared emergency powers that included the right to arrest and detain people without due cause; tapping phone lines and entering homes without warrants; establishing "rehabilitation and consolidation zones" retaken by the military; and limited or restricted foreign access to conflict areas. Uribe justified these measures as a means to fight terrorism and confront the growing guerrilla threat. What was unofficial policy became formalized. According to a government funded study by the "Commission on Ways to Overcome Violence," politically motivated deaths increased from ten per day in the early 1990s to fourteen per day in 1999, to more than twenty per day in 2002.[44] The commission was set up in the early 1990s following the elimination of the EPL, which aimed to identify the "perpetrators of violence" while ignoring the state.[45]

When unable to attack the guerrillas in the countryside, Colombian military and paramilitary forces worked together to punish and attack civilian supporters of the FARC. Human rights groups contend that the AUC and Colombian armed forces have been responsible for approximately 90 to 95 percent of all politically motivated killings, which have included massacres by chainsaw and other methods designed to terrorize the *campesinos* in rural areas under FARC control.[46] Others targeted in urban areas have included trade unionists,[47] university lecturers and students, human rights workers, Catholic priests, and anyone supporting or sympathizing with the guerrillas.[48]

Carlos Castaño of the AUC adopted the method of targeting selected civilian FARC supporters from General Van Martinez of the Colombian army in the early 1990s.[49] Castaño worked closely with another Colombian general, Ivan Ramirez Quintero, who had been a key intelligence source for the United States through the cocaine decade.[50] Trained in Washington, Ramirez became the first head of the narco-military network in Colombia, which was "designed by U.S. experts." According to the *Washington Post,* he also served as a paid informant for the CIA while maintaining "close ties to right-wing paramilitary groups."[51] Ramirez directed the state's war against Pablo Escobar and provided political protection for the Cali cartel.[52] At the center of this link between the United States and the cocaine trade were the CIA and the Pentagon.[53]

In 1993, Colombian legal authorities discovered that General Mario Montoya Uribe of the Colombian army had been involved in a 1978–79 bombing campaign by the AAA. The Colombian prosecutor general issued a scathing report regarding the conduct of the civil war under Montoya's command. The discovery of his AAA past led to further investigations by human rights groups and Montoya's eventual resignation in 2008 for what became known as the "false positives" scandal: "inflating body counts by shooting innocent civilians and claiming them as guerrillas killed in combat."[54] The Colombian prosecutor general reported how the "sea" was drained to isolate the FARC from their rural support base as part of the official counterinsurgency strategy:

[The security forces] act under the premise that gained currency in El Salvador, of "draining the sea," which means that a direct relationship is established, for example, between trade union or peasant movements and the subversive ranks. When counter guerrilla actions are carried out, these passive subjects are not identified as independent victims, but rather, as part of the "enemy."[55]

The AUC may not be a proxy army for the United States, but it functions as a vanguard force of the counterinsurgency strategy in the Colombian countryside.[56] "Draining the sea to kill the fish" has also been assisted by the Colombian army as well as large landowners who directly finance and run the paramilitary groups. In 2003, President Uribe initiated his policy of "democratic security," which created a "civil defense peasant militia" and a spy network of one million "civilian informers" in a nation where 69 percent of the population live below the poverty line with 87 percent in the countryside; 9.6 million are destitute; one in five children in rural Colombia is undernourished; and according to the UN High Commission for Refugees in 2005, two million Colombians were internally displaced by the war, overtaking Iraq (1.6 million), Pakistan (1.1 million), Sudan (1 million), and Afghanistan (912,000).[57]

President Uribe based the creation of civilian militias upon a RAND study called the "Colombian Labyrinth," which detailed a plan for a "civil defense" counterinsurgency structure made up of ordinary people.[58] The new "civil defense forces" were under direct army command.[59]

Under President Uribe's "civilian informers" strategy, more than half of the taxi drivers in Colombia became spies for the state, according to local reports.[60] In the country's regional airports, armed soldiers were seen wearing hoods to conceal their faces, a common military attire used by South American military juntas in the 1970s to intimidate foreign sympathizers.[61] The goal was to create a network of informers along the lines of the Convivir "civilian security groups" that Uribe had supported when he was the governor of Antioquia. The Convivir experiment allowed armed civilians to patrol and gather intelligence under local military command.[62] Under President Uribe's "democratic security" war plans, spies were given political blacklists with photos and state identification numbers.[63] In the same year of his presidential inauguration, Uribe argued that civilians should be provided with radios, vehicles, and possibly weapons: "Initially, [they] will not have guns because people will kill them to take the weapons, but the defense minister [his successor as president, Juan Manuel Santos] and the high commanders will study under what circumstances the use of arms could be authorized."[64]

The Uribe government pushed for a constitutional amendment that would reestablish some of the provisions of the Security Statute, which stripped citizens of their civil liberties in the 1970s and enabled the military to prosecute leftists with impunity.[65] Fernando Londoño, Colombia's justice and interior minister, stated that Colombians should be prepared to sacrifice all civil rights for greater security.[66] The AUC was allowed to infiltrate the administration, faculty, and student body at universities in Medellín and on the Atlantic coast and carry out assassinations.[67] The "law of silence" was applied in so many areas of Colombian life that a foreigner might think that ordinary Colombians were supportive of *los paramilitares* (the paramilitaries). According to the Australian organization Peace and Justice for Colombia, there were up to ten thousand political prisoners incarcerated in Colombian prisons living in inhumane conditions. Most were activists, but included academics, unionists, and ex-combatants.[68]

When the Uribe administration stepped up its civil war preparations in 2002, the U.S. government demanded cooperation in shielding U.S. forces stationed in-country from prosecution for war crimes.[69] The U.S. undersecretary of state for political affairs along with the deputy commander-in-chief of SOUTHCOM requested that the Colombian government sign an agreement not to turn any U.S. nationals over to the International Criminal Court in The Hague, Netherlands.[70] In some ways, U.S.-sponsored state terrorism in Colombia resembles the political repression in Latin America throughout the 1970s and 1980s,[71] and the continuing "democratic security" measures initiated by President Uribe can be seen as a means to legitimize state-terrorism by denying any knowledge of an existing narco-military network. After being extradited to the United States on charges of drug trafficking in 2008, the former AUC leader Salvatore Mancuso testified that one hundred politicians in Colombia's congress have direct links to existing paramilitary groups.[72] These revelations led to what became known as the *"Parapolitica"* scandal, implicating Uribe's intelligence service chief Jorge Noguera with a recent sentence of 25 years for collaborating with paramilitary groups.[73] One-third of Colombia's congressional representatives have come under investigation.[74] One hundred and thirty-three current and former members of Congress have been implicated.[75] Nearly all were members of President Uribe's governing coalition.[76] Uribe however has denied any involvement.

Billions of dollars in U.S. capital have been pumped into Colombia to restore order through U.S.-sponsored state terrorism. Throughout Uribe's term in office, the FARC's ability to build a base of mass support among the peasantry created a political and financial vacuum that rocked the narco-bourgeoisie with scandals, extraditions, and divisions among various paramilitary groups.[77] Drug traffickers competed with one another by establishing direct alliances with mid-level AUC leaders, who then challenged AUC commanders for control and "demobilized" the paramilitary organization in 2006.[78] With successor paramilitary groups such as the Black Eagles, increased internal warfare for territorial control between emerging factions plus the mysterious death of Mancuso's predecessor, Carlos Castaño, exposed serious weaknesses within the narco-bourgeoisie.[79] The state had "no interest in pursuing paramilitary groups or drug traffickers" while at the same time the AUC alongside the army were unsuccessful in disciplining dissident paramilitary groups.[80] Prior to the crisis surrounding the AUC leadership, the Colombian army deployed more than one thousand soldiers in an offensive against one group in the eastern department of Casanare in August 2004, that resulted in the deaths of twenty-one paramilitaries. The Colombian army used aircraft and helicopters, killing another thirteen and capturing thirty-two. Following the selective extraditions of paramilitary leaders Mancuso, Diego Murillo "Don Berna," Hernan Giraldo, and Rodrigo Tovar "Jorge 40," known for his annihilation of *Kankuamo* Indians in the northern Sierra Nevada de Santa Marta mountains, paramilitary groups have been in disarray and have weakened the state's central authority and military chain of command. By no small means, Colombia had become what Hernando Calvo Ospina described as a "laboratory of the extreme right."[81]

8. The Consequences of Relocation and Regionalization

In the midst of the civil war, the U.S.-Colombian counterinsurgency campaign to destroy Latin America's most powerful guerrilla army has become a nightmare for the campesinos, who live in an environment of state-controlled terror and political violence. One of the most devastating consequences has been the ecological destruction of peasant land with biochemical agents, which are sprayed over the rebel-held areas of coca cultivation. Washington and Bogotá justify the aerial fumigation strategy as a means to take away the source of cocaine, which they argue is the FARC. The spraying is part of a "relocation strategy" for the campesinos, designed to isolate the FARC guerrillas and separate them from their supporters. As the cocaine trade is regionalized, coca cultivation will remain under the control of Colombia's narco-military network before it reaches the global market.

Relocation

The U.S. Southern Command (SOUTHCOM), based in Miami, Florida, states that its aims in Latin America are to "conduct military operations and promote security cooperation to achieve U.S. strategic objectives," one of which is to lead "efforts to halt the flow of illegal drugs into the United States and to support host nation efforts to combat the narco-terrorism, threats to legitimate governments, dangers to their citizens associated with the production and sale of those drugs."[1] SOUTHCOM contends that the "impact of drug trafficking is a destabilizing factor to countries of the region, a threat to public security, and a threat to national security."[2] However, in assessing what the United States means by "strategic objectives," it is important to keep in mind that the former commander-in-chief of SOUTHCOM, General Peter Pace, argued in 2000 that vital U.S. interests include the preservation of capitalist socioeconomic relations and unhindered access to Latin American markets by American transnational corporations.[3]

Pace explained the real goal in Colombia was to maintain a "continued stability required for access to markets in the SOUTHCOM AOR [area of responsibility], which is critical to the expansion and prosperity of the United States."[4] Pace's successor, General James T. Hill, added that by 2010 "trade with Latin America is expected to exceed that with the European Economic Community and Japan combined" in order to cement the integration of Latin America with U.S. capital.[5] The comments made by SOUTHCOM highlight a reality between stated and real objectives, which involve the protection and security of operations of U.S. capital in Colombia.

To destroy the insurgency in Colombia and secure control of the hemisphere and its natural resources, the banner of the war on drugs and terror has been politically expedient. Leading CIA officials proposed a political use for the war on drugs. According to Michael Levine, an important DEA operative in Latin America in the 1980s, the idea was discussed about "how to make Americans surrender their own constitutional rights voluntarily," and going so far as to create a "horror drug," if necessary, that "Americans would be begging their government to take any rights they need to protect them."[6]

The U.S. counterinsurgency strategy in Colombia has consistently used the fear of cocaine to justify its controversial "drug war" in the Colombian countryside. The aerial spraying of biochemical agents over the rebel-held areas of coca cultivation forces the relocation of coca plantations to anywhere in Colombia under state control. American drug-law enforcement defines this function as "fumigation." According to a declassified CIA document, the aerial fumigation strategy was known to U.S. policymakers in 2000 when the first phase of Plan Colombia was put into effect. Such a strategy contradicted the stated aims of the plan, which were to promote the peace process with guerrillas, combat the narcotics industry, revive the Colombian economy, and strengthen democracy with mostly military assistance.[7] President George W. Bush's chief supporter of Plan Colombia was the Colombian president, Alvaro Uribe Velez, who spearheaded the aerial fumigation strategy. A declassified report by the U.S. Defense Intelligence Agency from 1991 ranked Uribe number 82 on a list of 104 "more important Colombian narco-traffickers contracted by the Colombian narcotics cartels for security, transportation, distribution, collection and enforcement of narcotics operations in both the U.S. and Colombia." The report describes him:

82. Alvaro Uribe Velez—A Colombian politician and senator dedicated to collaboration with the Medellín Cartel at high government levels. Uribe was linked to a business involved in narcotics activities in the U.S. His father was murdered in Colombia for his connection with the narcotics traffickers. Uribe has worked for the Medellín Cartel and is a close personal friend of Pablo Escobar Gaviria. He has participated in Escobar's political campaign to win the position of assistant parliamentarian to Jorge [Ortega]. Uribe has been one of the politicians, from the Senate, who has attacked all forms of the extradition treaty.[8]

The report lists mostly unknown members of the Colombian narco-bourgeoisie linked to the Medellín cartel, as well as a number of hit men used to assassinate leftists, including members of the Colombian Communist Party and the Union Patriotica (UP) linked to the FARC.[9]

Since 1978, small-scale coca cultivation in guerrilla zones has been the subject of a forced eradication policy from the air. The aerial spraying program in Colombia uses *Fusarium oxysporum*, sometimes described as Agent Green. A derivative of this fungus is Fusarium EN-4, a mycoherbicide that is the basis of chemical weapons developed by the United States, the former Soviet Union, Britain, Israel, and France.[10] The research conducted on Fusarium was considered controversial by the scientific community because of covert sources of funding. In the mid-1970s the Department of Plant Pathology at the University of California conducted research funded by the DEA on a strain of *Fusarium oxysporum* as a mycoherbicide. By 1983 the CIA was funding research on Fusarium in Hawaii and in Peru, where research on coca paste smoking and cocaine addiction had also been conducted.[11] Scientists under contract with the CIA experimented with *Fusarium oxysporum* and coca in Hawaii and worked with Hawaiian Fusarium in Peru.[12] The fungus occurs naturally, particularly in coca-growing soil, and can have disastrous effects on coca crops in large doses. The aim of the research and whether data between the scientists working on the Fusarium and those working on coca paste smoking and cocaine addiction was exchanged is not known, but the mono-crop drug *fincas* of the narco-bourgeoisie in Colombia were not sprayed. The fungal spraying was proposed only for the rebel-held areas of Colombia.[13]

In Hawaii, a coca test field established by the Coca-Cola Company (the largest importer of coca leaves in the world) was destroyed by Fusarium EN-4. The Agricultural Research Service (ARS) of the U.S. Department of Agriculture (USDA) laboratories further developed these experiments.[14] A scientist named David Sands repeated the CIA's clandestine work in trials conducted by the USDA/ARS, and by 1986 the ARS had developed biological agents. The program aimed to legitimize the research so that it would no longer be considered clandestine. In 1987 the USDA/ARS took over the Hawaiian site and the U.S. Department of Energy continued to conduct "other clandestine work."[15] At David Sands's private company, Agricultural and Biological Control (AgBio Con), and in the Department of Plant Science and Plant Pathology at Montana State University, Sands argued for spraying huge quantities of mycoherbicides using military cargo planes.[16]

Links among AgBio Con, high-ranking U.S. military personnel, and Jeb Bush were reported in 1999.[17] James McDonough, Florida's director of the Office of Drug Control, engineered the proposal to use mycoherbicides. Bush brought him to Florida from his position as Director of Strategy for the White House Office of National Drug Control Policy. Florida Republican Bill McCollum helped secure the first $23 million for mycoherbicide financing in his defense contractor's bill: the $2.3 billion Western Hemisphere Drug Elimination Act. Virtually all the money went to weapons purchases for SOUTHCOM and antidrug programs.[18] Title VIII of the Omnibus Consolidated Appropriations Act, P.L. 105–277, contains the Western Hemisphere Drug Elimination Act. This legislation authorized billions of dollars in funding during fiscal years 1999, 2000, and 2001 for the U.S. Customs Service, the U.S. Coast Guard, the U.S. Department of State, the U.S. Agency for International Development, the DOD, the DOA, and the DEA to enhance antidrug programs. The George W. Bush administration ensured that mycoherbicide research would continue in government laboratories. The Office of National Drug Control Policy Reauthorization Act of 2006 was passed through Congress, which required that mycoherbicides be deployed in Colombia and in its southwest Asian counterpart, Afghanistan.[19]

In the spring of 1999, the U.S. government passed on responsibilities to the United Nations to manage the mycoherbicide program in Colombia. The first approach was through the UN Drug Control Program (UNDCP), which proposed a project to establish a research station to conduct field trials. Klaus Nyholm, the UNDCP representative in Colombia, said the proposed arrangement of a U.S. presence in Colombia under the banner of the United Nations was not his idea.[20]

Fusarium and its mycotoxins are biological warfare agents that were used in Southeast Asia and sold in Iran, causing human deaths and dermal diseases.[21] In experimental animal studies at the U.S. Army Biomedical Research and Development laboratory at Fort Detrick, Maryland, this agent has penetrated through skin, causing symptoms ranging from erythema and skin lesions to death.[22] The American war on the processing and exporting of Colombian cocaine saw significant developments in U.S. biological and biochemical research, with a focus on striking the supply side of the drug trade.

In March 2002, the U.S. State Department revealed estimates of Colombia's coca crops. The aerial defoliation program and provision of military aid had failed to eradicate or even diminish the size of the illegal coca fields, despite ongoing displacement in the countryside. Colombia's coca crop had actually increased from 122,000 hectares in 1999 to 170,000 in 2001.[23] The U.S. and Colombian governments have discouraged independent investigation of the effects of aerial spraying and its sources.

The United States has used glyphosate (N-phosphonomethyl) as a herbicide for two decades for its imperialist counterinsurgency efforts. The biggest-selling commercial formulation of glyphosate is Roundup and Roundup Ultra, products of Monsanto, a chemical and biotechnology transnational corporation based in St. Louis, Missouri. Monsanto, the supplier of Agent Orange in Vietnam, has been the major provider of glyphosate in Colombia. Monsanto's herbicides have produced consistent health complaints from peasants in the Colombian countryside—ignored by both the White House and Monsanto. When interviewed by CorpWatch, a non-profit investigative research group, a U.S. State Department official described the relationship between the U.S. government and Monsanto as proprietorial "information between us and our supplier. It's exempt from the FOIA [Freedom of Information Act] requirements too, so I don't think you will be able to get it."[24]

The spraying of herbicides is a grave risk to humans and their environment. The chemicals' effects on Colombia's ecology remain unknown, yet the *Fusarium oxysporum* species contain over 250 enzymes that may be activated or deactivated, depending on environmental conditions.[25] The fumigation process is ineffective. The FARC informs campesinos when fumigations are coming, so that they can dig up their coca plants and hide them far from their plantations. When the fumigation is over, they let a little time pass and dig up the hidden plants again.[26] Coca is not eradicated. Even without the FARC, peasants can also cut down the coca shrubs to the roots before or shortly after the spraying so that they can grow back rapidly and yield more leaves than before. The salient question is whether the primary target of the chemical spraying program is the coca leaf in a civil war. The targets are, in truth, the peasants, their families, and their livestock because chemical warfare does not discriminate among living species.[27]

Between 1992 and 1998, 140,858 hectares of coca were drenched with 1,897,357 liters of glyphosate.[28] It is difficult to estimate the environmental damage of the spraying. Chemical pollution of soil and water in the fragile ecosystems of the Amazon rain forest and the Andean mountain cloud forests must be anticipated. Glyphosate is promoted as a mild defoliant, as it allegedly breaks down quickly. But in 1997 Monsanto was forced by New York's attorney general to remove the terms "biodegradable" and "environmentally friendly" from Roundup (glyphosate) advertisements.[29]

A broad-spectrum herbicide, Roundup has severely affected or killed numerous other plants in Colombia, including food crops like banana, yucca, cocoa, maize, and papaya. Eating these affected crops and drinking Roundup-polluted water has caused health complaints among the peasant population that involve vomiting, diarrhea, nausea, and headaches. The long-term effects are unknown. Farmland has turned completely yellow in color, meaning it is contaminated with Roundup, but is said to "recuperate" by its supporters.[30] Young cattle lose their hair after eating sprayed grass. Chickens die after drinking the contaminated water. Fish stocks have become extinct in heavily sprayed waterways.[31]

A new "super coca plant" has been cultivated in Colombia, according to media reports, which grows to more than twelve feet (ordinary plants grow up to five feet), grows faster, and produces more cocaine compound—between 97 and 98 percent; ordinary plants produce up to 25 percent. Jeremy Bigwood, a mycotoxicologist, contends that the percentiles of cocaine concentration seem extremely high.[32] Experts say that science could manipulate coca bushes to be resistant to the herbicide glyphosate. University of Missouri scientist Brant Sellers points out that given that Monsanto sells "Roundup Ready" corn, cotton, soybeans, and canola that are bioengineered to resist it, a coca plant could also be developed to resist it. If such a product were developed, coca farmers could spray Roundup to kill weeds without harming their coca plants. Sellers argues that, even without the manipulation, "if you spray any plant species over and over and over again," it can develop resistance to the herbicide.[33] There have been reports of large coca plants that go back a couple or more centuries, but having them grow too tall would require ladders for harvesting, which does not make economic sense. Bigwood says the reports of glyphosate or Roundup resistant coca are plausible but have not been substantiated. Coca plants resistant to glyphosate or Roundup are usually strains of plants that have been exposed to glyphosate over a long period of time.[34]

The narco-bourgeoisie's unending demand for control over coca production has forced many peasant families from their land. The narco-military network orchestrated this forced relocation through tactics such as fumigation backed by narco-state terror. Fleeing from war and lacking an alternative, hundreds of thousands escaped into uninhabited areas to grow coca. In 2010 the United Nations estimated that up to 3.7 million people have been displaced as a result of Washington's relocation strategy, the largest number of displaced people in the world, with Ecuador the largest recipient.[35] In Miraflores, a town in southeastern Guaviare department, a joint Colombian military and police so-called counterdrug operation provoked mass demonstrations, which according to the U.S. embassy in Bogotá, were sustained by funds from coca production. "Embassy officials saw 'these kinds of operations' as proof that—in cases where peasants and/or guerrillas threaten mission success—the participation of Colombian military forces is vital." Declassified 1996 documents illustrate one such relocation operation:

> The aim of the operation is to take over Miraflores, effectively shutting coca production out of that area. . . . Large numbers of residents have been displaced by the relentless push of the Army's Second Mobile Brigade [and] campesinos from surrounding areas have flocked to Miraflores in a show of solidarity.[36]

A follow-up cable states:

> An estimated 4,000 to 20,000 campesinos have descended on the town of Miraflores, blocking access to the local airstrip in protest of the Colombian government's counterdrug operations. Colombian police and Army troops from the Second Mobile Brigade have been deployed in the area to prevent guerrillas from overrunning and destroying the town as they did in August 1995.[37]

The cable goes on to note that the presence of army troops alongside the "anti-drug police" ensures that a guerrilla attack on the town would be met with "commensurate force." The Miraflores operation would result in "major damage to narcotraffickers and guerrillas in Guaviare."[38]

Many campesinos have been forced to migrate into the Andean mountain regions and the Amazonian basin as aerial spraying pursues their coca production. As in Afghanistan, equally "successful" manual eradication methods as well as ceremonial burning of drugs, are hailed as virtual proof that Colombia is not a narco-state. Meanwhile, swidden agricultural techniques are used to sow coca, which has resulted in widespread deforestation. According to the Mandala Project, an independent research group based at American University in Washington:

> At this rate, Colombia's woodlands will be depleted in forty years. Such deforestation has increased the rate of extinction for many plant and animal species, many of which are endemic to the country. Furthermore, the social and economic fabrics of indigenous peoples who inhabit the forests are rapidly being destroyed. . . . Colombia's total forest coverage accounts for 10 percent of the earth's biodiversity. Behind Brazil, the country is considered the most biodiverse in the world.[39]

Ostensibly, the aerial fumigation strategy is presented by Colombia and the United States as a method of destroying the illegal drug trade and the FARC. In reality, the supply of coca will be sustained as long as there are growing areas left and people willing to grow the crop. In this sense, the relocation strategy is a method to relocate coca for cocaine manufacture. If the peasants are driven off their particular land, the narco-bourgeoisie can either terminate coca production there or set up large-scale production sites elsewhere in the country. Coca production has added a new dimension to the decades-old struggle over land in Colombia.[40]

In the past, the potential growing area of Amazonia in Colombia seemed almost inexhaustible. The total area of the Colombian Amazon is 40 million hectares, of which 29 million are rain forest; the Orinoco basin covers 25 million hectares, with 3.5 million of them rain forest. There are significant numbers of impoverished and internally displaced people desperate enough to do anything to survive. "Every hectare fumigated means a hectare substituted," says Gloria Elsa Ramírez of the environmental section of the Defensoría del Pueblo, the governmental institution responsible for the promotion, implementation and dissemination of human rights.[41]

Drug-crop cultivation and chemical processing of the raw materials into cocaine cause substantial environmental damage. The U.S. rationale that the fumigation policy is an antidote to the environmental impact of illicit crops is flawed. Chemical spraying aggravates, directly and collaterally, the already negative environmental effects of the illicit crops. The continuous displacement of crops by fumigation multiplies the pace of deforestation of the Amazon and Andean mountain forests and spreads pollution throughout these fragile ecosystems.[42] By increasing fumigation, the United States has created the conditions for an ecological catastrophe, as the only viable crop will be coca. Human rights are continuously violated, the legitimacy of the government eroded, and the civil war extended with aerial spraying. Simultaneously, coca production fuels the civil war economy of both guerrilla and counterinsurgency forces, the U.S. war on drugs and terror, and the importance of the cocaine trade to Colombia. In 2000, the Colombian newspaper *El Tiempo* reported on the environmental destruction:

> The Colombian state should avoid deepening disastrous contradictions that erode its legitimacy, that intensify the conflict or that destroy the environment even more. If there are nowadays more than

100,000 hectares of coca and the Colombian Amazon disposes of 40 million of hectares for expanding the agricultural frontier, will this spiral of fumigations ever come to an end?[43]

Fernando Londoño, Alvaro Uribe's minister of interior, offered another perspective:

Colombia is the victim of an international conspiracy in which environmentalists and communists participate. . . . This diabolical conspiracy is also carried out when members of the armed forces are brought to court without any proof or evidence.... Political scientists tell us that communism is dead, but the communists are not and they continue to have their views and their will to fracture contemporary society. Frequently they dress green, so they are the Green Parties . . . they all come together to figure out where they are going to hit and they painfully hit the prestige and the livelihood of Colombians.[44]

Londoño's perspective demonstrates how the Colombian state has discouraged independent investigation of the effects of aerial spraying. The state continues the war against the FARC insurgency, but it also persecutes anyone—NGOs, members of the media, environmentalists, trade unionists, human rights groups—who might question or seek to challenge its authority. The Uribe administration promoted the dismantling of those NGOs with interests in labor and human rights issues, deeming them sympathetic to the FARC.[45] Most interestingly, the sociologist James Brittain's work has documented how the Colombian state has imitated the United States by simultaneously applauding specific NGOs for their work in condemning the FARC and supported increased U.S.-based counterinsurgency forces to be deployed throughout Colombia.[46] Human Rights Watch is influential in this condemnation of the FARC, along with paramilitary-funded NGOs in Colombia such as the Social Front for Peace (FSP), which is directly linked to the AUC.

Ultimately, fumigation serves to restore coca production. The fumigation strategy promotes coca production in areas not controlled by the guerrillas, where it can be processed for export as cocaine. The FARC contends that the only way to eliminate the drug problem in Colombia is to legalize drug consumption and develop a plan of alternative crops.[47] The sustainability of Colombia's natural environment does not seem to be a consideration by the Colombian state or its U.S. backers. Sustainability has become a voguish aim in the Western world, but in Colombia it has little meaning to the majority of its people. Ecocide is an unavoidable consequence of the partnership between the Colombian state and the United States through the counterinsurgency relocation strategy that includes, but is not limited to, fumigation.[48]

Regionalization

For American drug-law enforcement, the regionalization of the cocaine trade is most commonly known as the "balloon effect," in which production expands throughout the country but the balloon never pops. If planes are shot down, smugglers will use speedboats; if selective crops are eradicated in Colombia, growers will move to Bolivia or Peru. Regionalization has also been called the "push-down–push-up effect," to describe the pattern that occurs when coca is pushed down in one spot yet pops up in another not far away. And it has also been called the "hydraulic effect" to describe how it parallels the physical effect of incompressible fluids. If pressure is applied in one area, the fluid will shift toward the area of lower resistance.[49]

The regionalization of the cocaine trade began in the mid-1970s when Latin American fumigations were first carried out by CIA proprietary airlines. Mexico's Operation Condor in 1975 was the first example of aerial spraying on the continent. The CIA planes were from Evergreen International and flown by Mexican pilots and U.S. veterans of Vietnam. Evergreen acquired most of the assets of the CIA airline Intermountain Aviation. The company with the contract for all airplane maintenance in Mexico was E-Systems, which acquired the CIA airline Air Asia. However, the so-called antidrug program was a failure and not a single important trafficker was arrested.[50]

In the early 1970s there was political pressure from President Richard Nixon on the Southern Cone governments of Argentina, Uruguay, Paraguay, Chile, and Brazil to pass antidrug legislation to counter the growing heroin threat. Nixon's administration was the first to officially declare the U.S. "War on Drugs," which was crucial for U.S. drug diplomacy and Latin American relations at a time when Americans were increasingly alarmed at the high rate of drug consumption caused by the heroin epidemic that began in the 1960s.[51]

Nixon's war on drugs led to the inter-American cocaine drug trade. From the Andean region and beyond, the balloon continued to expand northward toward Brazil and southward throughout the Southern Cone awaiting future American presidencies. This war on drugs has dictated the course of policy, academic analysis, and journalistic interest in drug trafficking since American forces intervened in the Golden Triangle, as exemplified by President George H. W. Bush's drug war speech to the nation in September 1989 and the subsequent Andean Strategy and Drug Summits in Cartagena, Colombia (1990) and San Antonio, Texas (1992). Antidrug efforts to stem the flood of cocaine, however, were, as one critic put it, "like standing under a waterfall with a bucket."[52]

By 1987 the international press was reporting on the "balloon effect" with increased trafficking, corruption, and violence, linked to the drug trade in Brazil and Paraguay.[53] The Southern Cone became crucial for drug traffickers seeking new routes, locations for cocaine laboratories, and money-laundering centers.[54] The Reagan-Bush White House was instrumental in this aspect of regionalization. Officials in the enforcement section of the Treasury Department monitored the sharp increase of capital that entered Florida and later Los Angeles banks in the late 1970s and "connected it to the large-scale laundering of drug receipts."[55] Detailed information on money-laundering was brought to the DEA and Justice Department, and after some media exposés Reagan was forced to act. Operation Greenback was launched to prosecute the money launderers; however, according to the federal prosecutor, Bush "wasn't really too interested in financial prosecution" and the program was terminated. William Bennett, the first director of the Office of National Drug Control Policy (ONDCP), the position that became known as "Drug Czar," followed Bush's lead by implementing a historic "no-questions asked" policy for U.S. banks, making it possible for an estimated $8 billion surplus to be deposited into Miami and Los Angeles banks in that period.[56] A small bank in Panama was pressured to plead guilty, but Reagan dropped the criminal charges against its parent bank, Banco de Occidente, a major financial institution based in one of the centers of the Medellín drug cartel.[57] Throughout the cocaine decade, any attempt to investigate U.S. profits from the drug trade to prosecute money launderers was seriously undermined by the growing power of drug money that had been entering the United States since President Richard Nixon.

Drug processing requires ether and acetone, which are imported into the Crystal Triangle. Rafael Perl of the Congressional Research Service, the public policy research arm of the U.S. Congress, estimated that more than 90 percent of the chemicals used to produce cocaine come from the United States. In the nine months before the announcement of President George H. W. Bush's drug war in 1989, Colombian police reportedly seized 1.5 million gallons of precursor chemicals, many found in drums displaying American corporate logos.[58] A CIA study concluded that U.S. exports of these chemicals far exceeded the legal commercial purpose, and enormous amounts were being siphoned off to produce cocaine and heroin in Latin America. Chemical companies remain off-limits for investigation, and monitoring by drug-law enforcement appears to be politically and economically unacceptable to the United States. "Most DEA offices have only one agent working on chemical diversions," a U.S. official reported. Raids on the corporate headquarters of chemical companies in Manhattan are impossible because they are located in the financial center of the United States.[59]

From available evidence, five plausible factors may have contributed to the regionalization of the cocaine trade: 1) a massive and continuous U.S. propaganda campaign that the drug problem had to be resolved at the source rather than at its financial destination in the

United States; 2) discreet and incremental penetration of cocaine into regional economies and their societies; 3) consistent funding for supply-side strategies such as Plan Colombia rather than prevention, treatment, and education programs; 4) an intensification of both covert and overt economic operations; 5) the gradual sealing-off of investigations with outdated studies reflecting this. By the end of the cocaine decade, the *Boston Globe* reported just how political the debate over drugs had become:

> There are two camps on drug policy. One is made up of those who emphasize "supply-side" strategies to cut off the flow of drugs like cocaine before they reach the American public. This includes virtually all U.S. politicians, at least when they speak in public. The other is made up of people who have examined the results of past and present law enforcement efforts, considered the complexities of America's relationship with other countries and the power of capitalism and the marketplace, and conclude that supply-side strategies will not work. This group argues that the answer will be found in "demand-side" strategies that incorporate treatment and rehabilitation programs with a propaganda campaign to discourage drug use. One element would be an evaluation of the decriminalization of some drugs, possibly even dangerously addictive ones like heroin or cocaine, so that their use by adults is regulated and taxed. The decriminalizers stress the threats to democracy that come through the corruption of police, judges and politicians, through the melding of police and military forces in the name of "national security" and through special, "wartime" curtailment of civil liberties.[60]

Before the Bolivian cocaine coup of 1980, Paraguay was the first country in Latin America to be publicly exposed for its involvement in the drug trade. Paraguay in the early 1970s was a vital center for the Corsican mafia, leading to the development of a vast international heroin-trafficking network supplied from Turkey and based in Marseille, the infamous "French Connection."[61] Corsicans coordinated the transport of heroin from Marseilles to the United States via

Paraguay. The CIA used such networks as transit stops in transporting Asian heroin to the United States with the help of corrupt high-ranking government and military officials, as it did with the AAA cocaine, and as the AAA, in turn, did with their favored French Connection.[62] Paraguay's vast Chaco region, a virtually unpatrolled wilderness with over nine hundred clandestine airstrips, provided an ideal base for planes to land and take off. It is believed that over 50 percent of the chemicals used to process cocaine came through Paraguay after Bolivia's cocaine coup of 1980.[63] The institutionalization of cocaine in primarily Colombia, Bolivia, and Peru provided the ideal environment for the trade to regionalize. Hence, the contemporary narco-military network, composed of military and government officials with the active involvement of intelligence agencies and organized crime based in various Latin American, North American, and West European capitals, was founded with Miami as the point for congregation.[64]

Cocaine laboratories have been found in northern and western Brazil and in northwestern Argentina. Precursor chemicals are produced and transported through Argentina, Brazil, and Paraguay, and after the 1989 U.S. invasion of Panama, Uruguay and Chile became major financial centers for laundering drug money. A UN International Narcotics Control Board (INCB) report in 1994 cited Argentina and Chile, formerly classified as secondary or marginal transit and consumption points, as not only important transit countries but major consumption and money-laundering centers.[65] New cocaine routes emerged in Brazil that cut through Brazilian cities and into Europe, where cocaine consumption has increased. In the slums of Rio de Janeiro, crack cocaine has taken hold. Military-style police patrols armed with assault rifles have been repelled by drug gangs similar to those in Los Angeles. Multi-ton loads of cocaine are headed to Europe, and poor African countries have experienced a boom in trafficking and drug use.[66] The shift to Europe came as a result of the saturated U.S. market in the late 1980s and early 1990s, to yield much higher profits.

The Southern Cone continues to play the role as a transshipment point for cocaine produced in the Andean region destined for the U.S.

and European markets. The regionalization of the cocaine trade, which includes coca cultivation, cocaine processing, transportation, and money-laundering, can be considered as a Latin American component of U.S. finance imperialism. In classical economic terms, if supply at the source of the Crystal Triangle is restricted, then the commodity price will increase, and theoretically, consumer demand will decrease. By restricting supply, the price of cocaine on U.S. streets will increase and, in turn, reduce demand. Decades of organization and movement of capital, narcotics, and technology demonstrate that corporate finance capital has driven the global drug trade. Shortly before the global financial crisis the *Wall Street Journal* reported:

> The price of cocaine—the pure version, not crack—has kept falling. In the early 1980s, the price of a gram of cocaine was about $600. By the late 1990s the price had fallen to about $200. According to the Drug Enforcement Administration, the street price of a gram of cocaine in 2005 was $20-$25 in New York, $30-$100 in Los Angeles and $100-$125 in Denver.[67]

In the cocaine decade, a pure gram of cocaine sold for $600 in the United States. Since then, cocaine prices, regardless of quality, fell, making cocaine cheaper and more accessible than ever before. The global financial crisis in 2008, which saw a spike of about $160 for 2010, brought prices closer to 1990s levels. So far, the neo-liberal policies guiding the "War on Drugs" have neither stopped the cocaine trade nor undermined it in any substantial way. Globally, Washington's efforts appear to have stabilized cocaine markets, doubling demand in Europe over the past decade while sustaining the United States as the world's largest market for cocaine.[68] The relocation strategy in Colombia has had no meaningful impact on the price of cocaine or its consumption, according to a range of government, media, and independent sources.[69] A key measure of the strategy is also coca production. Given the counterproductive results of fumigation the amount of land under coca cultivation in South America, at approximately 200,000 hectares, provides a more realistic picture than those offered by official estimates.[70] As of 2004, Colombia has produced twice as much cocaine as its neighbors Peru and Bolivia, producing 80 percent of the world's cocaine supply and generating annual revenues estimated to be worth at least 2.2 billion dollars.[71] In 2001, the U.S. State Department reported that coca cultivation in Colombia had peaked. The State Department's annual International Narcotics Control Strategy (INCS) report expressed it this way: "The year's most noteworthy accomplishment was to keep the Andean coca crop from expanding significantly."[72]

Using U.S. State Department data, Table 1 illustrates how coca production in Bolivia, Peru, and Colombia simply relocated in the post-cartel narco-economy that emerged in the early 1990s.

Given the data produced by the U.S. State Department, the U.S. Council on Foreign Relations concludes that Andean coca production has not decreased. There is "an inability of the U.S. to assess the changing conditions in the Andes and reorient its policies."[73] The area of land under coca cultivation has increased in Bolivia and Peru, and in Colombia coca has also relocated beyond its borders.[74] Supply-side programs allow coca to be relocated, cocaine to be exported, and the trade to regionalize, suggesting there are hidden or unrecorded levels of coca cultivation and cocaine production within the Crystal Triangle as in other drug producing zones.

According to the ONDCP, the year 2006 witnessed the most intensive use of fumigation in Colombia's history: 157,200 hectares of coca cultivation areas were detected, 13,200 hectares more than in 2005, confirming Colombia's central role in the political economy of global cocaine production and trade. In the dynamics of quantitative/speculative/political assessments of the size and market value of the cocaine trade, the Uribe government insisted that fumigations had been effective and pointed to results from other surveys conducted by the UN Office on Drugs and Crime (UNODC), which are the only studies that gave Uribe's argument any credence. In U.S.-Colombian drug diplomacy, Colombia has accepted the UN survey data and not always those produced from U.S. government funded research.[75] The drug diplomacy between Colombia and the United

Table 1: Andean Coca Production (figures are in metric tons)

| | YEAR | | |
COUNTRY	2000	1997	1993
Bolivia	14,000	45,800	47,200
Colombia	136,200	79,500	39,700
Peru	34,200	68,800	108,800
TOTAL COCA	184,400	194,100	195,700

Source: International Narcotics Control Strategy (INCS) Report, March 2001.

States can be best understood as a negotiated relationship, that is, a quid pro quo between U.S. imperialism and the narco-bourgeoisie, based on a mutual dependency on cocaine exports and preserving existing economic conditions that are vital to their political and economic interests in cocaine thereby determining market share.

Figure 3 illustrates how the relocation strategy is officially represented by the U.S. government and the United Nations with hectare estimates to provide ample evidence that the "War on Drugs" is worth pursuing. However, it fails to demonstrate how American imperial strategies protect the privatized and decentralized agents of economic operations connected to the counterinsurgency strategy, that is, U.S. and Colombian agents who have a direct impact on coca production to cocaine exports.

According to the Transnational Institute (TNI) research group, "It is not just a case of coming to an agreement, rather, of disclosing the truth and coming to the logical conclusions that these results point to."[76] The U.S. government does not fail to read its own reports. The power and control of the narco-bourgeoisie in Colombia in the "destruction" of the drug cartels, "dismantling" of certain paramilitary militias achieved from "peace talks," and the imprisonment of some organized "crime bosses" has had no impact on the cocaine trade. Through the narco-military network, coca-growing areas are divided and restructured by the narco-state. Businessmen and foreign multinational corporations exploit Colombia under the ideological mask of the American war on drugs and terror where FARC is the principal enemy.

In recent developments, the Chiquita Brands International Company, the successor to the United Fruit Company, one of the best-known U.S. monopolies, pleaded guilty in March 2007 to providing more than $1.7 million in funding over seven years to the Colombian AUC in return for "protection."[77] According to Terry Collingsworth, a lawyer with International Rights Advocates who led a multimillion-dollar lawsuit against the transnational corporation, "This is a landmark case, maybe the biggest terrorism case in history."[78] Chiquita pleaded guilty to one count of doing business with a terrorist group and agreed to pay a fine of $25 million. Under the agreement, none of the company's executives were to face criminal charges. Between 1997 and February 2004, Chiquita made more than one hundred payments to the AUC, including over fifty payments totaling more than $850,000 after the State Department listed the AUC as a terrorist organization in September 2001. Prior to 1997, Chiquita had made payments to the FARC, but that was before FARC had been labeled a terrorist organization by the State Department and thus prompting the Colombian state to pardon Chiquita for its crimes. It is known that Chiquita made over $200 million in profits since the AUC was listed as a terrorist organization in 2001. Chiquita's fine amounted to less than half of the $51.5 million that it made from the 2004 sale of its Colombian subsidiary, Banadex.[79] This U.S. transnational corporation was barely punished for doing business with narco-terrorists.

Beyond the social, environmental, and economic impact of narco-colonialism, there are political implications for U.S. imperialism in Latin America. The BBC reported that the imperial project has spilled across the border into Ecuador, triggering fears of a "Colombianization" of the region.[80] Ecuadorians feared that if Colombia became "the next Vietnam," Ecuador could become "the next Cambodia." The Colombian narco-bourgeoisie has bought land

Figure 3: Colombian Coca Production Estimates by the U.S. Government
and the United Nations, 1998–2006

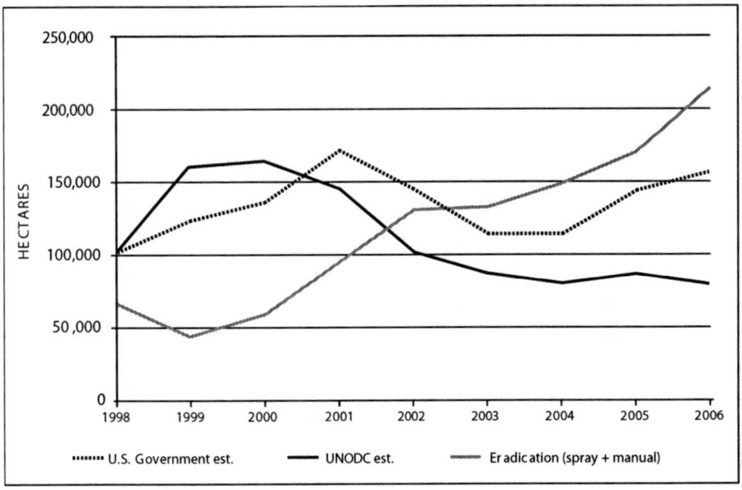

Source: Center for International Policy (CIP)

in the northern Ecuadorian provinces of Sucumbios and Carchi bordering Colombia. This increased the price of coca paste in northern Peru and facilitated the relocation of coca deeper into the Amazon.[81] In General Farfan and Puerto el Carmen, villages along the banks of the San Miguel River in Sucumbios, Ecuadorian farmers have reported damaged crops, sore eyes, and headaches, demonstrating the effects of the fumigation strategy in Ecuador.[82]

Fears of a Colombianization of Latin America with cocaine are substantiated with the development of cocaine and chemical-manufacturing laboratories, set up by Bolivian *compradores* throughout the Brazilian Amazon as well as in northwestern Argentina and northern Chile. A narco-bourgeoisie is emerging in countries outside the Crystal Triangle as well. In the inter-American drug trade, Colombian middlemen are being replaced by distributors in Mexico, where an increasing share of exports from Colombia are controlled.[83] In an effort to distract attention from the Colombian source, the past decade has seen the "Mexican drug war" (2006–present) become the apparent focus in drug war propaganda. Colombian cocaine laboratories situated near rivers and in thick tropical jungles are refining and exporting cocaine to transshipment Southern Cone countries.[84] To the powers that be in Washington, this may send mixed signals about imperial-*comprador* relations in Latin America. The gang-related violence in Rio de Janeiro—known euphemistically as the "White Republic" for the color of cocaine—and the involvement of government officials in the drug trade could lead to a possible Colombianization of Brazil.[85] Cocaine cartels, resembling the paramilitary militias of Colombia, have invaded small Amazonian towns, turning their inhabitants into drug addicts and cheap "mules," or drug couriers.[86] Growing market competition among the landowning and national business classes could lead to cocaine wars of the kind seen during the cocaine decade. The current drug wars in Mexico between drug cartels and security forces resemble Colombia during the 1980s.[87] If the political environment gives rise to new Pablo Escobars, it could bring yet another challenge for U.S. imperialism and the *compradores*.

The regionalization of cocaine has expanded to countries traditionally important to the interests of the United States, such as Argentina and Brazil, but also to other countries which have resisted narco-colonialism such as Bolivia under President Evo Morales of the Movement Toward Socialism (MAS) Party and Venezuelan president Hugo Chávez. In Bolivia, Morales has banned the DEA from his country citing the book *The Big White Lie* by Michael Levine. Such radical forces have the potential to create an "anti-imperialist" bloc in Latin America, on the one hand spearheaded by the armed struggle of the FARC in Colombia and on the other by Chávez and his 21st-Century Socialism. Gregory Wilpert writes:

> What, though, does Chávez mean by "21st Century Socialism"? After his initial announcement, at the January 2005 World Social Forum in Porto Alegre, Chávez often repeated the call, but did not provide much more details, other than a list of values upon which this new socialism would be based. These values can be characterized as involving the ideals of the French Revolution, of utopian socialism,

and of Christianity. "We have assumed the commitment to direct the Bolivarian Revolution toward socialism and to contribute to the socialist path, with a new socialism, a socialism of the 21st century, which is based in solidarity, in fraternity, in love, in justice, in liberty, and in equality," said Chávez in a speech in mid-2006. Also, this socialism is not pre-defined. Rather, said Chávez, we must "transform the mode of capital and move toward socialism, toward a new socialism that must be constructed every day."[88]

Resistance to U.S. imperialism has intensified in Colombia with Venezuelan president Hugo Chávez. His open support for the Cuban Revolution and the ratification by the Venezuelan Congress in 2008 that FARC be recognized as a legitimate political force and not a terrorist group has given rise to much controversy.[89] Despite his revolutionary overtones, Chávez distanced himself from the FARC soon after declaring "the guerrilla war is history." Chávez said, "At this moment in Latin America, an armed guerrilla movement is out of place."[90] Chávez's statement came after the Colombian Air Force bombed a FARC camp in Ecuador on March 1, 2008, killing the FARC emissary Raul Reyes and twenty-four foreign sympathizers (including four Mexicans and an Ecuadorian). The bombing raid detonated the worst crisis of inter-American diplomacy of the last decade, prompting Venezuelan and Ecuadorian security forces to the Colombian border.[91] For Chávez, the FARC's armed struggle strained Venezuelan-Colombian relations. In May 2004, however, Venezuelan security forces captured eighty-six Colombian paramilitaries. They were arrested wearing Venezuelan army uniforms in a country house near the outskirts of Caracas belonging to a "radical member of the opposition," an anti-Castro Cuban named Roberto Alonso who is believed to be residing in Miami. Chávez said the aborted plan entailed an invasion that was "thought up, planned and led by an international network—two of whose hubs are Miami, Florida, and Colombia—with the complicity of unpatriotic Venezuelans."[92]

Alongside Cuba and the FARC guerrillas, Venezuela remains a target in Washington's "Axis of Evil," which has serious political implications for U.S. imperialism in Latin America.[93] Further, the leftist government of President Rafael Correa in Ecuador could leave Colombia sandwiched between two leftist governments. Concerning the U.S. Manta air base on Ecuador's Pacific coast, Correa has argued that Washington must let him open a military base in Miami if the United States wants to keep using it. U.S. officials say the base is vital for counter-narcotics surveillance operations on Pacific drug-running routes.[94] Washington fears that if these two leftist governments move farther to the left it will lead to either accommodation or economic and political strangulation for Colombia. Since it depends on Venezuela for much of its agricultural exports, Colombia also fears support for Chávez's 21st-Century Socialism among Latin American countries.[95]

Under pressure from the George W. Bush administration, President Uribe neutralized Chávez's growing influence in the Colombian conflict by dismissing his mediating efforts that had commenced in 2007, preferring instead his close ally, the Catholic Church hierarchy, backed by the governments of France, Spain, and Switzerland, which have corporations with substantial investment interests in Colombia.[96] Since the Colombia-Ecuador border crisis Venezuelan-Colombian relations have normalized with Colombian president Juan Manuel Santos though scandals traced to his predecessor continue. They include the ongoing *Parapolitica* scandal in which Santos has repeatedly said Uribe will not be investigated under his government; an International Criminal Court investigation; an alleged war crime involving the use of the Red Cross emblem during a supposed "daring" and "perfect" military rescue operation against the FARC, apparently choreographed by the Colombian government and media;[97] an alleged assassination plot against President Chávez; the violation of Ecuadorian sovereignty; electoral fraud; doctoring police and judicial records to erase paramilitary cases; and the most serious of these traceable to Uribe: the "disappearances" of more than 250,000 Colombians in the last two decades, surpassing the recorded mass murders committed by the military juntas of Argentina (30,000), Chile (3,000), and Uruguay (600) in the previous century combined.[98] According to Colombian investigative journalist Azalea

Robles, the 250,000 figure has been systematically reduced with the use of crematory ovens and mass graves throughout the country resembling those used by the Nazis during the Second World War.[99] A written statement signed by a diverse range of social movements, left-wing organizations, and unions condemned February 2008 anti-FARC demonstrations that the Colombian left maintains were orchestrated by the Uribe government.[100]

When compared to the cartel-run narco-economy of the 1980s, which provided a degree of order and stability for the economic interests of the narco-bourgeoisie and U.S. imperialism, the regionalization of the cocaine trade has brought financial benefits but also increasing resistance to the privatization and decentralization of the Colombian economic system. The relocation and regionalization strategy prevails as U.S. imperialism works ferociously to isolate the FARC and undermine anti-imperialist politics in the region. Colombia was never a traditional coca-growing nation until U.S. imperialism and cocaine intersected. Regionalization is important to U.S. imperialist goals that were made possible through its supply-side programs and Plan Colombia. "The days when the vast majority of cocaine was bound for the United States are long gone," says a DEA official in Washington who works on policy in Colombia. "The cocaine trade has gone global."[101]

9. The War on Drugs:
Corporatization and Privatization

The counterinsurgency campaign against the FARC has not eliminated the drug trade in Colombia. Colombian cocaine continues to be produced and transported in large quantities for sale in the United States and Western Europe. This chapter examines the links between U.S. corporations and the private defense industry and how they profit from the drug trade via finance capital and banks that launder the proceeds of the cocaine trade.

State-Organized Crime

The networks of politicians, police, private security firms, and ordinary citizens investing in illegal enterprises for a high return can be described as state-organized crime.[1] Western governments smuggle arms and drugs, participate in assassinations, conspiracies, and terrorist acts to further their foreign policy objectives, acts defined by law as "criminal and committed by state officials in pursuit of their job as representatives of the state."[2] Criminologists point to piracy as an early form of state-organized crime, as virtually every European nation including the United States since Christopher Columbus's voyages to the New World have either established alliances with pirates to strengthen their borders or have financially benefited in their share of the profits. Today, it is likely to be carried out under the auspices of state agencies with investigative powers, such as the CIA, the FBI, and the Internal Revenue Service.[3] U.S. imperialism's political and economic interest in the drug trade reflects Marx's dictum that the internal logic of the capitalist system involves the continual expansion of production and profit, which, in Colombia, is achieved through narco-colonialism.

Profits from the drug trade far exceed what is needed to fund U.S. covert operations, wars, presidential campaigns, and other activities. Most of the profits from the drug trade are hidden, usually in offshore financial institutions, where corporations acquire these funds.[4] The use of American private corporations, whether wholly owned by the CIA as "proprietaries" or outsourced as "private contractors," has become a common practice in regions of conflict or "shatter zones." The operations of these private defense contractors in the counterinsurgency strategy in Colombia are crucial for corporations. Theodore Shackley, a former CIA operative wrote, in support of state-organized crime in Asia and Latin America during the Cold War:

> These, then, are all facets to what irregular warfare technocrats call— for better or worse—"the third option" to the persuasions of diplomacy and trade on the one hand and military force on the other. It also includes all aspects of covert action, which in some lexicons is defined as the influencing of people and the shaping of events through the use of political, economic or military factors, without the sponsor of this activity being identified in an attributable manner.[5]

Paradoxically, the cocaine trade involves the billions of dollars in U.S. military hardware used for the war on drugs and terror. This phenomenon has been described as the "military-industrial narcotics complex."[6] The Cold War saw the growth of this complex that involved companies outsourced by the CIA such as Air America, SAT, SETCO, DIACSA, Vortex, and Frigorificos de Puntarenas (a Costa Rican seafood company), all of which assisted in covert drug trafficking operations.[7] Counterinsurgency operations by the United States would not have been possible without the involvement of private defense contractors.

In October 2000, an important conference was held to discuss U.S. plans for Colombia in the twenty-first century that involved the U.S. Department of Defense, U.S. Department of State, the intelligence community, and the Colombian military.[8] Colombia was presented as "the linchpin of stability of the Andean region." The conference report stated that "prosecuting the war does not contradict the peace process [and] regaining control over the drug-producing areas of Colombia means wrestling territorial control from the insurgents, particularly the FARC." The report pointed out that "the self-defense groups popularly called 'paramilitaries' need to be included in the peace process because the population they represent is of such significant size."

To regain FARC-controlled drug-producing areas, U.S. private defense provides military assistance to the narco-bourgeoisie so that drug profits continue to flow to U.S. financial institutions, private banks, and transnational corporations (TNCs).[9] A major report from the UNDCP in 1998 revealed that with "increasing globalization," $2 trillion a day was being laundered through the "world's financial system," a "money launderer's dream."[10] Several hundred billion dollars are washed through the U.S. financial system each year virtually unchecked.[11] The annual profits from the global drug trade are estimated to be worth between $300 and $500 billion with an estimated flow of $250 billion going directly to U.S. banks each year.[12] Martin Woods, a former senior anti-money-laundering officer at Wachovia Bank (now Wells Fargo & Company), one of the largest in the United States, which investigators have recently found was laundering money for Mexican drug cartels, says, New York and London "have become the world's two biggest laundries of criminal and drug money, and offshore tax havens. Not the Cayman Islands, not the Isle of Man or

Jersey. The big laundering is right through the City of London and Wall Street."[13] This pattern of drug money-laundering banks is traceable to the Reagan and Bush eras.

Catherine Austin Fitts, who had been managing director of the now defunct Wall Street investment firm Dillon, Read & Co. before becoming assistant secretary of housing under George H. W. Bush, stated that somewhere between $250 and $300 billion from the importation of drugs from Colombia went to Florida, New York, Texas, and California.[14] According to Fitts, just a decade ago these "money-laundering" states provided 80 percent of presidential campaign funds. Fitts, who is now president of Solari, Inc., and managing member of Solari Investment Advisory Services claims that corporations have stock values based upon annual net profits known as "price earnings" or "the pop" and identify the multiples of income at which a stock trades, that is, stock value. The multiplier effect of stock values can reach a factor of thirty. Fitts estimated the figure for drug money entering America reaches up to six times $250 billion annually through money-laundering activities, resulting in an estimated $1.5 trillion per year in U.S. cash transactions from the global drug trade.[15]

Money deposited in the United States is not difficult to monitor. The U.S. Federal Reserve System registers any deposit over $10,000 as standard practice.[16] According to Salomon Kalmanovitz, an economist and member of Colombia's Central Bank board of directors, the estimated wealth of the Colombian narco-bourgeoisie in the early years of the post-cartel economy was $76 billion, which is about 30 percent of the country's total wealth, less than half of U.S. annual profits from the drug trade.[17] Robert Auerbach of the University of Texas was told by U.S. General Accounting Office inspectors in 2002 that the vaults of the Los Angeles Federal Reserve "have the second-most currency in the entire Federal Reserve System because of all the drug money flowing into California."[18] Auerbach observed that officials who run the Federal Reserve Bank bureaucracy fail to monitor money-laundering.[19] Auerbach estimates that $80 billion in cash from corrupt accounting practices in the Federal Reserve has been stored at its second-largest vault facility in Los Angeles, second only to New York in terms of the volume of cash transactions. Nevertheless, there is no conclusive evidence or precise figures that demonstrate drug money is being laundered through the U.S. financial system. The Colombian narco-economy allows narco-capital to flow to the United States and return. Colombian financial institutions are engaged in currency transactions involving international narcotics trafficking proceeds that include significant amounts of U.S. currency.[20] In Colombia, money-laundering has not been prosecuted and neither businesses nor assets have been seized (for examples, vehicles used to transport narcotics), nor have farms on which cocaine is grown or intangible property (bank accounts). This untouchability prevails throughout the Colombian banking and financial system, through contraband, real estate, and the *comprador* narco-bourgeoisie's own front companies.[21]

The Colombian narco-bourgeoisie's financial needs are accommodated through the New York Stock Exchange. In June 1999, news services reported that Richard Grasso, chairman of the Board of Governors of the Federal Reserve, and members of his executive staff flew to Colombia. Others who attended the meeting were unnamed, but Grasso's visit was organized by the Colombian government, in particular by Colombian ambassador to the United States Luis Alberto Moreno, said to be a close personal friend of Grasso.[22] "I invite members of the FARC to visit the New York Stock Exchange so that they can get to know the market personally," Grasso was quoted as saying. "I truly hope that they can do this," he added. Media reported that Grasso had asked to meet Raul Reyes of the FARC's high command to discuss foreign investment and the future role of U.S. businesses in Colombia.[23] The purpose of the meeting was to bring a message of cooperation from U.S. financial services and to discuss foreign investment and the future role of U.S. businesses in Colombia.[24] In retrospect, Grasso's trip served as a fact-finding mission concerning the FARC's alleged role in drug trafficking activities. However, no deal was brokered with the insurgency as the U.S. government does not accept the FARC applying tax revenues to nothing other than the American depository and investment system in which the Colombian narco-economy is linked. The FARC's long-held policy of legalization of drug consumption as a means to eliminate the drug trade was unacceptable to Grasso also.[25] According to Catherine Fitts, such Wall Street behavior is not uncommon:

> I raised tens of thousands of dollars for the George Bush presidential campaign in 1988. Nicholas Brady, who became George Bush's Treasury Secretary, had been my partner and boss at Dillon Read. When "Iran-Contra" came and went I was oblivious. I had no idea about the drugs. It never entered my mind. Yet today I am convinced that the illegal drug trade, the enormous cheap capital it generates, and the CIA's role as enforcer/protector for the profits of that trade is a dominant factor in the economy of this country. It is a factor which is destroying the entire American culture and is utterly out of control. As an investor and banker and as a former Cabinet-level appointee, I tell you this is true.[26]

Christian de Brie, in *Le Monde Diplomatique,* contends that financial crime is a system closely linked to the expansion of modern capitalism, based on an association of three partners: governments, transnational corporations, and mafiosi.[27] This form of crime is part of a "service industry in which the Americans have a considerable lead over their competitors, not only in know-how, but also in the vast financial and logistical resources they are able to make available to their multinationals; these include the secret services of the world's most powerful state apparatus [the CIA and other U.S. intelligence services], which, with the Cold War over, have moved into economic warfare."[28] De Brie names U.S. corporations from the Fortune 500 that he considers experts in the matter: Lockheed Martin, Boeing, IBM, General Motors, Exxon, General Electric, and Texaco. He describes the relationships:

> Big business complicity and political *laissez-faire* is the only way that large-scale organized crime can launder and recycle the fabulous proceeds of its activities. . . . Politicians are directly involved and their

ability to intervene depends on the backing and the funding that keep
them in power. This collusion of interests is an essential part of the
world economy. . . . All this would be impossible without the power
of the state and international and regional organizations, especially
their ability to keep restrictive regulations to a minimum, to abolish or
override such rules as do exist, to paralyze inquiries and investigations or put them off indefinitely, and to reduce or grant amnesty from
any penalties.[29]

Privatizing the War on Drugs for Profit

At the end of the Cold War, the use of U.S. private defense contractors began to replace much of the covert work that had been formerly conducted by the CIA. A transition was underway where private
defense corporations were formed and contractors were deployed
in Colombia and throughout the cocaine decade and well into the
implementation of Plan Colombia.[30] During the Clinton–Bush
(1993–2009) years and for most of the Pastrana–Uribe
(1998–2010) presidencies, the majority of the profits went to
American firms under the sponsorship of "Plan Colombia."
Lobbyists from big oil, arms manufacturing, and military defense
companies in the United States made $6 million in campaign con-
tributions to Congress in support of Plan Colombia. Of the $1.3
billion initially approved for the program just 13 percent went to
the Colombian government to combat the FARC—the rest flowed
to corporate America.[31] It is imperative to now investigate what
those companies did in Colombia.

The *comprador,* financially linked to international capital, organizes cocaine production locally, creating a powerful transnational class
of businessmen and investors with a common interest in "private military companies" (PMCs) and their megaprojects. PMC owners and
employees are current or former U.S. military or intelligence personnel, often with past combat experience, directly engaged in the counternarcotics counterinsurgency strategy.

The use of PMCs and their activities in Colombia as well as in Iraq, Afghanistan, and Libya most recently have been cloaked in secrecy.[32] Since the election of U.S. president Barack Obama in 2008 this secrecy has intensified with any discussion, research, or media commentary relating to the war on drugs now centered on Mexico's "Merida Initiative," initiated by President George W. Bush. In 2010 Secretary of State Hillary Clinton stated that Mexico and Central America were facing an "insurgency" that required the equivalent of Plan Colombia.[33] This switch in public focus has been one major outcome of the regionalization strategy; however, it has not reduced U.S. involvement in the Colombian conflict.

As in Mexico, the drug war in Colombia has increasingly become a privatized war that goes well beyond the context of Plan Colombia.[34] Just as George W. Bush had started in 2001, Obama has continued the fight against "narco-terrorism" by providing $600 million in military aid to protect "a potentially failed state under terrorist siege."[35] Like Obama's renamed "Overseas Contingency Operation," there is little reference to Plan Colombia unless government spokespeople are referring to Mexico in a controversial sense. The privatization of the war on drugs is primarily due to the changing character of the war on terror which stretched American military capabilities in Iraq and Afghanistan since 2003 and demanded a much greater role for PMCs in "shatter zones."[36]

The expansionist role of American military forces has posed a new security dilemma for U.S. imperialism that can only be achieved through the methods of narco-colonialism applied throughout the Cold War from the Golden Triangle to the Crystal Triangle in the 1980s and 1990s. According to a survey conducted by international humanitarian organizations, the use of PMCs is spreading rapidly across Latin America despite the lack of studies on the changing security situation on the continent and internationally.[37] It is not clear whether the increase in the number of PMCs in South America have been a direct result of Plan Colombia.[38]

In a recent press conference held in Bogotá, General Douglas Fraser, the head of SOUTHCOM, reiterated U.S. support for the "ongoing war on drugs and terrorism."[39] Fraser said, "I reiterate the commitment of the U.S. government and the Southern Command in support of Colombia's commitment to defend its democratic institutions, protect its citizens and improve the security, stability and rule of law throughout the country."[40] Although there was no mention of PMCs or military personnel, as in the cocaine decade, Fraser's comments were not mere empty words to Colombian officials. The Colombian state is facing a deteriorating security situation in its war on the FARC while struggling to discipline internal divisions amongst the narco-bourgeoisie.[41] President Juan Manuel Santos has replaced the entire military command except the national police director. These developments follow ongoing criticisms of increasing FARC attacks on the Colombian army, which Santos argues are signs of their weakness.[42] According to Leon Valencia, director of Fundación Arco Iris, an NGO which specializes on the Colombian conflict, the FARC have been extensively reorganizing and adjusting their politico-military strategy in the past few years. "They have a new structure and a new strategy that has given them good results."[43] Valencia explains there have been political debates over the level of morale within Colombian security forces as the FARC has become more resourceful with heavy recruiting and engagement with social movements: "they're putting more focus on conquering the [hearts and minds of the] population."[44]

According to *NACLA Report on the Americas*, an influential non-profit magazine which specializes in Latin America, it is "very difficult to calculate U.S. presence in Colombia."[45] The counterinsurgency effort has employed approximately six hundred U.S. military personnel in Colombia, plus thousands of paramilitary troops, with hundreds more hired from the United States and Latin America who do not count toward the official cap. Hundreds more work as "contract employees"—spray-plane and helicopter pilots, search-and-rescue personnel, mechanics, logistics personnel, radar-site operators, and instructors.[46] Information relating to their covert activities within Colombia's narco-military network is minimal, outdated, and difficult to obtain, as the Center for International Policy notes:

Public information about the contractors and their operations is limited—neither the government nor the companies release much information about their outsourcing. Basic information, such as the names of all companies hired for State Department and intelligence-agency contract work, is unavailable. Due to a lack of primary sources, our research on contractors depends heavily on journalistic reports.[47]

The role of PMCs is obscured by another layer of secrecy. The U.S. government is not required to release information about their covert activities and can use "national security" as grounds to withhold data. PMCs, in turn, can plead "corporate confidentiality." The reason for this obscurity is to protect the United States from prosecution for war crimes by the International Criminal Court (ICC) where approximately 90–95 percent of human rights violations are committed by the narco-military network.[48] The immunity of U.S. personnel was strengthened further in a binational agreement between Colombia and the United States on September 17, 2003, in the following terms:

For the aims in the present Agreement the expression "person of the United States of America" means any government employee, employee (including any contractor), or member of the army, present or past, member of the Government that enjoyed immunity against the penal jurisdiction by virtue of the international law, anyway is subject to the jurisdiction of the State that it sends (the United States of America).[49]

The use of PMCs enable Special Operations Forces under the coordination and command structure of SOUTHCOM to work alongside private contractors for covert operations. Most importantly, PMCs decentralize covert operations by decreasing the U.S. government's official level of involvement as privatized armies or "special operations teams."[50] These teams are the same ones that assist the Colombian narco-military network in their war on the FARC but extend beyond counterinsurgency purposes. The number of foreign

PMCs in Colombia and details regarding their services are top-secret with public records and registrations outlining their presence sealed in the obscurity. This situation creates ambiguity with respect to the transnational corporations that operate in Colombia and the number of contracts that can be traced to them.[51] The imperial-*compradore* arrangement allows U.S. transnational corporations direct access to exploit the Colombian narco-economy with total immunity.

A significant proportion of the transnational PMCs in Colombia have their headquarters in the United States or the United Kingdom.[52] The top thirty-five, however, are among the most profitable transnational corporations in the United States. The *Los Angeles Times* reports that the U.S. Congress is notified only of contracts worth more than $50 million due to "conflicting views of what is in the U.S. interest."[53] When a license is granted, there are "no reporting requirements or oversight of work that typically lasts years and takes the firms' employees to remote, lawless areas." Huge PMCs that operate in Colombia are L-3 Military Professional Resources Incorporated, best known by its acronym MPRI, located in Alexandria, Virginia, and owned by L3 Communications; Kellogg Brown & Root, the Texas company that funded both Lyndon Johnson's political career and Dick Cheney's corporate career and is a subsidiary of the Halliburton[54] Corporation; DynCorp Aerospace Technology of Reston, Virginia; and Science Applications International Corporation (SAIC) of San Diego.[55]

In 1998, the American air freight company Southern Air Transport (SAT), which was active in the cocaine decade, declared bankruptcy. However, investigators found that $32 million of the company's assets had been moved before SAT filed, the very same day the CIA inspector general issued a report outlining allegations of SAT drug running. Proceeds from the sale of SAT assets were deposited in the personal bank account of the wife of the company's owner, James Bastian, a former CIA lawyer from Miami.[56] By 1999, other air cargo airlines were competing with SAT's successor, Southern Air, to gain access to SAT's designated U.S.-Colombia all-cargo scheduled service, which operated throughout the cocaine decade until its bankruptcy.[57] These airlines were Polar Air Cargo, Kitty Hawk Aircargo Incorporated, and Taiwan's EVA Air, former CIA proprietary Evergreen Air's successor.[58] The *Journal of Commerce* commented:

> Air cargo executives from around the globe have been invoking Latin America like a mantra for the past two years as one of the most promising areas for their industry. The optimism was muted at times due to the volatile situation in some countries, but overall, it has steadily gathered momentum. Today, with traditionally buoyant routes across the Pacific showing deteriorating yields, the region is even more regarded as the emerging "El Dorado" for air freight.[59]

Information about the cargo carried by these airlines is difficult to retrieve, but their operations were immensely profitable as components of the U.S.-outsourced special operations teams in the war on drugs and terror. Two PMCs, DynCorp and MPRI, are of particular significance. According to the State Department, since 2007 DynCorp, among other companies such as Lockheed Martin and ARINC, Inc., have been the major beneficiaries of Plan Colombia.[60] DynCorp, a "technology and services company" with over $1.8 billion in annual revenues and more than 23,000 employees worldwide, was the largest PMC operating in Colombia. Its contracts with U.S. government agencies account for 98 percent of its market share. DynCorp has been under U.S. State Department contract in Colombia since 1991, and in 1998 it was awarded a $170 million five-year contract.[61] DynCorp's planes and military helicopters are used in the relocation missions that involve chemical and biological warfare. In 2000, DynCorp helicopters were also involved in sixty reported gun battles with the FARC, according to the State Department.[62]

Richard Boucher, a State Department spokesman, has claimed that guerrillas fired at private contractors involved in a relocation mission. His comments to the press were made after admitting that "private U.S. citizens" had been involved in a battle with FARC rebels on the weekend of February 20, 2000. DynCorp personnel have provided logistical support and training for the Colombian army's "anti-narcotics" battalions, carrying troops into battle and rescuing shot-down pilots. DynCorp contract employees include military personnel with experience in Vietnam, the Middle East, and throughout Latin America (particularly covert operations against Cuba and in Central America) and are paid up to $10,000 a week and $200,000 a year.[63]

CorpWatch reported that the DynCorp "mission deployments may be made to any worldwide location, including, potentially, outside of Central and South America."[64] DynCorp has participated in "eradication missions, training, and drug interdiction" and "air transport, reconnaissance, search and rescue, airborne medical evacuation, ferrying equipment and personnel from one country to another, as well as aircraft maintenance." DynCorp is the same private company that the Reagan-Bush administration used to run arms and drugs during the cocaine decade.[65] In 1998, a U.S. reporter who attempted to talk to DynCorp pilots at San Jose del Guaviare said he was threatened with exclusion from the U.S. embassy if he ever attempted to approach DynCorp personnel again. Another reporter said he was banned from embassy-sponsored briefings after the reporter quoted a guerrilla leader as saying that U.S. military advisers would now be targeted for attack.[66]

Eagle Aviation Services and Technology (EAST), a subcontractor of DynCorp, has flown U.S. State Department planes such as armed UH-1H Iroquois, Bell-212 Huey-type helicopters, and T-65 Thrush crop dusters in top-secret missions in Colombia for at least fifteen years.[67] Current and "former" State Department officials have argued that EAST's interest in Colombia has nothing to do with its controversial past. Jonathan Winer, Senator John Kerry's aide during Iran-Contra, said in 2001, "That was 15 years ago. . . . the issue is what they're doing, not what they did."[68] In 2011, strenuous efforts to block any attempt by the public to investigate secret operations remain as proactive as they were during the cocaine decade.

Employees of DynCorp have been involved in drug trafficking as well as consuming heroin, cocaine, and amphetamines. On May 12, 2000, Colombian authorities intercepted a parcel containing a sample of liquid heroin in two bottles, which had been sent from DynCorp's

Colombian office to its Florida air base.[69] This again was only a random inspection check, and the matter was covered up quickly and clumsily, according to *Nation* reporter Jason Vest, who broke the story. Vest said that DynCorp, the Colombian National Police, the DEA, and the U.S. State Department could not stick to a single account of what occurred. In 1994, a DynCorp pilot stationed on the Tres Esquinas military base in southern Colombia died of a cocaine overdose; in 1999, the Colombian state prosecutor launched an investigation into amphetamine smuggling. Documents relating to all these cases have mysteriously disappeared and the issue of drug trafficking has been abandoned by both Colombian and American authorities.[70]

Richard Gadd, a retired U.S. Air Force officer, founded DynCorp during the cocaine decade. General Richard Secord, who directed SETCO and SAT during that time, recruited agents for DynCorp delivery operations. A former CIA agent, Herbert S. "Pug" Winokur, was chairman of the board of DynCorp from 1988 to 1997. According to Daniel Guttman's classic 1978 book *The Shadow Government,* he had been a permanent fixture in the Washington old-boy network of the Cold War years. Winokur was a member of the U.S. Council on Foreign Relations, "a clearinghouse for the really choice frauds," according to Lt. Commander Al Martin, a former CIA operative who testified before Senator John Kerry's congressional committee during Iran-Contra.[71] When Winokur was director of Harvard Management Company and a member of Harvard Corporation, funding dramatically increased from $5 billion to $19 billion in six years. Winokur also sat on the board of directors of Enron, the company that declared bankruptcy only after paying "corporate insiders" hundreds of millions of dollars for their "services."[72]

Catherine Austin Fitts believes that Winokur was responsible for destroying the economic research she undertook in 1996, which began to illuminate how the drug trade generates profits for Wall Street through the subsidized housing and urban development (HUD) market where Harvard Corporation is a major investor. Cases such as these suggest that there may be more to the failure of companies when bankruptcy is declared than simply bad management. The director of DynCorp since 1988, Dudley Mecum, is also the managing director of Winokur's Capricorn Holdings Inc. and of CitiGroup, which was implicated in money-laundering activities in 1998 along with its consumer banking arm, Citibank, for Raul Salinas (the brother of former Mexican president Carlos Salinas, 1988–94).[73] At the time of DynCorp's contract in 1998 with the U.S. State, Treasury, and Commerce departments, the company received a contract with the CIA and NASA to provide intelligence for the United States.[74] Whether this contract was linked to Plan Colombia is not known but it became common knowledge that DynCorp acted as a front company on behalf of the CIA, hiring mercenaries and "assets" for covert operations in Colombia.[75]

L-3 MPRI is a military consultancy and supplies pilots and Special Forces elite training and security services worldwide. Many of its contract employees serve on the U.S. Council on Foreign Relations.[76] An inside joke is that MPRI has more generals than the Pentagon.[77] While DynCorp-EAST is responsible for the skies, MPRI, with over a thousand elite military and law enforcement officers, has been responsible for the groundwork. Primarily, this means engaging FARC guerrillas in direct combat, and protecting cocaine distribution routes that have been undermined by the FARC. MPRI has worked with the Colombian armed forces and the national police in areas of planning; operations, including PSYOPS; training; logistics; intelligence; and personnel management. General Edward Soyster, an MPRI spokesman, compared his company with other U.S. TNCs operating overseas. We're "like Coca-Cola," he said.[78]

In 2000, MPRI signed a $4.3 million one-year contract with the U.S. Defense Department to carry out a "force modernization" of the Colombian armed forces and produced a report that, according to several analysts, provided "few new ideas for combating the FARC." The contract was not renewed in 2001. This may have been for two reasons. First, MPRI's poor results in engaging the FARC may have prompted the U.S. government to replace the PMC; and second, U.S. needs for oil and energy resources to sustain overseas deployments in a growing number of world hot spots (The Middle East, Central Asia, and North Africa).[79]

Military companies provide active assistance involving combat, which has a strategic impact on the political and security environments of the countries in which they operate. Sanho Tree, an expert on South America at the U.S. Institute for Policy Studies, says, "Congress has little oversight of what PMCs are doing in Colombia," and "this is how the Pentagon wants it, because they can put more troops in Colombia than they are [legally] allowed." Tree concludes that the United States encourages the Colombian military, one of the least transparent and most abusive in the world, to be even more opaque. Not merely passive trainees, they fight alongside a client's military forces and routinely rotate with U.S. advisers in Colombia. "We have a database of more than 10,000 former soldiers who want to have military-related jobs," boasts the MPRI spokesman, General Soyster. A former congressional staffer described MPRI's activities as a "non-sexy but far bigger Oliver North-style enterprise."[80]

Alongside DynCorp and MPRI, Florida-based Airscan has been contracted by the Pentagon to monitor movements of drug supply through rural Colombia. Airscan of Rockledge, Florida, was formed in 1984 by former U.S. Air Force commandos Walter Holloway and John Mansur. Airscan specializes in airborne surveillance, security operations, surveillance systems, terrain surveys, and training, and is one of very few companies in the world that can operate unmanned aerial vehicles. Airscan is perhaps the most secretive PMC about its operations and the value of its contracts, choosing to remain vague, citing privacy, and speaking mostly of infrared "deer surveys" and "polar bear trackings" in Colombia and other war theaters.[81]

Airscan uses multi-spectrum cameras to pinpoint coca plantations under FARC control for relocation missions flown by DynCorp pilots. In areas targeted for aerial fumigations, paramilitaries working with the Colombian army arrive in helicopter gunships to "clear the ground" so that the planes, often piloted by Americans, are not shot at by militant campesinos. Day-to-day operations are overseen by a clique of officials in the U.S. State Department's Narcotics Affairs Section (NAS) and the State Department's "Air Wing." In 1998, Airscan was responsible for bombing the northern town of Santo

Domingo where at least eighteen people were killed and at least thirty injured. The Colombian military blamed the FARC; most of the victims were unarmed Colombian Communist Party activists.[82] *Time* magazine describes this as a "standard eradication mission" of which dozens are flown every year.[83]

Airscan's website lists the U.S. Forest Service as a client.[84] Since 1987, private contractors to the U.S. Forest Service have turned up all over the world in covert operations, some of them involved in drug trafficking. According to a lawsuit filed by whistleblower Gary Eitel, a pilot, aviation consultant, and aircraft broker, President Reagan moved as many as fifty C-130s into private contracts for use in a variety of covert operations that included drug smuggling and the direct enrichment of a number of private contractors and investors. A December 8, 1989, memorandum to George Leonard, the U.S. Forest Service associate chief, from Kenneth Cohen, the assistant general counsel, stated, "Apparently, [Department of Defense] thinks that by having the Forest Service as the intermediary, if any future aircraft are used in drug smuggling, the Forest Service and not DOD will suffer the adverse publicity."[85] These operations, although given presidential approval, would appear to violate U.S. federal law.

According to Lawrence Houston, the CIA's former general counsel, the primary company responsible for all CIA covert air operations was the holding company Pacific Corp, also known as Pacific Power & Light, Pacificorp, and Pacific Harbor Capital. Pacific Corp owned CIA companies such as Air America, SAT, and Intermountain Air. By the end of the cocaine decade, the CIA had made all of its aircraft available for use by private contractors working for the U.S. government. "We just didn't need them anymore, and it was fairly hard to keep them going as legitimate businesses," Houston said. "So we decided to sell them off."[86]

Northrop Grumman is another PMC that has been under contract to the U.S. government. Described as an "aerospace and defense services company," it has seventy-five thousand employees and projected revenues of $34.8 billion for 2010.[87] In a similar vein with Airscan, it provides an unknown number of contract employees in

Colombia. In 1998, the U.S. Air Force Combat Command awarded Northrop Grumman's technical services a contract to operate and maintain its "Counter Narcotics Surveillance and Control System." The five-year contract was extended and included performance maintenance, system operations, and logistic support of seven radar sites and ten associated ground satellite stations in Colombia, Peru, Venezuela, and Panama.[88]

Five of Northrop Grumman's radar stations are located in eastern and southern Colombia to monitor the country's cocaine distribution routes and traffic patterns. This has allowed American and Colombian airplanes, both private and military, as identified by U.S. intelligence, to fly safely in and out of Colombia and within the country, enabling them to carry narcotics, narcotics-manufacturing chemicals and equipment, weapons, and proceeds from the illegal sale of narcotics. The radar can employ a multiple beam to illuminate aircraft many times during a single antenna scan. The system has a range of 275 miles and can cover targets at up to 100,000 feet.[89] Airplanes not identified by U.S. intelligence are simply shot down by the Colombian air force and participating "interdiction program" countries. A law passed by Congress in 1994 exempts U.S. government officials and "employees" from liability for any "mistakes" committed while cooperating with "another country's shoot-down policy." President Bill Clinton named it the "Air Bridge Strategy."[90]

On February 2003, Northrop made world headlines when a U.S. spy plane carrying four CIA agents and one Colombian intelligence officer was shot down by the FARC in rebel-held territory. The CIA agents became prisoners of war. The remaining two were shot for resisting arrest. The crew members were contract employees of California Microwave Systems—a subsidiary of Northrop Grumman. The plane was essential to U.S. "intelligence-gathering" in Colombia, according to SOUTHCOM. The data it collected was popular among covert agencies that needed up-to-the-minute data on coca production, drug laboratories, and the movements of the product, including the CIA, the DEA, the military, and Customs Service. According to official sources, between 1998 and 2003 the FARC shot down twenty-one

U.S.-government-titled aircraft connected to Lockheed Martin, DynCorp, Northrop Grumman, California Microwave Systems, Matcom, and Arinc. According to a U.S. State Department official, four were under contracts with the aerial division of the State Department that owns Broncos and other important aircraft. Lesser-known firms such as the Rendon Group provide public relations support for the Colombian army; Science Application International Corp. assists in imagery analysis.[91]

On October 30, 2009, Obama and Uribe signed a military agreement that gave Washington access to seven new military bases in Colombia. White House and Colombian officials maintained the agreement was aimed at fighting drug traffickers and guerrillas within Colombian borders. A U.S. Air Force document states the agreement offered a "unique opportunity" for "conducting full-spectrum operations" in the region against various threats, including "anti-U.S. governments."[92] The Pentagon sought access to the bases in Colombia after Ecuadorian president Rafael Correa cancelled the lease for the U.S. military base in Manta, Ecuador.[93] However, with the United States already engaged in two major theaters of war (Iraq and Afghanistan/Pakistan) the immediate priorities for U.S. militarism lay elsewhere.

Plan Colombia—in practice—is alive and well and has no interest in eradicating cocaine. PMCs assist the Colombian narco-bourgeoisie in gaining a monopoly over cocaine production and for this to occur they must defeat the FARC. Narco-colonialism is big business for corporate America, as in other places and time-frames where drug producing zones provided a profit-making opportunity for U.S. finance capital and money-laundering banks.

The contemporary situation is reminiscent of how the CIA and the Argentine Anticommunist Alliance during the Cold War overthrew left-wing governments, fought communist insurgencies, and installed narco-militarists "friendly" to U.S. interests. The growing U.S. intervention in the Colombian conflict is a twenty-first-century version that aims to foster a deeper Latin American dependency on imperial America via its most important client state on the continent.

In a nutshell, the war on drugs and terror is part of a counterrevolutionary strategy designed to maintain rather than eliminate the economic conditions that allow the drug trade to thrive. From Reagan to Obama, U.S. covert intervention has, paradoxically, only accentuated the social violence and systematized the production and distribution of cocaine. Colombia has been transformed into a narco-state increasingly dependent upon a privatized and corporatized U.S. war on drugs and terror.

U.S. Narco-Colonialism and Colombia

In contemporary Colombia, the cocaine trade is seemingly no longer a state security problem. The "evil hour" has passed. Opponents claim to see many signs that the FARC is a diminished force unable to bring fundamental change to Colombia. The FARC's legendary leader, Manuel Marulanda (Tiro Fijo), is dead. Like every government since 1964, the governments of Alvaro Uribe and his successor and former defense minister, Juan Manuel Santos, are said to have waged sustained and successful military campaigns against the FARC, accelerating its demise. Venezuelan president Hugo Chávez has urged the FARC to free its political hostages and end the armed struggle. Venezuela has proven it is not to be the storm center of revolution in Latin America. In 2007 and 2008, Chávez offered to mediate a ceasefire between the Colombian military and the FARC, which was rebuffed by Uribe following pressure from Washington as well as Colombia's military leaders and ruling class. Plan Colombia was seen to be working, with Uribe winning the war against the revolutionary forces. In 2008, costs for U.S. military aid and training of the Colombian army and police had reached nearly $4.9 billion. Since 2008, Israel has been a large supplier of military aid and technology to

Colombia. Washington, a close ally of Tel Aviv and Bogotá, sees both Israel and Colombia as shatter zones. Through militarized power, imperial America believes it can maintain its dominance within both the Middle East and Latin America.

However, the reality of the FARC situation is more complex. For one thing, the real number of the FARC's fighting forces is unknown, as the PSYWAR reaches Orwellian proportions, and in 2011 those celebrations that followed the "famous moment" of Colombian politician Ingrid Betancourt's rescue or Operacion Jacque (in English "check" for "checkmate") in 2008 appear to have been premature. Second, Chávez believes that the Colombian situation could lead to the "Vietnamization of the whole region," implying that the FARC is far from defeated. Camilo Gómez, the top government negotiator under President Andres Pastrana says, "The FARC has an institutional structure that is stronger than any of its leaders."[1] In fact, in 2009 and 2010 more Colombian soldiers and police were killed by the FARC than in 2002 by using smaller and more effective hit-and-run guerrilla tactics.[2] The Uribe-Santos regime is in essence an American proxy government to prevent Venezuela, Ecuador, and Bolivia breaking free of U.S. imperialism. Within Colombia, the newly elected Bogotá mayor Gustavo Petro, a former M-19 guerrilla, may be a reflection of the worsening security situation which has incited calls amongst the urban middle class for peace and reconciliation with the FARC. Although Plan Colombia under Uribe's presidency was counted as a success in curbing the guerrilla war, bringing a decline in violence on the streets of Bogotá and Medellín, the FARC remains active throughout the countryside, mountains, and remote territories in the Amazon, and the Colombian state forces and the paramilitary death squads clash over control of the cocaine trade.

In 2008, America's first African-American president promised change for Colombia. In his presidential debate with Republican rival John McCain, Barack Obama argued, "The history in Colombia right now is that labor leaders have been targeted for assassination on a fairly consistent basis and there have not been prosecutions."[3] So far, the United States has not yet constructed its seven new military bases—

three air force, two naval, and two army stretching from the Pacific to the Caribbean—and reactivating its fourth Fleet. Washington may believe it has contained the insurgency in Colombia. The construction of new bases may simply be postponed rather than abandoned completely. Meanwhile, 4.9 million Colombians have been made refugees in their own country, and by conservative estimates nearly 69 percent of the population survives below the poverty line. Colombia is the only major country in Latin America where the gap between the rich and poor has markedly widened in recent years, according to the UN Commission on Latin America. At the height of the global financial crisis in 2008–2009, drug money worth billions of dollars permeated the financial system. Antonio Maria Costa, the head of the UN Office on Drugs and Crime, has acknowledged that the majority of the $352 billion of drug profits that were generated was absorbed into the global economic system: "It is understood that evidence that drug money has flowed into banks came from officials in Britain, Switzerland, Italy and the U.S."[4] U.S. narco-colonialism with the support of the international bourgeoisie has kept the financial system afloat.

The American war on drugs and terror in Colombia has neither reduced the amount of coca grown nor the cocaine exported. Though Washington claims its military aid and assistance to Bogotá has destroyed the Colombian drug cartels, cocaine remains a vital export commodity in Colombia's political economy. Colombia's cocaine is now largely controlled by competing factions within the narco-bourgeoisie, the military, the police, and paramilitary forces. It is transported to Mexico where competing drug cartels wage war for its control. According to a Jesuit priest, Father Javier Giraldo, Plan Colombia's war on drugs and terror has left Colombia a "compliant country," torn apart by a war for cocaine, and open to exploitation by American corporations of its raw materials, including oil and coal, which leaves a desperate workforce willing to accept barely subsistence wages and conditions.[5]

This study has delved into the Crystal Triangle and the political economy of Colombia, cocaine, and U.S. imperialism. It has revealed the dynamics, structure, and context of the Colombian cocaine trade and its dependency upon the United States. The U.S. war on drugs and terror has left Colombia saturated by drugs, misery and violence, as well as open to the possibility of revolutionary change. This war as decreed by successive Washington administrations was, is, and remains its opposites: a war *for* drugs and a war *of* terror. The fever of the escalating U.S.-sponsored counterinsurgency engulfs Colombia, immiserating its people, as cocaine flows to the U.S. and other global markets. Even though the drug war has apparently moved to Mexico, deep inside Colombia the "forgotten" popular struggle is busy being born as the old order is dying.

Bibliography

Adams, Nathan. "The Hunt for Andre." *Reader's Digest*, March 1973; "Heroin: Now It's the Latin Connection," *Newsweek*, January 24, 1972.

Agencia de Noticias Nueva Colombia. "President Blamed for the Killing of 10 Prisoners." May 14, 2003.

———. "Top US Official Lied About Al Qaida-FARC Link," September 12, 2002.

———. "UN Confirms: Colombian Army Implicated in Bojaya Tragedy." May 24, 2002.

———. "The Wrong Pig on Trial," June 2, 2003.

Allman, T.D. "Blow Back," *Rolling Stone*, May 9, 2002.

Ambrose, Stephen E., and Douglas G. Brinkley. *Rise to Globalism: American Foreign Policy Since 1938*, 8th ed. London: Penguin Books, 1997.

Amnesty International. *Colombia: Human Rights Developments—"Death Squads" on the Defensive?* New York: Amnesty International Publications, 1989.

———. "President Clinton Must Order Investigation into Allegations of U.S. Collusion with Colombian Death Squads." April 25, 2001. www.amnestyusa.org/news/2001/colombia04252001_2.html.

Anderson, Jack, and Dale Van Atta. "The Kings of the Medellin Cartel," *Washington Post.* August 24, 1988.

Anderson, Scott, and Jon. L. Anderson. *Inside the League: The Shocking Exposé of How Terrorists, Nazis, and Latin American Death Squads Have Infiltrated the World Anti-Communist League.* New York: Mead, 1986.

Andreas, Peter, and Coletta Youngers. "U.S. Drug Policy and the Andean Cocaine Industry." *World Policy Journal* 6 (Summer 1989): 529–62.

An Honest Citizen. Episode: "Map: Colombia, Cocaine and Cash: Colombia."
    Wide Angle. PBS Television Documentary Series, Directed by Angus
    Macqueen, Aired June 15, 2008, www.pbs.org/wnet/wideangle/episodes/
    an-honest-citizen/map-colombia-cocaine-and-cash/colombia/536/.

Anonymous, "Detenidos otros cinco Congresistas por caso de la parapolítica."
    La República.. February 16, 2007.

———. "Money Laundering on the Rise." *Internal Auditor* 55 (August 1998): 12.

———. "Profile: Colombia." *NACLA Report on the Americas* 36
    (September–October 2002): 13.

———. 2004.

Anslinger, Harry J., and Will Oursler. *The Murderers.* New York: Farrar, Straus
    & Cudahy, 1961.

Arango, Mario. *Los Funerales de Antioquia La Grande.* Medellin: Editorial J. M.
    Arango, 1990.

Arango, Mario, and Jorge Child. *Los Condenados de la Coca.* Medellin: Editorial
    J. M. Arango, 1985.

Archila, Mauricio, and Mauricio Pardo, *Movimientos Sociales, Estado y
    Democracia en Colombia.* Bogotá: Centro de Estudios Sociales,
    Universidad Nacional de Colombia, 2001.

Archive of Global Protests. "Colombia-Country Profile," *Archive of Global Protests,*
    www.nadir.org/nadir/initiativ/agp/free/colombia/colombia.htm,
    (12 October 2007).

———. "Megaprojects and Neocolonialisation in Colombia." *Archive of Global
    Protests,* January 2001, www.nadir.org/nadir/initiativ/agp/free/colom-
    bia/mega.htm.

Arenas, Jacobo. *Cese el Fuego: Una Historia Politica de las FARC.* Bogotá: Oveja
    Negra, 1985.

Aroyo, Tania. "Drug War: Faster and More Furious – Analysis." *Eurasia
    Review: News & Analysis,* September 30, 2011.

Arrington, Vanessa. "Colombians Protest Car Bomb Attack." Associated Press.
    February 9, 2003.

Associated Press. "Altered Coca Plants, a New Possible Threat in Drug War,
    Said to Lurk in Colombia's Jungles." September 1, 2004.

———. "Colombia Rebels Admit to Killings." March 10, 1999.

———. "U.S Asks for Immunity in Colombia." August 15, 2002.

Association d'Études Geopolitiques des Drogues. "Peru: The Unsaid in the
    Montesinos Scandal." *Geopolitical Drug Newsletter,* December 2000.

Auberbach, Robert D. *Deception and Abuse at the Fed: Henry B. Gonzalez
    Battles Alan Greenspan's Bank.* Austin: University of Texas Press, 2008.

———. Email message to authors. 15 December 2007.

Avant, Deborah. "Private Military Companies Part of US Global Reach."
    Foreign Policy in Focus, May 2002. http://www.fpif.org/progresp/vol-
    ume6/v6n17.html.

Avant, Deborah D. and Renee de Nevers. "Military Contractors & the American Way of War. (The Modern American Military." *Daedlus.* 140. Summer 2011, 88–99.

Bagley, Bruce. "Colombia and the War on Drugs." *Foreign Affairs* 67 (Fall 1988): 70–92.

Banerjee, Neela, and Reed Abelson. "Enron's Many Strands: College Reaction; Watchdog Group Wants Investigation on Harvard Official." *New York Times,* February 1, 2002.

BBC News. "End Struggle, Chavez Urges FARC." *BBC News,* June 9, 2008.

BBC World News. "Chiquita Admits Paying Fighters." *BBC World News,* March 14, 2007.

———. "Chiquita Sued Over Colombia." *BBC World News,* June 7, 2007.

———. "Colombian Drug Lords to Go Free," *BBC World News,* November 2, 2002.

———."Colombia Rebels Deny Club Attack." *BBC World News,* March 11, 2003.

———."Ecuador Hit by Colombia Conflict." *BBC World News,* July 20, 2001.

Beaty, Jonathan, and Sam C. Gwynne. *The Outlaw Bank: A Wild Ride into the Heart of BCCI,* Reprint. Washington DC: Beard Books, 2004.

Beckley, Paul A. "Maintaining the Violent Status Quo: The Political Economy of the Colombian Insurgency." Master's thesis, U.S. Navy Postgraduate School, Monterey, CA, 2002.

Belanger, Francis W. *Drugs, the U.S., and Khun Sa.* Bangkok: Editions Duang Kamol, 1989.

Bergen, Peter L. *Holy War, Inc.: Inside the Secret World of Osama bin Laden.* New York: Free Press, 2001.

Bergman, Lowell. "U.S. Companies Tangle in Web of Drug Dollars." *New York Times,* October 10, 2000.

Bergquist, Charles, Ricardo Penaranda, and Gonzalo Sanchez. *Violence in Colombia 1990–2000: Waging War and Negotiating Peace.* Wilmington: Rowman & Littlefield, 2003.

Bernards, Neal. *War on Drugs: Opposing Viewpoints.* San Diego: Greenhaven Press, 1990.

Berrigan, Frida. "Sky High: The Military Busts the 2003 Federal Budget." *In These Times,* March 18, 2002.

Bertram, Eva, Morris Blachman, Kenneth Sharpe, and Peter Andreas. *Drug War Politics: The Price of Denial.* Berkeley: University of California Press, 1996.

Betancourt, Dario, and Martha L. Garcia. *Contrabandistas, Marimberos y Mafiosos: Historia Social de la Mafia Colombiana (1965–1992).* Bogotá: Tercer Mundo Editores, 1994.

Bigwood, Jeremy. "Doing the US's Dirty Work: The Colombian Paramilitaries and Israel." *Narco News Bulletin.* April 8, 2003.

———. "Drug Warriors Push Eye-Eating Fungus." *In These Times.* June 6, 2006.

———. "The Drug War's Fungal 'Solution' in the Amazon." Lecture delivered at the Society for the Anthropology of Lowland South America, Annapolis, MD, June 8, 2002. www.jeremybigwood.net/Lectures/SALSA/Annapolis2002.htm.

———. "DynCorp in Colombia: Outsourcing the Drug War." *CorpWatch Investigative Report.* May 23, 2001.

———. Email message to authors, October 26, 2007.

———. Email message to authors, October 27, 2007.

———. "Toxic Drift: Monsanto and the Drug War in Colombia." *CorpWatch.* June 21, 2001. http://www.corpwatch.org/article.php?id=669.

Block, Alan. *Masters of Paradise: Organized Crime and the Internal Revenue Service in the Bahamas.* Piscataway, NJ: Transaction Publishers, 1991.

Bloomberg News. "USA: Government Ties Helped Cheney and Halliburton Make Millions." *Bloomberg News,* October 6, 2000.

Blum, William. *Rogue State: A Guide to the World's Only Superpower.* Monroe, ME: Common Courage, 2005.

Boville, Belen. *The Cocaine War in Context: Drugs and Politics.* New York: Algora Publishing, 2004.

Bowden, Mark. "Colombia: Killing Pablo—A Deadly Manhunt Guided by the US." *Philadelphia Inquirer.* November 12, 2000.

———. *Killing Pablo.* New York: Atlantic Monthly Press, 2001.

Brancoli, Fernando. "A New Security Dilemma: Plan Colombia and the Use of Private Military Companies in South America." *The London School of Economics and Political Science (LSE) Ideas,* November 16, 2010, http://blogs.lse.ac.uk/ideas/2010/11/a-new-security-dilemma-plan-colombia-and-the-use-of-private-military-companies-in-south-america/.

Brittain, James, J. "The FARC-EP in Colombia: A Revolutionary Exception in an Age of Imperialist Expansion." *Monthly Review* 57 (2005): 20–34.

———. "FENSUAGRO's Struggle for Social Justice." *Peace Review: Journal of Social Justice* 19 (2007): 417–26.

———. "Government, NGOs and the Paramilitary: A Colombian Contradiction." *Development* 50 (2007): 122–27.

———. "War, Evil, and the End of History: Review Essay of Bernard-Henri Lévy's Book Concerning the Global Shift toward Apolitical Conflict." *Rethinking Marxism* 19 (2007): 1–3.

———. *Revolutionary Social Change in Colombia: The Origin and Direction of the FARC-EP.* New York: Pluto Press, 2010.

Brook, Timothy, and Bob T. Wakabayashi, *Opium Regimes: China, Britain, and Japan, 1839–1952.* Berkeley: University of California Press, 2000.

Bruno, Kenny, and Jim Valette. "Cheney & Halliburton: Go Where the Oil Is." *Multinational Monitor,* May 2001. http://multinationalmonitor.org/mm2001/01may/may01corp10.html.

Bucchi, Kenneth C. *C.I.A. Cocaine in America?: A Veteran of the C.I.A. Drug Wars Tells All.* New York: S.P.I. Books, 1994.

————. *Operation Pseudo Miranda: A Veteran of the CIA Drug Wars Tells All.* Granite Bay, CA: Penmarin Books, 2000.

Buendia, Hernando G. *Violencia, Narcotrafico y Produccion Agropecuaria en Colombia.* Bogotá: Instituto de Estudios Liberales, 1989.

Burt, Jo-Marie. "Wall Street Chief Meets with Colombian Rebels." *NACLA Report on the Americas, 33* (July–August 1999): 2–5.

Buxton, Julia. *The Political Economy of Narcotics: Production, Consumption and Global Markets.* New York: Zed Books, 2006.

Cabrera, Irene, and Antoine Peret. "Colombia: Regulating Private Miiltary and Secuirty Companies in a 'Territorial State.' " PRIV-WAR Report – Colombia, National Report Series 19/09. University of Externado of Colombia, November 15, 2009;

Caldwell, Dan, and Robert E. Williams Jr. *Seeking Security In An Insecure World.* New York: Rowman & Littlefield Publishers, 2011.

Campbell, Duncan. "The Bush Dynasty and the Cuban Criminals." *The Guardian.* December 2, 2002.

————. "War on Error: A Spy Inc. No Stranger to Controversy." Center for Public Integrity, June 12, 2002.

Carlsen, Laura. "A Plan Colombia for Mexico." *Foreign Policy in Focus,* September 10, 2010, http://www.fpif.org/articles/a_plan_colombia_for_mexico.

Carpenter, Ted G. *Bad Neighbor Policy: Washington's Futile War on Drugs in Latin America.* New York: Palgrave Macmillan, 2003.

Carrigan, Ana. "War or Peace? Colombia's New President Must Choose between Washington and His Own People." *In These Times.* August 2, 2002.

Carroll, Rory. "Hillary Clinton: Mexican Drug Wars is Colombia-style Insurgency." *The Guardian,* September 9, 2010.

Castañeda, Jorge. *Utopia Unarmed: The Latin American Left after the Cold War.* New York: Alfred Knopf, 1993.

Castillo III, Celerino, and Dave Harmon. *Powderburns: Cocaine, Contras & the Drug War.* London: Sundial, 1994.

Castillo, Fabio. *Los Jinetes de la Cocaina.* Bogotá: Editorial Documentos Periodisticos, 1987.

————. *Los Nuevos Jinetes de la Cocaina.* Bogotá: Editorial Oveja Negra, 1996.

Carey, David. "Plan Colombia's Potential Impact on the Andean Cocaine Trade: An Examination of Two Scenarios of Plan Colombia Was the Massive Aerial Spraying of the Chemical Glyphosate on Illicit Crops in Colombia." September 19, 2000.

————. Testimony to House International Relations Committee on International Organized Crime. January 31, 1996. www.cia.gov/news-information/speeches-testimony/1996/carey_13196.html.

Center for International Policy. "Plan Colombia and Beyond. " http://www.cip-col.org/;

———. "Special Operations Forces, Latin America and the Caribbean."
    http://www.ciponline.org/facts/sof.htm.
———. "US Contractors in Colombia." November 2001. http://www.cipon-
    line.org/colombia/contractors.htm.
———. "U.S. Military and Police Aid." http://www.ciponline.org/colombia/aid-
    prop.htm.
Center for the Study of Responsive Law. "The Federal Reserve: Reality vs.
    Myth." Forum Conference—The Economic Policy Institute, National
    Press Club, Washington D.C., January 7, 2002.
Chambliss, William J. *On the Take: From Petty Crooks to Presidents*.
    Bloomington: Indiana University Press, 1988.
———. "State-Organized Crime." *Criminology* 27 (May 1989): 183–208.
Chennault, Anna C. *Chennault and the Flying Tigers*. New York: Eriksson, 1963.
Chomsky, Noam. "An American Addiction: Drugs, Guerrillas,
    Counterinsurgency: U.S. Intervention in Colombia." Produced by
    David Barsamian, Alternative Radio, May 12, 2000.
———. *Rogue States: The Rule of Force in World Affairs*. Cambridge, MA:
    South End Press, 2000.
Chossudovsky, Michel. *America's War on Terrorism*. Montreal: Global
    Research, 2005.
CNN. "The Drug War: Where Should the Battle Lines Be Drawn?" *The Point
    with Greta Van Susteren*. April 23, 2001.
Cockburn, Alexander, and Jeffrey St. Clair. *Whiteout: The CIA, Drugs and the
    Press*. New York: Verso, 1998.
Cockburn, Leslie. *Out of Control*. New York: Atlantic Monthly Press, 1987.
Cohen, Kenneth. "Letter from Assistant Counsel Kenneth Cohen to Forest
    Service Chief George Leonard." www.fromthewilderness.com/free/pan-
    dora/forest_service_c130s_large.gif.
Coll, Steve. *Ghost Wars: The Secret History of the CIA, Afghanistan, and Bin
    Laden, from the Soviet Invasion to September 10, 2001*. New York:
    Penguin Press, 2004.
Collett, Merrill. *The Cocaine Connection: Drug Trafficking and Inter-American
    Relations*. New York: Foreign Policy Association Headline Series, Fall
    1989.
———. "Colombia's Drug Lords Waging War on Leftists." *Washington Post*.
    November 14, 1987.
Collier, Paul, and Anke Hoeffler. *Greed and Grievance in Civil War*.
    Washington DC: World Bank, 2000.
———. "Justice-Seeking and Loot-Seeking in Civil War." Paper presented at the
    Civil Conflicts, Crime and Violence in Developing Countries, World
    Bank Workshop, London, April 26–27, 1999.
Collins, Larry. *Black Eagles*. New York: Harper Collins, 1993.
Colombia Solidarity.org. http://www.colombiasolidarity.org.uk/.

———. "Peace and Justice for Colombia." http://colombiasolidarity.net/.

Comision de Superacion de la Violencia. "Pacificar la Paz." Instituto de
    Estudios Politicos Relaciones Internacionales (IEPRI), Universidad
    Nacional de Colombia, Bogotá: IEPRI/CINEP/Comision Andina de
    Juristas/CECOIN, 1992.

———. "Panorama de Derechos Humanos y Derecho Humanitario." Instituto
    de Estudios Politicos Relaciones Internacionales, Universidad Nacional
    de Colombia, Bogotá: IEPRI/CINEP/Comision Andina de
    Juristas/CECOIN, 2001.

Congresso de La Republica. *Programa de Fortalecimiento Legislativo, Oficina
    de Asistencia Tecnica Legislativa,* May 26, 2005, Bogotá,
    http://www.secretariasenado.gov.co/estudios-ARD/036%20REFOR-
    MA%20AGRARIA.pdf.

Contreras, Joseph, and Fernando Garavito. *Biografía No Autorizada de Álvaro Uribe Vélez:
    El Señor de las Sombras.* Bogotá: Editorial Oveja Negra, 2002.

Cooley, John K. *Unholy Wars: Afghanistan, America, and International
    Terrorism.* London: Pluto, 2000.

Corporacion Colectivo de Abogados Jose Alvear Restrepo. *Terrorismo o
    Rebelion?* Bogotá: Intermedio Editores, 2001.

Corradi, Juan E., Patricia Weiss Fagen, and Manuel Antonio Garreton, eds. *Fear
    at the Edge: State Terror and Resistance in Latin America.* Riverside:
    University of California Press, 1992.

Corson, William R. *The Armies of Ignorance: The Rise of the American
    Intelligence Empire.* New York: Dial Press, 1977.

Corto, Jhony. "Fears of War between Colombia and Venezuela." *Agencia de
    Noticias Nueva Colombia (ANNCOL),* April 16, 2004.

Cottin, Heather. "Human Rights Watch Cover Up." In *War in Colombia: Made
    in the U.S.A.,* edited by Toledo et al., 99–109. New York: International
    Action Center, 2003.

Council on Foreign Relations, Independent Task Force. "Andes 2020: A New
    Strategy for the Challenges of Colombia and the Region." April 1–June
    30, 2004.

Council on Hemispheric Affairs. "Washington Report on the Hemisphere,"
    September 27, 1989.

Crandall, Russell. *Driven by Drugs: US Policy toward Colombia.* Boulder, CO:
    Lynne Rienner Publishers, 2002.

Cumings, Bruce. *The Origins of the Korean War.* Princeton: Princeton
    University Press, 1990.

Dabringhaus, Erhard. *Klaus Barbie: The Shocking Story of How the US Used
    This Nazi War Criminal as an Intelligence Agent.* Washington DC:
    Acropolis Books, 1984.

Dangl, B. "U.S. Bases in Colombia Rattle the Region." *The Progressive,* March
    2010. http://www.progressive.org/danglmarch10.html.

Dao, James. "US Company to Take Over Karzai Safety." *New York Times,*
    September 19, 2002.
Darling, Frank C. *Thailand and the United States.* Washington, DC: Public
    Affairs Press, 1965.
Davenport-Hines, Richard. *The Pursuit of Oblivion: A Global History of
    Narcotics 1500–2000.* London: Weidenfeld & Nicolson, 2004.
De Brie, Christian. "Thick as Thieves." *Le Monde Diplomatique,* May 4, 2001.
De la Garza, Paul, and David Adams. "Colombia: US Military Aid from the
    Private Sector." *St. Petersburg Times,* December 2, 2000.
Department of the U.S. Air Force. "Military Construction Program."
    Justification Data Submitted to U.S. Congress, May 2009.
    http://www.centrodealerta.org/documentos_desclasificados/original_in
    _english_air_for.pdf.
Departamento Nacional de Planeacion. *La Paz: El Desafio para el Desarrollo.*
    Bogotá: TM Editores, 1998.
De Vries, Lloyd. "Cali Cartel Drug Kingpins Plead Guilty." CBS News,
    September 26, 2006.
DeYoung, Karen. "Behind U.S-Peru Pact, a History of Division." *Washington
    Post,* April 25, 2001.
———. "Colombia's Non-Drug Rebellion." *Washington Post,* April 17, 2000.
DeYoung, Karen and Claudia J. Duque. "U.S. Aid Implicated in Abuses of
    Power in Colombia." *The Washington Post,* August 20, 2011;
Dinges, John, and Saul Landau, *Assassination on Embassy Row.* New York:
    Pantheon Books, 1980.
Dobson, Alan P., and Steve Marsh. *US Foreign Policy since 1945.* New York:
    Routledge, 2001.
Donahue, Sean. "The Life and Crimes of General Montoya Uribe." *School of the
    Americas Watch,* May 22. http://www.soaw.org/about-the-
    soawhinsec/colombia/2709.
———. "Mano Firme, Corazon Pequeño: Uribe Takes Hardline in Colombia
    with Bush's Blessing." *Counterpunch.* August 22, 2002.
    http://www.counterpunch.org/donahue0821.html.
Dowbenko, Uri. Part One: Dirty Tricks, Inc. The DynCorp-Government
    Connection." *Online Journal,* 20 March 2002. http://www.onlinejour-
    nal.com/archive/03-20-02_Dowbenko-Pt_1.pdf.
———. "Part Two: Dirty Tricks, Inc. DynCorp Drug Trafficking and Cover-
    up?" *Online Journal,* March 27, 2002. www.onlinejournal.com/archi-
    ve/03-27-02_Dowbenko-Pt_2.pdf.
Downes, Richard. *Landpower and Ambiguous Warfare: The Challenge of Colombia
    in the 21st Century.* Carlisle, PA: Strategic Studies Institute, 1999.
Drug Enforcement Administration (DEA). *Changing Dynamics of Cocaine
    Production in the Andean Region.* Drug Intelligence Brief. June 2002.
    http://www.usdoj.gov/dea/pubs/omte;/02033/02033p.html.

———. *The Drug Trade in Colombia: A Threat Assessment*. DEA Intelligence Division. March 2002. http://usregsec.sdsu.edu/docs/DEAMarch2002.pdf.

———. "Illegal Drug Price and Purity Report." April 2003. http://www.usdoj.gov/dea/pubs/intel/02058/02058.html.

———. "January 17, 1998 Shipment of 10,000 Kilograms of Potassium Permanganate, December 16, 1997, Shipment of 20,000 Kilograms of Potassium Permanganate and November 17, 1997 Shipment of 20,000 Kilograms of Potassium Permanganate; Suspension of Shipments." Notice by Donnie R. Marshall. August 3, 2000. http://federalregister.gov/a/00-21482.

———. *DEA Congressional Testimony before the Senate Caucus on International Narcotics Control* (statement of Donnie R. Marshall, Administrator of the Drug Enforcement Administration). February 28, 2001. http://www.justice.gov/dea/pubs/cngrtest/ct022801.htm.

———. *DEA Congressional Testimony before the House International Relations Committee, Subcommittee Regarding Western Hemisphere* (statement of James Milford, Deputy Administrator of the Drug Enforcement Administration). July 16, 1997. www.justice.gov/ dea/pubs/cngrtest/ct970716.htm.

Drugwar.com. "Drug War: Covert Money, Power and Policy: LSD." Drugwar.com, http://www.drugwar.com/lsd.shtm.

Dwyer, Paula. "The Citi That Slept." *Business Week*, November 2, 1998.

Economist, The. "The Americas: Spectres Stir in Peru; Drugs in the Andes." *The Economist*, February 16, 2002.

———. "Stopping It: How Governments Try—and Fail—to Stem the Flow of Drugs." *The Economist*. July 28, 2001.

———. "Survey: Talks of Peace, Acts of War." *The Economist*, April 21, 2001.

EcoNoticias. "Ministro del Interior acusa a ecologistas de 'complot mundial.'" *EcoNoticias*, July 16, 2002.

Eddy, Paul, Hugo Sabogal, and Sara Walden. *The Cocaine Wars*. London: Century, 1988.

Ehlers, Scott. "Drug Trafficking and Money Laundering." *Foreign Policy in Focus*. June 1, 1998. www.fpif.org/reports/drug_trafficking_and_money_laundering.

Ehrenfeld, Rachael. *Narcoterrorism*. New York: Basic Books, 1990.

———. *Narcoterrorism and the Cuban Connection*. Miami: Cuban American National Foundation, 1988.

———. *Narcoterrorism: The Kremlin Connection*. New York: Heritage Foundation, 1986.

El Espectador. "Olor a desierto en la Amazonia y Orinoquia." *El Espectador*, September 16, 1998.

Ellison, Katherine. "Alleged Drug Ties Rattle Brazil's Already Beleaguered Government." *Miami Herald*, April 9, 1994.

El Mercurio. "FARC Aprovechan Zona del Despeje para Lanzar Ataques." *El Mercurio*, July 27, 1999.

El Nacional."Medellin: epicentro de la mafia." *El Nacional*, January 16, 1985.

El Pais. "Vicente Castaño habría matado a su hermano."*El Pais*, February 1, 2007.

El Tiempo. "Editorial: De la fumigacion a la sustitución." *El Tiempo*, March 1, 2000.

Enqvist, Maria. "US Casualties on the Rise in Colombia." Agencia de Noticias Nueva Colombia, August 3, 2003.

Farah, Douglas, and Laura Brooks. "Colombian Army's Third in Command Allegedly Led Two Lives; General Reportedly Served as a Key CIA Informant while Maintaining Ties to Death Squads Financed by Drug Traffickers." *Washington Post*, August 11,1998.

Feigenblatt, Hazel. "US Says Coca Area Up in Bolivia and Down in Peru." Reuters, November 18, 2003.

Fernandez, Augusto C."Feast of Lies: The Supposed Reduction in Colombian Coca Crops in 2002." *Narco News Bulletin*, May 22, 2003.

Fidler, Stephen, and Thomas Catan. "Private Companies on the Front Line." *Financial Times*, August 12, 2003.

Fitrakis, Bob. "Spook Air: How a CIA-Connected Airline Landed in Columbus." *Columbus Dispatch*, August 25, 1999.

Fitts, Catherine A. "Former Bush Assistant Secretary for HUD Reveals 'Ethnic Cleansing' Connected to CIA Drug Dealing in Los Angeles." Dillon Read website. http://www.dunwalke.com/resources/events.htm.

———. "Narco-Dollars for Beginners (Part 2)." *Narco News Bulletin*, October 31, 2001.

———. "Tapeworm Economics." *The Solari Report*. http://solari.com/articles/tapeworm_economics/.

Foreign Broadcast Information Service (FBIS). *Joint Study Sums Up FARC, ELN Earnings*. Document No. FTS199990517001601. CIA Directorate of Science and Technology. Virginia. May 1999.

Forero, Juan. "Hide-and-Seek among the Coca Leaves." *New York Times*, June 9, 2004.

———. "Prosperous Colombians Flee, Many to US, to Escape War." *New York Times*, April 10, 2001.

Garamone, Jim. "Special Operations Part of US-Colombia Plan to Reinforce Success." *American Forces Press Service*, April 1, 2004.

Garamone, Jim. "U.S., Colombia Will Continue Pressure on Narcoterrorists." *American Forces Press*, Apr. 12, 2005.

Garcia-Godos, Jemima, and Knut Andreas O. Lid. "Transitional Justice and Victims' Rights before the End of a Conflict: The Unusual Case of Colombia." *Journal of Latin American Studies* 42 (2010): 487–516.

Gardner, Dan. "Losing the Drug War." *Ottawa Citizen*, September 6, 2000.

Gedicks, Al. "Colombia 'Drug War' a Sham." *Abu Saleh*, September 16, 2002.

Gibler, John. *To Die in Mexico: Dispatches from Inside the Drug War*. San Francisco, CA: City Lights Foundation, 2011.

Gibson, Arthur C. "Freud's Magical Drug." *The Mildred E. Mathias Botanical Garden UCLA Website*. http://www.botgard.ucla.edu/html/botanytext-books/economicbotany/Erythroxylum/index.html.

Gilmore, William C., and Alastair N. Brown. *Drug Trafficking and the Chemical Industry: Chemical Precursors and International Criminal Law*. Edinburgh: Edinburgh University Press, 1997.

Gilpin, Raymond. "Crime, Violence and Economic Development." United States Institute of Peace, August 2009, http://www.securitytransformation.org/images/even_wor_des/Raymond_Gilpin_presentation.pdf.

Giordano, Al. "Bush Ups Ante on Plan Colombia." *The Lindesmith Center–Drug Policy Foundation*, March 13, 2001.

Giraldo, Javier. *The Genocidal Democracy*. Monroe, ME: Common Courage Press, 1996.

Goff, Stan. "Blurring of the Lines." In *War in Colombia: Made in U.S.A.*, edited by Toledo et al., 77–83. New York: International Action Center, 2003.

Golden, Tim, and Steven L. Myers. "U.S. Plans Big Aid Package To Rally a Reeling Colombia." *New York Times*. September 15, 1999.

Gordon, Gretchen, and Noah Smith. "Truth Behind Bars: Colombian Paramilitary Leaders in U.S. Custody." International Human Rights Clinic, University of California, Berkeley, School of Law, February 2010, http://www.law.berkeley.edu/files/IHRLC/Truthbehindbars.pdf.

Griffin, Michael. *Reaping the Whirlwind: The Taliban Movement in Afghanistan*. London: Pluto, 2001.

Griffith, Ivelaw L. *The Political Economy of Drugs in the Caribbean*. New York: Palgrave Macmillan, 2000.

Grosse, Robert E. *Drugs and Money: Laundering Latin America's Cocaine Dollars*. London: Praeger, 2001.

Guaraca, Jaime. *Colombia y Las FARC-EP: Origen de la Lucha Guerrillera*. Tafalla, Spain: Txalaparta, 1999.

Guggenheim, Ken. "Drug Fight in Colombia Questioned." Associated Press, June 5, 2001, 2.

Gugliotta, Guy, and Jeff Leen. *Kings of Cocaine: An Astonishing True Story of Murder, Money and International Corruption*. New York: Simon and Schuster, 1990.

Guillen, Gonzalo, and Steven Salisbury. "Ex-General: DEA Agents Were Involved in Murders in Colombia." *Miami Herald*. December 10, 2003.

Guillermoprieto, Alma. "Mexico's Shocking New Saints." *National Geographic*, May 2010.

Guizado, Alvaro C., and Alvaro G. Barney. *Colombia: Cuidad y Violencia*. Bogotá: Foro Nacional, 1990.

Hargreaves, Clare. *Snowfields: The War on Cocaine in the Andes.* London: Zed Books, 1992.

Harris, David. *Shooting the Moon: The True Story of an American Manhunt Unlike Any Other, Ever.* New York: Back Bay Books, 2002.

Hildebrand, Donald C., and Arthur H. McCain, "The Use of Various Substrates for Large-Scale Production of Fusarium oxysporum f. sp. cannabis Inoculum." 68 *Phytopathology* (July 1978): 1099–1101.

Hill, James T."Posture Statement." U.S. Southern Command, House Armed Services Committee, March 12, 200

Hilton, Isabel. "A Dark Underbelly of Mass Graves and Electoral Fraud." *The Guardian,* March 8, 2007.

Hinckle, Warren, and William Turner. *The Fish Is Red.* New York: Harper & Row, 1981.

Hinterseer, Kris. *Criminal Finance: The Political Economy of Money Laundering in a Comparative Legal Context.* London: Kluwer Law International, 2002.

Hiro, Dilip. *War Without End: The Rise of Islamic Terrorism and the Global Response.* New York: Routledge, 2003.

Holsen, Sarah, José Egas, and Laura Glynn,."Plan Colombia—Definition and Funding." http://www.derechos.net/cedhu/plancolombia/PLAN-COLOMBIAINGLES.html.

Houtart, Francois. "Nicaragua: A Revolution Forgotten." *Le Monde Diplomatique,* December 13, 2001.

Human Rights Watch. "Colombia's Killer Networks: The Military-Paramilitary Partnership and the United States." November 1996. http://www.hrw.org/reports/1996/killertoc.htm.

———. "The Ties that Bind: Colombia and the Military-Paramilitary Links." February 2000, http://www.hrw.org/reports/2000/colombia/.

———. "Colombia: Human Rights Watch Testifies before the Senate," Testimony of José Miguel Vivanco, New York, April 24, 2002, http://reliefweb.int/sites/reliefweb.int/files/reliefweb_pdf/node-103491.pdf.

———. "You'll Learn Not to Cry: Child Combatants in Colombia." September 2003, http://www.hrw.org/reports/2003/colombia0903/.

Hylton, Forrest. "Colombia's Three-Year Truce Ends: From 'Peace' to War." Countercurrents.org. April 28, 2002, http://www.countercurrents.org/hylton280402.htm.

———. *Evil Hour in Colombia.* London: Verso Books, 2006.

———. "An Evil Hour: Uribe's Colombia in Historical Perspective." *New Left Review* 23 (September–October 2003): 51–93.

Idels, Marcel. "The Political Economy of a Narco-Terror State: Colombia and Corporate Profits." *Bluegreenearth,* August 14, 2002. http://www.bluegreenearth.us/archive/article/2002/idels2.html.

———. "Part Two: Dirty Tricks, Inc."

Inciardi, James A. "Beyond Cocaine: Basuco, Crack, and Other Coca Products." *Contemporary Drug Problems* (Fall 1987): 461–92.

———. "Crack Cocaine in Miami." In *The Epidemiology of Cocaine Use and Abuse,* edited by Susan Schober and Charles Schade, 263–75. Washington, DC: U.S. Government Printing Office, 1991.

Intelligence Online. "Business Intelligence and Lobbying Firms." *Intelligence Online,* No. 469, January 30, 2004. http://www.intelligenceonline.com/ps/AN/Arch/INT/INT_469.asp?ru b=archives.

International Consortium of Investigative Journalists. "Making a Killing: The Business of War." Center for Public Integrity, eleven-part series, October 28, 2002. http://www.publicintegrity.org/bow/report.aspx?aid=147.

International Labor Rights Forum. "Colombian Unravels Government-Paramilitary Ties." March 20, 2007, http://www.laborrights.org/end-violence-against-trade-unions/news/10862.

International Press Institute. "Colombia: World Press Freedom Review." http://www.freemedia.at/cms/ipi/freedom_detail.html?country=/KW00 01/KW0002/KW0016/&year=2000.

Isacson, Adam. "'Getting in Deeper': The United States' Growing Involvement in Colombia's Conflict." Center for International Policy. February 2000. http://www.ciponline.org/coipr/coipr002.htm (June 15, 2006).

———. "The State Department's Data on Drug-Crop Cultivation." Center for International Policy Press Release. March 22, 2004. http://www.cipon-line.org/colombia/040322coca.pdf.

Isacson, Adam, and Ingrid Vaicius, "International Policy Report–Plan Colombia's 'Ground Zero.'" Center for International Policy. March 9–12, 2001. http://www.ciponline.org/colombia/0401putu.htm.

———. "Plan Colombia's 'Ground Zero,'" Center for International Policy, March 9–12, 2001. http://www.ciponline.org/colombia/0401putu.htm.

Isenberg, David. "Combat for Sale: The New, Post-Cold War Mercenaries." *USA Today,* March 2000.

———. "There's No Business like Security Business." *Asia Times,* April 30, 2003

———. "Security for Sale in Afghanistan." *Asia Times,* January 6, 2003.

Israel, Jared. "Washington: Parent of the Taliban and Colombian Death Squads." Emperor's Clothes.com. June 5, 2001. http://emperors-clothes.com/articles/jared/mis.htm.

Izaguirre, Ada K. *Private Participation in Infrastructure: Trends in Developing Countries in 1990–2001.* Washington DC: World Bank Publications, 2003.

Jackson, Derrick Z. "Our Fraudulent War on Drugs." *Boston Globe,* September 13, 1996.

James, Ian. "Chávez Chews Coca Leaves at Summit, Saying 'Coca Isn't Cocaine.'" *Dallas Morning News.* January 27, 2008.

Jelsma, Martin. "Vicious Circle: The Chemical and Biological War on Drugs." Paper presented at Transnational Institute, Amsterdam, March 2001. http://www.xs4all.nl/~tni/archives/jelsma/viciouscircle-e.pdf.

Jervis, Robert. *System Effects Complexity in Political and Social Life* . Princeton: Princeton University Press, 1999.

Just the Facts.org. "U.S. Aid to Colombia, All Programs, 2006–2011." http://justf.org/Country?country=Colombia.

———. "Quick Data: U.S. Military and Police Aid Grants by Country (Total Aid since 1996)." http://justf.org/.

Kaihla, Paul. "The Technology Secrets of Cocaine Inc." *Business 2.0.* July 2002.

Kalmanovitz, Salomon. http://www.unam.mx/cronica/1996/a8096/int006.html.

Kawell, Jo Ann. "The Addict Economies." *NACLA Report on the Americas* 22 (March 1989): 33–40.

Kenney, Michael C."Intelligence Games: Comparing the Intelligence Capabilities of Law Enforcement Agencies and Drug Trafficking Enterprises." *International Journal of Intelligence and Counterintelligence* 16 (2003): 212–43.

Kirk, Robin. *More Terrible than Death: Massacres, Drugs and America's War in Colombia.* New York: Public Affairs, 2003.

Knoester, Matthew. "Washington's Role in Colombian Repression." *Z-Magazine,* January 1998. http://www.zcommunications.org/title-washingtons-role-in-colombian-repression-by-matthew-knoester.

Koen, Ross Y. *The China Lobby in American Politics.* New York: Macmillan, 1960.

Kraar, Louis, and Jonas Blank. "The Drug Trade." *Fortune,* June 20, 1988.

Kraul, Chris. "Colombia General Gen. Mario Montoya Resigns." *Los Angeles Times,* November 5, 2008.

Krause, Kristin S."Good-bye Southern Air." *Traffic World* 256 (October 1998): 34.

Kruger, Henrick. *The Great Heroin Coup: Drugs, Intelligence, and International Fascism.* Boston: South End Press, 1980.

Kurlantzick, Joshua. "Outsourcing the Dirty Work: The Military and Its Reliance on Hired Guns." *The American Prospect,* May 2003.

Lamb, Christina. "Colombian Rebels Plan for Cocaine War." *Telegraph,* September 3, 2000.

Landau, Saul. *The Dangerous Doctrine: National Security and US Foreign Policy.* Boulder, CO: Westview Press, 1988.

Larios, Nelson V. *FENSUAGRO–CUT–FSM: 30 Años 1976–2006 Organizacion, Lucha y Resistencia.* Bogotá: Impreso en Colombia, 2006.

Larmer, Brook. "US, Mexico Try to Halt Chemical Flow to Cartels." *Christian Science Monitor,* October 23, 1989.

Laurent, Frederic. *L'orchestre noir.* Paris: Stock, 1978.

Lee, Matthew. "Albright Pleased by Bolivian Fight, Unable to Promise Aid." Agence France Presse, August 18, 2000.

Lee III, Rensselaer W., "Perverse Effects of Andean Counternarcotics Policy." *Orbis* 46 (Summer 2002): 537–54.

———. *The White Labyrinth: Cocaine and Political Power.* New Brunswick, NJ: Transaction, 1998.

Lee III, Rensselaer W. and Patrick Clawson. *The Andean Cocaine Industry.* New York: St. Martin's Press, 1998.

Leech, Garry M. "Colombian Army Selectively Targets Paramilitaries." *Colombia Journal,* October 4, 2004. http://colombiajournal.org/colombian-army-selectively-targets-paramilitaries.htm.

———."Informers for a Day." *Colombia Journal,* April 7, 2003. http://colombiajournal.org/informers-for-a-day.htm.

———."An Interview with FARC Commander Simon Trinidad." *NACLA Report on the Americas* 34 (September–October 2000): 24–25.

———."Is the Colombian Government Guilty of War Crimes?" *Colombia Journal,* July 17, 2008, http://colombiajournal.org/is-the-colombian-government-guilty-of-war-crimes.htm.

———. *Killing Peace: Colombia's Conflict and the Failure of U.S. Intervention.* New York: Information Network of the Americas, 2002.

———."Slap on the Wrist for Corporate Sponsors of Terrorism." *Colombia Journal,* March 19, 2007, http://colombiajournal.org/slap-on-the-wrist-for-corporate-sponsors-of-terrorism.htm.

Le Grand, Catherine. *Frontier Expansion and Peasant Protest in Colombia 1850–1936.* Albuquerque: University of New Mexico Press, 1986.

Lenin, Vladimir I. "The Dual Power."In *Lenin Collected Works,* vol. 24. Moscow: Progress Publishers, 1917.

———. "Imperialism, the Highest Stage of Capitalism." In *Lenin Selected Works,* vol. 1. Moscow: Progress Publishers, 1917.

LeoGrande, William M. *Our Own Backyard: The United States in Central America, 1977–1992.* Chapel Hill: University of North Carolina Press, 1998.

Lernoux, Penny. *In Banks We Trust: Bankers, and Their Close Associates, the CIA, the Mafia, Drug Traders, Dictators, and the Vatican.* New York: Anchor/Doubleday, 1984.

Levine, Michael. *Deep Cover.* New York: Delacorte Press, 1990.

———. *The Triangle of Death.* New York: Delacorte Press, 1996., 234–40.

Levine, Michael, and Laura Kavanau-Levine. *The Big White Lie: The CIA and the Cocaine/Crack Epidemic.* New York: Thunder's Mouth Press, 1993.

Libertad-prensa.org. "Entrevista con Ignacio 'Nacho' Gómez, reciente ganador del Premio Internacional de Libertad de Prensa del Comité Mundial para la Protección de los Periodistas (CPJ)." *Medios y Libertad de Expresion en las Americas.* November 25, 2002,. http://www.libertad-prensa.org/nacho.html.

Lifshultz, Lawrence. "Inside the Kingdom of Heroin." *The Nation,* November 14, 1988.

Linklater, Magnus, Isabel Hilton, and Neal Ascherson. *The Nazi Legacy.* New York: Holt, Rinehart, and Winston, 1984.

Livingstone, Grace. *Inside Colombia: Drugs, Democracy, and War.* New Brunswick, NJ: Rutgers University Press, 2003.

Lobe, Jim. "US Punishes 35 Countries for Signing Onto Int'l Court." Inter Press Service Agency, July 1, 2003.

Los Angeles Times. "Complete Final Debate Transcript: John McCain and Barack Obama." *Los Angeles Times,* October 15, 2008. http://latimes-blogs.latimes.com/washington/2008/10/debate-transcri.html.

Lupsha, Peter A. "Towards an Etiology of Drug Trafficking and Insurgent Relations: The Phenomenon of Narco-Terrorism." *International Journal of Comparative and Applied Criminal Justice* 13 (Fall 1989): 60–74.

———. "Transnational Narco-corruption and Narco Investment: A Focus on Mexico." *Transnational Organized Crime* (Spring 1995): 87.

MacDonald, Scott. "The Next Wave of the Latin Drug Trade." *Times of the Americas,* June 27, 1990.

MacGregor, Felipe E. *Coca and Cocaine: An Andean Perspective.* Westport, CT: Greenwood Press, 1993.

Mandala Project. "Deforestation in Colombia." Trade and Environment Database (TED), School of International Service, American University. http://www1.american.edu/ted/ (June 17, 2008).

Mao Tse-tung. "Analysis of the Classes in Chinese Society." In *Selected Works of Mao,* vol. 1. Peking: Foreign Languages Press, 1926.

Markey, Patrick. "Hope for US hostages after 5 years." Reuters, February 12, 2008.

Marks, Thomas. *Colombian Army Adaptation to FARC Insurgency.* Carlisle, PA: Strategic Studies Institute, 2002.

Marquez, Gabriel G. *News of a Kidnapping.* London: Penguin, 1998.

Marquez, Humberto. "Venezuela: Chávez Says 'Invasion' Planned in Miami and Colombia." *Global Information Network,* May 13, 2004.

Marshall, Jonathon. "Opium and the Politics of Gangsterism in Nationalist China, 1927–1945." *Bulletin of Concerned Asia Scholars* (July–September 1976): 19–48.

Marshall, Jonathon, Peter D. Scott, and Jane Hunter. *The Iran-Contra Connection.* Montreal: Black Rose Books, 1987.

Martin, Al. *The Conspirators: Secrets of an Iran Contra Insider.* Pray, MT: National Liberty Press, 2002.

Masciandaro, Donato. *Global Financial Crime: Terrorism, Money Laundering, and Off Shore Centres.* London: Ashgate Publishing, 2004.

Mathers, Chris. *Crimes School: Money Laundering: True Crime Meets the World of Business and Finance.* New York: Firefly Books, 2004.

McClintock, Michael. *Instruments of Statecraft.* New York: Pantheon, 1992.

McCoy, Alfred W. *The Politics of Heroin: CIA Complicity in the Global Drug Trade.* Chicago: Lawrence Hill Books, 2003.

McCue, Andy. "IT Myths: Colombian drugs gang's mainframe-assisted assassinations?" Silicon.com. July 10, 2003. http://www.silicon.com/technology/hardware/2003/07/10/it-myths-colombian-drugs-gangs-mainframe-assisted-assassinations-10005093/.

McDermott, Jeremy. "New Super Strain of Coca Plant Stuns Anti-Drug Official." *The Scotsman,* August 27, 2004.

McFarlane, Anthony. *Colombia before Independence: Economy, Society, and Politics under Bourbon Rule.* Cambridge: Cambridge University Press, 1993.

McQuaid, John. "Fatal Mission." *Times–Picayune,* November 9, 2003.

Medellin Civico. "Del pueblo Colombiano." *Medellín Cívico,* March 1984.

———. "En la mitad del camino." *Medellín Cívico,* March 1984.

———. "Estamos con la patria." *Medellín Cívico,* March 1981.

———. "Pablo es La Paz." *Medellín Cívico,* March 1984, 7.

———. "Una leccion de educacion civica de Pablo Escobar a la Secretaria de Educacion." *Medellín Cívico,* March 1984.

Medina, Gallegos. *Autodefensas, Paramilitares y Narcotrafico en Colombia Origin, Desarrollo y Consolidacion el Caso Puerto Boyaca.* Bogotá: Editorial Documentos Periodisticos, 1990.

Messick, Hank. *Of Grass and Snow: The Secret Criminal Elite.* Englewood Cliffs, NJ: Prentice-Hall, 1979.

Miami Herald. "Airline Does Job—Quietly Miami Company Used to Secrecy." *Miami Herald,* December 10, 1986, 2.

Michaels, Julia. "Brazil's Drug War Extends to Its Congress." *Christian Science Monitor,* September 10, 1991.

Michelsen, Alfonso L., and Enrique Calderon, *Palabras Pendientes: Conversaciones Con Enrique Santos Calderon.* Bogotá: El Ancora Editores, 2001.

Miller, Alan. "Wall Street Bullish on the Spoils of War; The Global Private Military Industry Is Changing How Nations Fight." *Christian Science Monitor,* August 14, 2003.

Miller, Christian. "Use of Foreign Pilots Avoids Congressional Limits." *Los Angeles Times,* August 18, 2001.

Mills, James. *The Underground Empire: Where Crime and Governments Embrace.* New York: Doubleday, 1986.

Milne, Seumas. "Can the US Be Defeated?" *The Guardian,* February 15, 2002.

Mintz, Sidney W. "The Forefathers of Crack." *NACLA Reports on the Americas* 22 (March 1989): 31–32.

Mitnick, Kevin D., and William L. Simon. *The Art of Deception: Controlling the Human Element of Security.* New York: Wiley, 2003.

Molano, Alfredo. "The Evolution of the FARC: A Guerrilla Group's Long History." *NACLA Report on the Americas* 34 (Sept–Oct 2000): 23–31.

———. "Peor el remedio." *El Espectador.* September 1, 2002.

Molloy, Ivan. *Rolling Back Revolution: The Emergence of Low Intensity Conflict.* London: Pluto Press, 2001.

Momento. "Colombia Displaces and Ecuador Receives Refugees by Violence." *Momento 24,* November 9, 2010.

Montalvo, Michael L. "Investigative Report: Politics and Covert Operation Policy in the Drug War." *We the People.* http://www.wethepeople.la/montal1.htm.

Mora, Frank O. "Brazil and the Southern Cone: An Annotated Bibliography." In *Drug Trafficking Research in the Americas,* edited by Bruce Bagley, 249–97. Boulder, CO: Lynne Rienner Publisher, 1996.

———. "Paraguay International Drug Trafficking." In *Drug Trafficking in the Americas,* edited by Bruce Bagley and William Walker, 351–73. New Brunswick, NJ: Transaction Publishers, 1994.

———. "Victims of the Balloon Effect: Drug Trafficking and US Policy in Brazil and the Southern Cone of Latin America." *Journal of Social, Political, and Economic Studies* 21 (Summer 1996): 115–40.

Morley, Jefferson. "The Great American High: Contradictions of Cocaine Capitalism." *The Nation,* October 2, 1989.

Moroney, Robin. "Cocaine Keeps Getting Cheaper and Cheaper." *Wall Street Journal Blogs,* June 6, 2007. http://blogs.wsj.com/informedreader/2007/06/06/cocaine-keeps-getting-cheaper-and-cheaper/.

Morris, Ruth. "UN Tries to Avert War in Colombia." *The Independent,* January 13, 2002.

Mortimer, Golden W. *History of Coca: The Divine Plant of the Incas.* San Francisco: And/Or Press, 1974.

Murillo, Luis E. *The Noriega Mess: The Drugs, the Canal, and Why America Invaded.* London: Verso, 1995.

Murphy, Helen, and Blake Schmidt. "Colombia's Spy Scandal Turns Uribe Against Former Ally Santos." *Bloomberg,* September 15, 2011, http://www.bloomberg.com/news/2011-09-15/colombia-s-spy-scandal-turns-uribe-against-former-ally-santos.html.

Murrillo, Mario A. *Colombia and the United States: War, Unrest and Destabilization.* New York: Seven Stories Press, 2004.

Naím, Moises. "The Five Wars of Globalization." *Foreign Policy,* January 1, 2003.

Narco News Bulletin. October 25, 2004.

National Public Radio. "Cocaine Prices Have Fallen Steeply since 1980s." National Public Radio (NPR), May 15, 2007.

National Security Archive, George Washington University. "New National Police Chief Appointed, U.S. Embassy Bogotá Cable." December 20, 1993. www.gwu.edu/~nsarchiv/NSAEBB/NSAEBB243/19931220.pdf.

———. "US Embassy Colombia Cable, Aerial Eradication in Guaviare, Caqueta and Putumayo." July 16, 1996.
http://www.gwu.edu/~nsarchiv/NSAEBB/NSAEBB69/col44.pdf.

———. "U.S. Embassy Colombia Cable, Protesting Coca Growers Continue Stand-Off." July 24, 1996.
http://www.gwu.edu/~nsarchiv/NSAEBB/NSAEBB69/col45.pdf.

———. "U.S. Intelligence Listed Colombian President Uribe among 'Important Colombian Narco-Traffickers in 1991.'" September 23, 1991.
http://www.gwu.edu/~nsarchiv/NSAEBB/NSAEBB131/index.htm.

Navarro, Mireya. "Russian Submarine Drifts into Center of a Brazen Drug Plot." *New York Times,* March 7, 1997.

Naylor, Robin T. *Hot Money and the Politics of Debt.* New York: Simon & Schuster, 1987.

Neville, Robert C. *The Human Condition: A Volume in the Comparative Religious Ideas Project.* Albany: State University of New York Press, 2002)

New York Times. "Colombian Rebels to Leave Enclave as Talks Fail." *New York Times,* January 23, 2002.

Noriega, Manuel, and Peter Eisner. *America's Prisoner: The Memoirs of Manuel Noriega.* New York: Random House, 1997.

Noss, Heather, and David Spencer. "Colombia: Strategic End State, Goals and Means." Workshop Report, Center for Strategic Studies, November 6, 2000; The CNA Corporation, Arlington, 9-14.

Noto, David. "Is Colombia Losing Its War against Rebels and Drug Gangs?" Fox News Latino, September 26, 2011, latino.foxnews.com/latino/news/2011/09/26/is-colombia-is-losing-its-war-against-rebels-and-drugs-gangs/.

Novak, Robert D. "Terrorism Close to Home." *Washington Post,* April 19, 1999.

Nuevo Herald. "Narcotrafico invade pueblos amazonios." *Nuevo Herald,* April 15, 1996.

O'Conner, Dermot. "The Political Economy of Colombia's Cocaine Industry." *Papel Politico* 14 (January–June 2009), 81–106.

Office of the Superintendent of India. *Report on East Indian Finances—Papers Relating to the Opium Question.* Calcutta: Office of the Superintendent of Government Printing, 1872.

Oneworld.net. "Colombian Demonstrations Warning" Oneworld.net, January 28, 2008.

Oppenheimer, Andres. "Uribe Being Driven a Lot Closer to Chávez." *Miami Herald,* October 4, 2007.

Orozco, Jorge E. *Lehder . . . El Hombre* (Bogotá: Plaza y Janes, 1987).

Ospina, Hernado C. *Colombia, Laboratorio de Embrujos: Democracia y Terrorismo de Estado.* Madrid: Ediciones Aka, 2008.

Pace, Peter. "Advance Questions for Lieutenant General Peter Pace: Defense Reforms." U.S Senate Committee on Armed Services, 2000. http://www.senate.gov/~armed_services/statemnt/2000/000906pp.pdf.

Padgett, Tim. "Taking the Side of the Coca Farmer." *Time,* May 8, 2002. http://www.time.com/time/magazine/article/0,9171,332053,00.html.

Passage, David. *The United States and Colombia: Untying the Gordian Knot.* Carlisle, PA: Strategic Studies Institute, 2000.

Pastrana, Andres, A. *La Palabra Bajo Fuego.* Bogotá: Planeta, 2005), 48, 51.

Patrick, Stewart. *Weak Links: Fragile States, Global Threats, and International Security.* New York: Oxford University Press, 2011.

Pearce, Jenny. *Colombia: Inside the Labyrinth.* London: Latin America Bureau—Research and Action, 1990.

Penhaul, Karl. "IRA Suspects Set Free in Colombia." CNN, June 16, 2004.

———. "Outlaw Role Seen in Colombia." *Boston Globe,* March 28, 2001.

People's Weekly World. "Colombia's Uribe Mired in Paramilitary Scandal." *People's Weekly World,* February 24, 2007.

Percy, Sarah. "Amid Libya Slaughter, Let's Stop Mercenaries." *USA Today,* February 25, 2011.

Pereira, Anthony W. *Political (In)Justice: Authoritarianism and the Rule of Law in Brazil, Chile, and Argentina.* Pittsburgh: University of Pittsburgh Press, 2005.

Petras, James. "Bolivia: Between Colonization and Revolution." *Canadian Dimension* 38 (January–February 2004): 33–36.

———. "Colombia: The FARC and the Trade Unions." *Rebelion,* December 11, 2001. http://rebelion.org/petras/english/farcunions010102.htm.

———. "Dirty Money: Foundation of US Growth and Empire." *La Jornada,* May 19, 2001.

———. "The FARC Faces the Empire." *Latin American Perspectives* 27 (September 2000): 134–43.

———. "The Geopolitics of Plan Colombia." *Monthly Review* 53 (May 2001): 30–49.

———. "Interview with Professor James Petras: Behind Colombia's Civil War." *Committees in Solidarity with Latin America & the Caribbean.* March 25, 2002. http://www.mail-archive.com/marxist-leninist-list@lists.econ.utah.edu/msg02521.html.

———. *The New Development Politics: The Age of Empire Building and New Social Movements.* London: Ashgate Publishing, 2003.

———. "Non-Governmental Organizations in a Conjuncture of Conflict and

War Psychosis." *Rebelion*, December 4, 2001. http://rebelion.org/
petras/english/ngo170102.htm.

———. "The Revolutionary Armed Forces of Colombia—People's Army (FARC-
EP): The Cost of Unilateral Humanitarian Initiatives." March 16, 2008.
http://petras.lahaine.org/articulo.php?p=1728&more=1&c=1.

Petras, James, and Morris Morley. *US Hegemony under Siege: Class, Politics and
Development in Latin America*. London: Verso, 1990.

Petras, James, and Henry Veltmeyer. *Globalization Unmasked: Imperialism in
the 21st Century*. London: Zed Books, 2001.

Podur, Justin. "How Would Drug Legalization in the United States Affect
Colombia?" *Colombia Journal*. March 17, 2003, http://colombiajour-
nal.org/how-would-drug-legalization-in-the-united-states-affect-colom-
bia.htm.

Podur, Justin, and Manuel Rozental. "Prepare for 4 Years of the Uribe Model:
Change and Continuity after Colombia's Elections." *Z-Magazine*, May
30, 2002. http://www.zmag.org/content/Colombia/podur_rozental-
uribemodel.cfm.

Posada, Alejandro R. "Compras de Tierra por Narcotraficantes." In *Drogas
Illicitas en Colombia, su Impacto Economico, Politico y Social*, edited by
Francisco Thoumi, 280–346. Bogotá: PNUD/DUE/Ariel Ciencia
Politica, 1997.

———. "Conflicto armado y territorio en Colombia." In *Colonizacion del Bosque
Humedo Tropical*, edited by Humberto Rojas Ruiz, 112–33. Bogotá:
Corporacion Aracuara, 1989.

Potter, Gary W., and Bruce Bullington. "Drug Trafficking and the Contras: A
Case of State-Organized Crime." Paper presented at annual meeting of
the American Society of Criminology, Montreal, 1987.

Quintanilla, Jacob. "The 'Invisible' U.S. War in Colombia." *Resource Center of
the Americas*, June 29, 2004.

Rabasa, Angel, and Peter Chalk. *Colombian Labyrinth: The Synergy of Drugs
and Insurgency and Its Implications for Regional Stability*. Santa
Monica, CA: Rand Corporation, 2001.

Rabine, Mark. "The War on Drugs." *Z-Magazine*, January 1989.
http://www.zcommunications.org/the-war-on-drugs-rabine.

Radu, Michael Radu. "The Perilous Appeasement of Guerrillas." *Orbis* 44
(Summer 2000): 363–82.

Ramo, Joshua C. "America's Shadow Drug War." *Time*, May 7, 2001.

Randall, Stephen. J. *Colombia and the United States: Hegemony and
Interdependence*. Athens: University of Georgia Press, 1992.

Reason, Tim. "The Corporate Connection: How Drug Money Is Finding Its
Way to the Bottom Line." *CFO Magazine*. March 1, 2001.

Reinarman, Craig, and Harry G. Levine. *Crack in America: Demon Drugs and
Social Justice*. Berkeley: University of California Press, 1997.

Rempe, Dennis. *The Past as Prologue? A History of US CI Policy in Colombia, 1958–66*. Carlisle, PA: Strategic Studies Institute, 2002.

Renacientes.org. "Colombia Monthly Report 1997." Cited in *Plan Colombia & Proceso de Comunidades Negras (PCN)*. www2.renacientes.org:8080/renacientes.

Reuters. "Colombia Blames Rebels for Bogotá Club Bomb." February 8, 2003;
———. May 15, 2001.
———. "NYSE Chief Meets Top Colombia Rebel Leader." June 26, 1999.
———. "Peace Czar Says FARC Not Responsible for Necklace Bomb." May 21, 2000.

Revista Nota Economica. "Los Paras Ganan La Guerra." *Revista Nota Economica*. November 17, 1997.

Revolutionary Armed Forces of Colombia—People's Army (FARC-EP). "Colombia: Legalization of Drug Consumption, the Only Serious Alternative for the Elimination of the Narcotics Traffic." Secretariat of the Central General Staff, Plenum of the Central General Staff, Mountains of Colombia. March 29, 2000.
———. "Communiqué." Mountains of Colombia. March 10, 1999.
———. "The Demilitarized Zone, A Laboratory of Peace." *Resistencia International* 26 (2001).
———. *FARC-EP: Historical Outline*. Toronto: International Commission, 2000.
———. "Paramilitarismo Como Politica Contrainsurgente de Estado." Mountains of Colombia, January 1999.

Reyes, Alejandro. "La Compra de Drogas en Colombia: Su Impacto Economico, Politico y Social." In *Direccion Nacional de Estupefacientes and UNDP,* edited by Francisco Thoumi, 279–346. Bogotá: Editorial Planeta, 1997.

Richani, Nazi. Email message to authors. August 12, 2005.
———. *Systems of Violence: The Political Economy of War and Peace in Colombia*. New York: State University of New York Press, 2002.

Richards, James R. *Transnational Criminal Organizations, Cybercrime, and Money Laundering: A Handbook for Law Enforcement Officers, Auditors, and Financial Investigators*. Boca Raton, FL: CRC Press, 1998.

Robberson, Tod. "U.S. Launches Covert Program to Aid Colombia Military, Mercenaries Hired, Sources Say." *Dallas Morning News,* August 19, 1998.

Robbins, Christopher. *Air America: The True Story of the CIA's Mercenary Fliers in Covert Operations from Pre-War China to Present Day Nicaragua*. London: Corgi Books, 1988.

Robinson, Eugene. "Cocaine Operations Shift Southward: Drugs Processed in Bolivia Shipped from Argentina to Europe." *Washington Post,* June 6, 1991.

Robinson, Linda. "America's Secret Armies: A Swarm of Private Contractors Bedevils the US Military." *US News & World Report*, November 4, 2002.

———. "The Fugitive: An Account of the Search for the Head of the Medellin Drug Cartel." *New York Times*, June 17, 2001.

Robinson, Matthew B., and Renee G. Scherlen. *Lies, Damned Lies, and Drug War Statistics* . Albany: State University of New York Press, 2007.

Robles, Azalea. "250 mil desaparecidos claman justicia, y Falsimedia confunde para seguir desapareciendo la verdad." *Rebelion*, March 22, 2011, http://www.rebelion.org/noticia.php?id=122896

Robles, Frances. "Cocaine No Longer the Drug of Choice." *The Sacramento Bee*, September 19, 2011.

Rocha, Ricardo. "The Colombian Economy after 25 Years of Drug Trafficking." United Nations Drug Control Program (UNDCP) 2000, Bogotá Country Office. http://www.undcp.org/colombia/rocha.html.

Rogers, Paul, Simon Whitby, and Malcolm Dando. "Biological Warfare against Crops." *Scientific American* (June 1999): 70–76.

Rohter, Larry. "Colombia Adjusts Economic Figures to Include Its Drug Crops." *New York Times*, June 27, 1999.

———. "Former Smuggler Ties Top Officials of Cuba and Nicaragua to Drug Ring." *New York Times*, November 21, 1991.

Ronfeldt, David. *Tribes, Institutions, Markets, Networks: A Framework about Societal Evolution*. Santa Monica, CA: Rand Corporation, 1996.

Roskin, Michael G. "Crime and Politics in Colombia: Considerations for US Involvement." *Parameters: US Army War College Quarterly* (Winter 2001–2002): 126–34.

Ross, Jeffrey I. *Controlling State Crime*. Piscataway, NJ: Transaction Publishers, 2000.

Roston, Aram. "It's the Real Thing: Murder. US Firms Like Coca-Cola Are Implicated in Colombia's Brutality." *The Nation*, September 3, 2001.

Royce, Knut, and Nathaniel Heller. "Cheney Led Halliburton to Feast at Federal Trough." *Center for Public Integrity Report*, August 2, 2000.

Ruiz, Bert. *The Colombian Civil War*. London: McFarland & Company, 2001.

Russell, Dan. "Agent Green: McCollum's 'Silver Bullet' in the Head." Drugwar.com. 23 February 2001. http://www.drugwar.com/fusarium.shtm.

———. *Drug War: Covert Money, Power & Policy*. Camden, New York: Kalyx, 2000.

Ryan, Randolph. "Shifting the Drug War." *Boston Globe*, March 10, 1989.

Ryder, Nicholas. *Financial Crime in the 21st Century: Law and Policy*. Cheltenham: Edward Elgar, 2011.

Sabbag, Robert. "Hot Crime: Money Laundering." *Rolling Stone*, August 21, 1997.

Salazar, Alonso, and Ana M. Jaramillo. *Medellin: Las Subculturas del Narcotrafico, Coleccion Sociedad y Conflicto.* Bogotá: CINEP, 1992.

Salgado Tamayo, Manuel. "The Geostrategy of Plan Colombia." *CovertAction Quarterly.* 71, Winter 2001), 37-40.

Sanchez, Gonzalo. *Ensayos de Historia Social y Politica del Siglo XX.* Bogotá: El Ancora Editores, 1984.

Saunders, Frances S. *Who Paid the Piper: The CIA and the Cultural Cold War.* London: Granta Books, 1999.

Schneider, Cathy L. "Violence, Identity and Spaces of Contention in Chile, Argentina and Colombia." *Social Research* 67 (Fall 2000): 773–802.

Schneier, Bruce. *Secrets and Lies: Digital Security in a Networked World.* New York: Wiley, 2004.

School of the Americas Watch. "Notorious Graduates from Colombia." http://www.soaw.org/index.php?option=com_content&id=235.

Schoultz, Lars. *National Security and United States Policy toward Latin America.* Princeton: Princeton University Press, 1987.

Schrader, Esther. "US Companies Hired to Train Foreign Armies." *Los Angeles Times,* April 14, 2002.

Schulte-Bockholt, Alfredo. *The Politics of Organized Crime and the Organized Crime of Politics: A Study in Criminal Power.* Lanham, MD: Lexington Books, 2006.

Scott, Peter D. , "Colombia: Washington's Dirtiest 'War on Drugs.'" *Tikkun* 12 (May–June 1997): 27–31.

———. *Deep Politics and the Death of JFK.* Berkeley: University of California Press, 1993.

———. *Drugs, Oil, and War: The United States in Afghanistan, Colombia, and Indochina.* New York: Rowman & Littlefield Publishers, 2003.

Scott, Peter Dale. *American War Machine: Deep Politics, the CIA Global Drug Connection, and the Road to Afghanistan.* New York: Rowman & Littlefield, 2010.

Scott, Peter D., and Jonathan Marshall. *Cocaine Politics: Drugs, Armies, and the CIA in Central America.* Reprint. Berkeley: University of California Press, 1998.

Secretariat of the Central General Staff, FARC-EP. Plenum of the Central General Staff, International Commission. "Colombia: Legalization of Drug Consumption. The Only Serious Alternative for the Elimination of the Narcotics Traffic." Mountains of Colombia, March, 29 2000; Revolutionary Armed Forces of Colombia—People's Army, *FARC-EP: Historical Outline* (Toronto: International Commission, 2000).

Semana. "Los Nuevos Narcos," *Semana,* May 8, 2001.

Shackley, Theodore. *The Third Option: An American View of Counterinsurgency Operations.* New York: McGraw Hill, 1981.

Shannon, Elaine. *Desperados: Latin Drug Lords, US Lawmen, and the War America Can't Win.* New York: Viking Press, 1988.

Sharma, Sohan, and Surinder Kumar. "The Military Backbone of Globalization," *Race and Class 3* (January–March 2003): 23–39.

Shifter, Michael. "A Decade of Plan Colombia: Time for a New Approach." *Inter-American Dialogue,* June 21, 2010, www.thedialogue.org/page.cfm?pageID=32&pubID=2407.

Siegel, Ronald K. "History of Cocaine Smoking." *Journal of Psychoactive Drugs* 14 (Oct–Dec 1982): 277–99.

Silverstein, Ken. "Privatizing War: How Affairs of State Are Outsourced to Corporations beyond Public Control." *The Nation,* July 28, 1997.

Silvestrini, Elaine. "'Express' Tracking Colombian Cocaine." *Tampa Tribune.* July 4, 2004.

Simon, Jose L. "Narcotrafico via Paraguay irrita a Washington." *Sendero,* January 15, 1988.

Singer, Peter W. *Corporate Warriors: The Rise of the Privatized Military Industry.* Ithaca, NY: Cornell University Press, 2004.

Sklar, Holly. *Washington's War on Nicaragua.* Boston: South End Press, 1988.

Slack, Edward. *Opium, State, and Society: China's Narco-Economy and the Guomindang, 1924–1937.* Honolulu: University of Hawaii Press, 2001.

Smith, Michael L., and Charunee Normita Thongtham. *Why People Grow Drugs: Narcotics and Development in the Third World.* London: Panos, 1992.

Smith, Rebecca, and John R. Emshwiller. "Internal Probe of Enron Finds Wide-Ranging Abuses—Unanswered in Board Report Are Some Big Questions Regarding Legal Liability." *Wall Street Journal,* February, 2002.

Social Justice Colombia.org, http://www.socialjusticecolombia.org/.

Solberg, Victoria B., et al. "Penetration of (sup 3 H) T-2 Mycotoxin through Abraded and Intact Skin and Methods to Decontaminate (sup 3 H) T-2 Mycotoxin from Abrasions." 28 *Toxicon* (January 1990): 803–11.

Spencer, Christopher P., and Visweswaran Navaratnam. *Drug Abuse in East Asia.* Kuala Lumpur: Oxford University Press, 1981.

Steiner, Roberto. "Hooked on Drugs: Colombian-US Relations." In *The United States and Latin America: The New Agenda,* edited by Victor Bulmer-Thomas and James Dunkerley, 159–76. London: Institute of Latin American Studies, 1999.

Stewart, Phil. "Ecuador Wants Military Base in Miami." Reuters, October 22, 2007.

Stich, Rodney. *Drugging America: A Trojan Horse.* California: Diablo Western Press, 1999.

———. *Defrauding America: Encyclopedia of Secret Operations by the CIA, DEA, and Other Covert Agencies.* 3rd ed. California: Diablo Western Press, 2001.

Stokes, Doug. *America's Other War: Terrorizing Colombia*. New York: Zed Books, 2005.

Storrs, Larry K., and Nina M. Serafino. "Andean Regional Initiative (ARI): FY 2002 Assistance for Colombia and Neighbors." *Congressional Research Service Report*. Washington DC: Library of Congress Congressional Research Service, February 14, 2002.

STRATFOR. "The Splintering of Colombia's AUC." Basic Global Intelligence Brief, October 8, 2004.

Strong, Simon. *Whitewash: Pablo Escobar and the Cocaine Wars*. London: Macmillan, 1995.

Suarez, Alfredo Rangel. *Colombia: Guerra en el Fin de Siglo*. Bogotá: TM Editores, 1998.

———. *Guerreros y Politicos: Dialogo y Conflicto En Colombia, 1998–2002*. Bogotá: Intermedio Editores, 2003.

Summers, Anthony, and Robbyn Swan. *The Arrogance of Power: The Secret World of Richard Nixon*. New York: Viking Press, 2000.

Syal, Rajeev. "Drug Money Saved Banks in Global Crisis, Claims UN Advisor." *The Guardian*, December 13, 2009. http://www.guardian.co.uk/global/2009/dec/13/drug-money-banks-saved-un-cfief-claims.

Sydney Morning Herald. "Jailed Drug Dons' $2.8b Comedown." *Sydney Morning Herald*, September 27, 2006.

Takáts Előd. "A Theory of 'Crying Wolf': The Economics of Money Laundering Enforcement." *Journal of Law, Economics, and Organization*. 27, April 2011, 32–78;

Tamayo, Juan O. "Colombia: Private Firms Take On US Military Role in Drug War." *Miami Herald*, May 22, 2001.

Tate, Winifred. "Colombia: The Right Gathers Momentum." *NACLA Report on the Americas* 35 (May–June 2002): 13–17.

———. "Repeating Past Mistakes."

Taussig, Michael. *Law in a Lawless Land: Diary of a 'Limpieza' in Colombia*. New York: New Press, 2003.

Tayacan. *Psychological Operations in Guerrilla Warfare: The CIA's Nicaragua Manual*. New York: Vintage Books, 1985.

Thompson, Matthew. "The Secret War of Colombia." *Sydney Morning Herald*, August 17, 2008.

Tickner, B. Arlene, "Colombia and the United States: From Counternarcotics to Counterterrorism." *Current History* 102 (February 2003): 77–85.

Thoumi, Francisco. "Corruption and Drug Trafficking: General Considerations and References to Colombia." Unpublished conference paper presented at the U.S. War College Conference on Colombia, December 1998, Carlisle, Pennsylvania.

———. *Illegal Drugs, Economy, and Society in the Andes*. Washington DC: Woodrow Wilson Center Press, 2003.

———. *Political Economy and Illegal Drugs in Colombia*. London: Lynne Rienner, 1995.

Tokar, Brian. "Monsanto: A Checkered History." *The Ecologist* 28 (September–October 1998): 254–60.

Toledo, Rebecca, Teresa Gutierrez, Sara Flounders, and Andy McInerney, eds. *War in Colombia: Made in U.S.A.* New York: International Action Center, 2003.

Transnational Institute. "Colombia Coca Cultivation Survey Results, A Question of Methods." Drug Policy Briefing No. 22, Transnational Institute, Amsterdam, June 2007. http://www.tni.org/detail_page.phtml?act_id=17020.

———. "Super Coca?" Drug Policy Briefing No. 8, Transnational Institute, Amsterdam, September 2004. http://www.tni.org/detail_page.phtml?page=policybriefings_brief8.

Treaster, Joseph. "Cocaine Manufacturing Is No Longer Just a Colombia Monopoly." *New York Times*, June 30, 1991.

Trebat, Nick. "Drugs Replace Communism as the Point of Entry for US Policy on Latin America." Council on Hemispheric Affairs, August 24, 1999. http://www.icdc.com/~paulwolf/colombia/hemisphr.htm.

Trento, Joseph J. *The Secret History of the CIA*. New York: Forum/Crown/ Random House, 2001.

Trocki, Carl A. *Opium and Empire: Chinese Society in Colonial Singapore, 1800–1910*. London: Cornell University Press, 1990.

———. *Opium, Empire and the Global Political Economy: A Study of the Asian Opium Trade 1750–1950*. New York: Routledge, 1999.

Truell, Peter, and Larry Gurwin. *False Profits: The Inside Story of BCCI, the World's Most Corrupt Financial Empire*. Boston: Houghton Mifflin, 1992.

Turnbull, Constance M. *The Straits Settlements: From Indian Presidency to Crown Colony, 1824–1867*. Singapore: Oxford University Press, 1975.

Uesseler, Rolf. *Servants of War: Private Military Corporations and the Profit of Conflict*, trans. Jefferson Chase. New York: Soft Skull Press, 2008.

UN Drug Control Program. "Global Illicit Drug Trends Survey 2002." http://www.unodc.org/pdf/report_2002-06-26_1/report_2002-06-26_1.pdf.

UN High Commissioner for Human Rights. *Report on the Human Rights Situation in Colombia*. New York: United Nations Publications, 2001.

UN High Commissioner for Refugees. "2005 Global Refugee Trends: Statistical Overview of Populations of Refugees, Asylum-Seekers, Internally Displaced Persons, Stateless Persons, and Other Persons of Concern to UNHCR." June 9, 2006. http://www.unhcr.org/cgi-bin/texis/vtx/home/opendocPDFViewer.html?docid=4486ceb12&query=global trends 2005.

UN International Narcotics Control Program. "International Narcotics Control Board, 1994 Report." http://www.incb.org/pdf/e/ar/incb_report_1994_1.pdf.

UN Office on Drugs and Crime. *Drugs and Development,* vol. 6, June 1994. www.unodc.org/pdf/Alternative%20Development/Drugs_Development.pdf.

———.*Drug Therapy Instead of Criminalizing Drug Addicts.* Committee paper presented at Vienna International Model United Nations, August 4–8, 2002.

———. "World Drug Report 2010." www.unodc.org/unodc/en/data-and-analysis/WDR-2010.html.

U.S. Army. June 16, 2007. http://www.army.mil/.

U.S. Congress. Senate Committee on Foreign Relations, Subcommittee on Terrorism, Narcotics and International Operations Report, Drugs, Law Enforcement, and Foreign Policy. Washington DC: U.S. Government Printing Office, 1989.

———. Senate Select Committee on Improper Activities in the Labor or Management Field, Hearings, 85th Cong. 2d sess. Washington DC: U.S. Government Printing Office, 1959.

U.S. Court of Appeals for the DC Circuit Division for the Purpose of Appointing Independent Counsel, *Final Report of the Independent Counsel for Iran/Contra Matters,* vol. 1: *Investigations and Prosecutions, Lawrence E. Walsh, Independent Counsel.* Washington DC: U.S. Government Printing Office, 1993.

U.S. Department of Defense. *Dictionary of Military and Associated Terms.* Washington DC: U.S. Government Printing Office, 1987.

U.S. Department of Justice. *Colombian Narco-Terrorist Extradited to United States.* December 31, 2004. http://www.america.gov/st/washfile-english/2005/January/20050103142132ASrelliM0.8359339.html.

U.S. Department of Justice, National Drug Intelligence Center. *National Drug Threat Assessment,* August 2011, Washington DC, http://www.justice.gov/ndic/pubs44/44849/44849p.pdf.

U.S. Department of State. "Fact Sheet on Plan Colombia." March 14, 2001. http://www.state.gov/p/wha/rls/fs/2001/1042.htm.

———. *Foreign Relations of the United States, 1961–1963,* vol. 2: *American Republics* (Washington DC: U.S. Government Printing Office, 1996).

———. *International Narcotics Control Strategy Report 2001.* www.state.gov/p/inl/rls/nrcrpt/2001/.

———. *International Narcotics Control Strategy Report 2004.* Bureau for International Narcotics and Law Enforcement Affairs. www.state.gov/g/inl/rls/nrcrpt/2003/.

———. *International Narcotics Control Strategy Report 2008.* Bureau for International Narcotics and Law Enforcement Affairs. http://www.state.gov/p/inl/rls/nrcrpt/2008/index.htm.

U.S. Department of Transport. Docket OST-96 – 1153,
http://www.airlineinfo.com/ost-html2/347.htm.

U.S. Department of Treasury. "Bank Secrecy Act/Anti-Money Laundering –
Comptroller's Handbook." December 2000.

U.S. Department of the Treasury. *Financial Crimes Enforcement Network 2000-
2005 Strategic Plan.* Washington DC: U.S. Government Printing
Office, 2000.

U.S. General Accounting Office. *Drug Control: Narcotics Threat from Colombia
Continues to Grow.* Washington DC: U.S. Government Printing Office,
1999.

———. *Drug Control: U.S. Supported Efforts in Burma, Pakistan, and
Thailand.* U.S. General Accounting Office Report. Washington DC:
U.S. Government Printing Office, 1988.

———. *Drug Control: The Department of State's Contract Award for Its
Counternarcotics Aviation Program, U.S. General Accounting Office
Report.* Washington DC: U.S. Government Printing Office, 2001.

———. *U.S. Assistance to Colombia Will Take Years to Produce Results.*
Washington DC: U.S. Government Printing Office, 2000.

U.S. Naval War College. "Maoist Strategic Theory and the Chinese Civil War."
Newport, Rhode Island. http://www.nwc.navy.mil/defaultf.htm.

U.S. Southern Command. http://www.southcom.mil/AppsSC/index.php.

"US Reaffirms Support for Colombia's War on Drugs." *Colombia Reports,*
October 7, 2011.

USA-Colombia Bi-national Agreement regarding the Surrender of Persons to
the International Criminal Court, September 17, 2003.

Valentine, Douglas. *The Strength of the Wolf: The Secret History of America's
War on Drugs.* New York: Verso, 2004.

Van Biema, David. "Sweet,Sweet Surrender: A Cali Cartel Chief Proposes to
Give Up under Conditions So Lenient that They May Strain US-
Colombian Relations." *Time,* November 7, 1994.

Van Dongen, Rachel. "US's 'Private Army' Grows: In Colombia and around the
World, Civilians Are Doing Work Formerly Done by the Military."
Christian Science Monitor, September 3, 2003.

Vargas, Ricardo. "The Anti-Drug Policy, Aerial Spraying of Illicit Crops and
their Social, Environmental and Political Impacts in Colombia."
Journal of Drug Issues 32 (Winter 2002): 11–60.

———. *Drogas, Poder y Region en Colombia.* Bogotá: CINEP, 1994.

———. *Fumigación y Conflicto: Políticas Antidrogas y Deslegitimación del
Estado en Colombia.* Bogotá: Tercer Mundo Editores, 1999.

———. "The Revolutionary Armed Forces of Colombia (FARC) and the Illicit
Drug Trade." Transnational Institute, June 1999,
http://www.tni.org/briefing/revolutionary-armed-forces-colombia-farc-
and-illicit-drug-trade.

Vest, Jason. "DynCorp's Drug Problem." *The Nation*, July 3, 2001.

Villar, Oliver, Drew Cottle, and Angela Keys. "The Kill for Drugs Policy? Ecocide in Rural Colombia." Paper presented at the 14th Ecopolitics Conference of the Ecopolitics Association of Australasia, RMIT University, Melbourne, November 27–29, 2003.

Vivanco, Jose Miguel Vivanco. Director of Human Rights Watch Americas Division, testimony before U.S. Senate, Subcommittee on the Western Hemisphere, April 24, 2002. http://hrw.org/english/docs/2001/07/11/colomb184.htm.

Vulliamy, Ed. "Going Backwards: US Prepares to Spray Genetically-Modified Herbicides on Colombians." London *Observer*, July 2, 2000.

——. "US Sprays Poison in Drugs War." *Observer International*, July 2, 2000.

——. Vulliamy, Ed. "How a Big US Bank Lundered Billions from Mexico's Murderous Drug Gangs." *The Observer*, April 3, 2011.

Waghelstein, John D. "Latin American Insurgency Status Report." *Military Review* 67 (February 1987): 42–47.

Waisbord, Silvio. "Grandes Gigantes: Media Concentration in Latin America." February 27, 2002, http://www.opendemocracy.net/media-globalmediaownership/article_64.jsp.

——. *Watchdog Journalism in South America, News Accountability and Democracy*. New York: Columbia University Press, 2001.

Washington Office on Latin America. "Data Shows Record Low Prices of Cocaine and Heroin." November 1, 2004, http://www.wola.org/index.php?option=com_content&task=viewp&id =397.

Way IV, Pennington. "Colombia to Receive New Radar System from US." *Defense Daily*, March 14, 2000.

Wayne, Leslie. "America's For-Profit Secret Army." *New York Times,* October 13, 2002.

Webb, Gary. *Dark Alliance: The CIA, the Contras, and the Crack Cocaine Epidemic*. New York: Seven Stories Press, 1998.

Weekly News Update on the Americas. "US Covert Program Exposed in Colombia." *Weekly News Update on the Americas,* August 23, 1998, http://www.colombiasupport.net/wnu/wnu082398.html.

Weiner, Tim. *Blank Check: The Pentagon"s Black Budget*. New York: Warner Books, 1990.

——. *Legacy of Ashes: The History of the CIA*. London: Penguin Books, 2008.

White House Office of National Drug Control Policy. *National Drug Control Strategy 2008 Annual Report*. www.whitehousedrugpolicy.gov/publications/policy/ndcs08/index.html.

White House Office of National Drug Control Policy. *Pulse Check: Trends in Drug Abuse,* January 2004, http://www.whitehousedrugpolicy.gov/publications/drugfact/pulsechk/january04/index.html/.

White, Josh. "Iraq War Cost Put at $1.7 Trillion." *The Age*, November 14, 2007.

Whittaker, David J. *The Terrorism Reader*, 2nd ed. New York: Routledge, 2002.

Williams, Phil. "The Nature of Drug-Trafficking Networks." *Current History*, 97 (April 1998), 154–159.

Williams, Phil, and Carl Florez. "Transnational Criminal Organizations and Drug Trafficking." *United Bulletin on Narcotics* 46 (January 1994): 14.

Wilpert, Gregory. "Chávez's Venezuela and 21st-Century Socialism." *Research in Political Economy* 24 (Spring 2007): 23.

Wilson, Scott. "Coca Trade Booming Again in Peru: U.S.-Sponsored Eradication Plans Spark Peasant Protests." *Washington Post*, March 22, 2003.

———."Commander of Lost Causes." *Washington Post*, July 6, 2003.

———. "US Seeks Court Immunity for Troops in Colombia, US Trying to Protect Nationals from International Courts." *Washington Post*, August 15, 2002.

Wise, David, and Thomas B. Ross. *The Invisible Government*. New York: Random House, 1964.

Wolf, Paul. "America's Dirty War in Colombia." August 25, 1998. http://www.icdc.com/~paulwolf/colombia/whde.htm.

———. "FARC Not a Terrorist Group." *Colombia Journal*, January 12, 2008. http://colombiajournal.org/farc-not-a-terrorist-group.htm.

———. "United States and Colombia." *Z-Magazine*, March 1999. http://www.thirdworldtraveler.com/US_ThirdWorld/United%20States_Colombia.html.

Woods, Brett F. *The Art & Science of Money Laundering: Inside the Commerce of the International Narcotics Traffickers*. Boulder, CO: Paladin Press, 1998.

"World: Americas Citbank Censured over Money Laundering." *BBC News*, November 9, 1999, http://news.bbc.co.uk/2/hi/americas/511951.stm.

World Organization against Torture. *El Terrorismo de Estado en Colombia*. Brussels: Editorial NCOS, 1992.

World Public Opinon.org. "Latin American Publics Are Skeptical about US—but not about Democracy." World Public Opinion.org, March 7, 2007. http://www.worldpublicopinion.org/pipa/articles/brlati-namericara/328.php?nid=&id=&pnt=328&lb=brla.

Wyss, Jim. "Colombian Ex-Spy Chief Gets 25-Year Sentence." *Miami Herald*, September 14, 2011.

Youngers, Coletta, and Eileen Rosi. *Drugs and Democracy in Latin America: The Impact of U.S. Policy*. Boulder, CO: Lynne Reinner Publishers, 2005.

Zagaris, Bruce, and Scott Ehlers. "Drug Trafficking & Money Laundering." *Foreign Policy in Focus*, May 2001. http://www.fpif.org/briefs/vol6/v6n18launder.html.

Zamosc, Leon. *The Agrarian Question and the Peasant Movement in Colombia.*
    Cambridge: Cambridge University Press, 1986.
Zarate-Laun, Cecilia. "CIA, Cocaine, and Death Squads." *Covert Action*
    Quarterly (Fall/Winter 1999): 16–17.
Zill, Orina, and Lowell Bergman. "The Bell Helicopter Case." *Frontline,*
    October 2000. www.pbs.org/wgbh/pages/frontline/shows/drugs/spe-
    cial/bell.html.
———. "U.S. Business and Money Laundering." *Frontline,* October 2000.
    http://www.pbs.org/wgbh/pages/frontline/shows/drugs/special/us.html.
Zion, Sidney. "Seizing Drugs, Seizing Property." *Journal of Commerce* (July
    1996): 101–2.

Notes

FOREWORD

1. U.S. Army Special Warfare School, "Subject: Visit to Colombia, February 26, 1962," Declassified Documents Reference Series (Arlington, VA: Carrollton Press, 1976), 154D; Michael McClintock, *Instruments of Statecraft: U. S. Guerrilla Warfare, Counterinsurgency, and Counterterrorism* (New York: Pantheon, 1992), 222. In 1959, even before Kennedy was elected, the United States dispatched to Colombia Colonel Charles Bohannan, a veteran of the bloody Philippine counterinsurgency after the Second World War. See McClintock, *Instruments,* 143.

2. McClintock, *Instruments,* 223.

3. *1963 Field Manual on U. S. Army Counterinsurgency Forces* (FM 31–22), 82–84; quoted in McClintock, *Instruments,* 252.

4. *Reglamento de Combate,* 317; quoted in McClintock, *Instruments,* 252; see also 223.

5. McClintock, *Instruments,* 193, citing Office of Public Safety, International Police Academy, syllabus for Course no. 6. Nineteen Colombians took the course, the largest group from any single country.

6. The revolutionary organization M-19 evolved from a group of nonviolent student activists whose efforts to organize the employees of U.S. firms led to some of their group being murdered. See Aña Carrigan, *The Palace of Justice: A Colombian Tragedy* (New York: Four Walls Eight Windows, 1993). For another U.S. oil company's use of a major international mafia figure, see Peter Dale Scott, *Deep Politics and the Death of JFK* (Berkeley: University of California Press, 1996), 202–4.

7. *San Francisco Chronicle*, June 15, 2001. It is common for oil companies abroad to become involved with local security forces who then commit atrocities in which the oil companies are implicated. In Aceh, Indonesia, Exxon-Mobil has maintained what Bloomberg.com has called a "less than arm's-length detachment from the military" ("a long-term miscalculation"), which has tortured civilians on or near company facilities (Bloomberg.com, March 25, 2001, quoted in Robert Jereski, "The Conflict in Aceh," www.preventconflict.org/portal/main/research/jereski.htm). In September 2002, victims of Myanmar military atrocities committed in connection with security for a Unocal pipeline won the right to sue for damages in a U.S. court (*Los Angeles Times*, September 19, 2002).

8. Peter Dale Scott and Jonathan Marshall, *Cocaine Politics* (Berkeley: University of California Press, 1991), 89.

9. Human Rights Watch, *State of War: Political Violence and Counterinsurgency in Colombia*, www.hrw.org/reports/1993/stateofwar1.htm.

10. Human Rights Watch, *Colombia's Killer Networks: The Military-Paramilitary Partnership and the United States*, www.hrw.org/hrw/reports/1996/killer1.htm.

11. Frank Smyth, *Progressive*, June 1998: "These death squads killed trade unionists, peasant leaders, human-rights workers, journalists, and other suspected 'subversives.' The evidence, including secret Colombian military documents, suggests that the CIA may be more interested in fighting a leftist resistance movement than in combating drugs."

12. Human Rights Watch, *The Ties that Bind: Colombia and Military-Paramilitary Links*, http://www.hrw.org/reports/2000/colombia; Alma Guillermoprieto, "Our New War in Colombia," *New York Review of Books*, April 13, 2000.

13. Guillermoprieto, "Our New War": "In 1995, according to a recent report by the U.S. State Department, Bolivia had 48,600 hectares of coca under cultivation. In 1999 there were only 21,800. Even more dramatic are the figures for Peru, where production peaked at 115,300 hectares in 1995, and shrank four years later to barely 38,700. But if one takes the total combined figures for hectares of coca under cultivation in Colombia, Bolivia, and Peru in 1995, and again in 1999, the picture is somewhat different. In 1995 the estimated total was 214,800 hectares. In 1999 it was 183,000." See also *Chicago Sun-Times*, January 21, 2001: "Peru and Bolivia began major anti-coca efforts of this type in the 1990s. Peru's coca cultivation is down 66 percent in the last four years (helped in part by a fungus that attacked Peru's coca bushes). Bolivia's has fallen 55 percent in 2 1/2 years. Colombia's coca production rose rapidly at the same time, but not as much as these drops, meaning there was a net reduction in the total amount of coca grown. Or so the authorities thought. Further analysis showed that

Colombian cocaine productivity was 2 1/2 times higher than previously believed. It's impossible to say for how long the United States has been underestimating South American cocaine production. Once the 1998 and 1999 figures for Colombia were adjusted accordingly, the major drop in cocaine production vanished."

14. Scott and Marshall, *Cocaine Politics*, 81–84.
15. *New York Times*, October 25, 1997.
16. Aña Carrigan, *Irish Times*, August 23, 2000. By late 1989, the Cali cartel had become "the principal source of information to the [Colombian] security agencies." Patrick Clawson and Rensselaer W. Lee III, *The Andean Cocaine Industry* (New York: St. Martin's, 1996), 57.
17. Mark Bowden, *Killing Pablo* (New York: Atlantic Monthly Press, 2001), 184–225. In April 2001, Amnesty International USA filed a lawsuit to obtain CIA records on Los Pepes. AIUSA alleged that its investigation pointed to "an extremely suspect relationship between the U.S. government and the Castaño family—at a time when the U.S. government was well aware of that family's involvement in paramilitary violence and narcotics trafficking." (Amnesty International USA press release, April 25, 2001; http://www.amnestyusa.org/news/2001/colombia04252001_2.html.)
18. *Washington Post*, July 21, 1996 (for reports); Bowden, *Killing Pablo*, 186, 263, 268. According to the respected Colombian writer Aña Carrigan, the DEA in 2000 still regarded Castaño as a potential ally: "Serious allegations have emerged that agents of the U.S. Drug Enforcement Agency (DEA) have offered to subsidise the 'paramilitary' leader, Carlos Castaño, in return for his support in combating the traffickers. Speaking on national television from his northern fiefdom, Castaño said he did not know whether a request for his help reflected U.S. policy or came from agents acting on their own initiative. A DEA informant, who says he acted as translator at meetings between DEA agents, traffickers and members of Castaño's paramilitaries, claims it was agreed that U.S. officials should meet Castaño to conclude a deal" (Carrigan, *Irish Times*, August 23, 2000). Carrigan believed that Castaño intended by sustained military activity to divert middle-class hopes away from the peace process and toward a military-civilian "national unity government," with himself at its head.
19. *New York Times*, November 23, 1996.
20. *Time*, November 29, 1993, http://www.time.com/time/magazine/article/0,9171,979669,00.html: "The shipments continued, however, until Guillen tried to send in 3,373 lbs. of cocaine at once. The DEA, watching closely, stopped it and pounced."
21. Mike Wallace, CBS News transcript, *60 Minutes*, November 21, 1993.
22. *Wall Street Journal*, November 22, 1996. The information about the drug activities of Guillén Davila had been published in the U.S. press years

before the indictment. It is probable that, had it not been for the controversy aroused by Gary Webb's Contra-cocaine stories in the August 1996 *San Jose Mercury News*, Guillén would have been as untouchable as other kingpins in the global CIA drug connection, such as Miguel Nassar Haro in Mexico.

23. Chris Carlson, "Is the CIA Trying to Kill Venezuela's Hugo Chávez?" *Global Research*, April 19, 2007.

24. Douglas Valentine, *The Strength of the Pack: The People, Politics and Espionage Intrigues that Shaped the DEA* (Springfield, OR: TrineDay, 2009), 400; *Time*, November 23, 1993. McFarlin had worked with anti-guerrilla forces in El Salvador in the 1980s. The CIA station chief in Venezuela, Jim Campbell, also retired.

25. This was at the time that the CIA was plotting, successfully, to bring down Pablo Escobar, chief of the Medellín cartel, with the assistance of the drug-trafficking death squad leader Carlos Castaño.

26. Peter Dale Scott, *Drugs, Oil, and War* (Lanham, MD: Rowman & Littlefield, 2003), 89, quoting Paul Eddy, *The Cocaine Wars* (New York: W. W. Norton, 1988), 342.

27. Peter Dale Scott, *American War Machine* (Lanham, MD: Rowman & Littlefield, 2010), 63–119, 134–40.

28. Ibid., 20–21 (Gladio), 56 (Brigada Blanca).

29. Ibid., 24–25; quoting from Ruth Goring, "Executing Justice: Which Side Are We On? An Interview with Colombian Human Rights Activist Padre Javier Giraldo, S.J.," Equipo Nizkor, April 2003, www.derechos.org/nizkor/colombia/doc/giraldo1.html.

30. See chapter 6.

31. Alain Labrousse, interview with *Pulso* (Bolivia), www.narconews.com/pressbriefing21september.html. Labrousse also agreed "absolutely" with the statement by Carlos Fuentes that for each dollar earned in the business of drugs, two-thirds stays in the banks of United States.

32. *Guardian*, April 3, 2011, www.guardian.co.uk/world/2011/apr/03/us-bank-mexico-drug-gangs.

33. Rajeev Syal, "Drug Money Saved Banks in Global Crisis, Claims UN Advisor,"*Observer*, December 13, 2009, www.guardian.co.uk/global/2009/dec/13/drug-money-banks-saved-un-cfief-claims.

INTRODUCTION: A WAR OF MANY WARS

1. Galeano interviewed in *Democracy Now*, http://www.democracynow.org/.

1. FROM COCA TO COCAINE

1. Ian James, "Chávez Chews Coca Leaves at Summit, Saying 'Coca Isn't Cocaine,'" *Dallas Morning News,* January 27, 2008.
2. Ibid.
3. Tim Padgett, "Taking the Side of the Coca Farmer," *Time,* May 8, 2002, www.time.com/time/magazine/article/0,9171,332053,00.html.
4. Golden W. Mortimer, *History of Coca: The Divine Plant of the Incas* (San Francisco: And/Or Press, 1974).
5. Leon Zamosc, *The Agrarian Question and the Peasant Movement in Colombia* (London: Cambridge University Press, 1986), 9.
6. Clare Hargreaves, *Snowfields: The War on Cocaine in the Andes* (London: Zed Books, 1992), 42.
7. Arthur C. Gibson, "Freud's Magical Drug," *The Mildred E. Mathias Botanical Garden UCLA Website,* www.botgard.ucla.edu/html/botanytextbooks/economicbotany/Erythroxylum/index.html.
8. Hargreaves, *Snowfields.*
9. Ibid, 42.
10. Anthony McFarlane, *Colombia before Independence: Economy, Society, and Politics Under Bourbon Rule* (Cambridge: Cambridge University Press, 1993).
11. Robert C. Neville, *The Human Condition: A Volume in the Comparative Religious Ideas Project* (Albany: State University of New York Press, 2002), 13.
12. Zamosc, *The Agrarian Question and the Peasant Movement in Colombia,* 11.
13. Catherine Le Grand, *Frontier Expansion and Peasant Protest in Colombia 1850–1936* (Albuquerque: University of New Mexico Press, 1986).
14. Nazih Richani, *Systems of Violence: The Political Economy of War and Peace in Colombia* (New York: State University of New York Press, 2002).
15. Jenny Pearce, *Colombia: Inside the Labyrinth* (London: Latin America Bureau—Research and Action, 1990), 31; Grace Livingstone, *Inside Colombia: Drugs, Democracy, and War* (New Brunswick, NJ: Rutgers University Press, 2003); Revolutionary Armed Forces of Colombia—People's Army, *FARC-EP: Historical Outline* (Toronto: International Commission, 2000).
16. Tim Weiner, *Legacy of Ashes: The History of the CIA* (London: Penguin Books, 2008); FARC-EP, *Historical Outline;* Marcel Idels, "Colombia and the New Latin America: Keys to US and Global Lies," *Blue,* November 8, 2002, http://www.bluegreenearth.us/archive/article/2002/idels5.html.
17. Pearce, *Inside the Labyrinth.*
18. David J. Whittaker, *The Terrorism Reader,* 2nd ed. (New York: Routledge, 2002), 184; Richani, *Systems of Violence.*

19. Pearce, *Inside the Labyrinth,* 169; FARC-EP, *Historical Outline*

20. Ibid.

21. Robin Kirk, *More Terrible than Death: Massacres, Drugs and America's War in Colombia* (New York: Public Affairs, 2003), 48–55; Pearce, *Inside the Labyrinth,* 64; Cathy L. Schneider, "Violence, Identity and Spaces of Contention in Chile, Argentina and Colombia," *Social Research* 67 (Fall 2000): 773–802; Angel Rabasa and Peter Chalk, *Colombian Labyrinth: The Synergy of Drugs and Insurgency and Its Implications for Regional Stability* (Santa Monica, CA: Rand Corporation, 2001).

22. Ibid.

23. Ibid.

24. Pearce, *Inside the Labyrinth,* 58.

25. Forrest Hylton, *Evil Hour in Colombia* (London: Verso Books, 2006).

26. Stephen. J. Randall, *Colombia and the United States: Hegemony and Interdependence* (Athens: University of Georgia Press, 1992).

27. Alfredo Molano, "The Evolution of the FARC: A Guerrilla Group's Long History," *NACLA Report on the Americas* 34 (Sept–Oct 2000): 23–31; Jacobo Arenas, *Cese el Fuego: Una Historia Politica de las FARC.* (Bogotá: Oveja Negra, 1985). Marulanda, like most FARC rank-and-file members, came from the poor peasantry; Jacobo Arenas came from the urban proletariat. Arenas (top left) and Marulanda (top right) appear on the FARC's website http://www.farcejercitodelpueblo.org/.

28. FARC-EP, *Historical Outline,* 26.

29. Congreso de La Republica, *Programa de Fortalecimiento Legislativo, Oficina de Asistencia Tecnica Legislativa,* May 26, 2005, Bogotá, http://www.secretariasenado.gov.co/estudios-ARD/036%20REFOR-MA%20AGRARIA.pdf; Alejandro Reyes, "La Compra de Drogas en Colombia: Su Impacto Economico, Politico y Social," in *Direccion Nacional de Estupefacientes and UNDP,* ed. Francisco Thoumi (Bogotá: Editorial Planeta, 1997), 279–346.

30. Matthew Knoester, "Washington's Role in Colombian Repression," *Z-Magazine,* January 1998, www.zcommunications.org/title-washingtons-role-in-colombian-repression-by-matthew-knoester.

31. James Brittain, "The FARC-EP in Colombia: A Revolutionary Exception in an Age of Imperialist Expansion," *Monthly Review* 57 (2005): 4.

32. Charles Bergquist, Ricardo Penaranda, and Gonzalo Sanchez, *Violence in Colombia 1990–2000: Waging War and Negotiating Peace* (Wilmington: Rowman & Littlefield, 2003); Richani, *Systems of Violence.*

33. Brittain, "The FARC-EP in Colombia," 25.

34. Ibid.; Richani, *Systems of Violence.*

35. Brittain, "The FARC-EP in Colombia."

36. Peter A. Lupsha, "Towards an Etiology of Drug Trafficking and Insurgent Relations: The Phenomenon of Narco-Terrorism," *International Journal of Comparative and Applied Criminal Justice* 13 (Fall 1989): 67.

37. Ehrenfeld wrote the following books: *Narcoterrorism: The Kremlin Connection* (New York: Heritage Foundation, 1986); *Narcoterrorism and the Cuban Connection* (Miami: Cuban American National Foundation, 1988); and *Narcoterrorism* (New York: Basic Books, 1990). Ehrenfeld is also a member of the Committee on the Present Danger (CPD), a neo-conservative lobby group chaired by former CIA director James Woolsey. CPD was the first to allege the Saddam Hussein-al Qaeda link after September 11. Notably, Ehrenfeld was a participant in a series of Western intelligence conferences that were held in Israel in 2003.

38. Rebecca Toledo et al., eds., *War in Colombia: Made in U.S.A.* (New York: International Action Center, 2003); Marcel Idels, "The Political Economy of a Narco-Terror State: Colombia and Corporate Profits," *Bluegreenearth,* August 14, 2002, www.bluegreenearth.us/archive/article/2002/idels2.html.

39. U.S. Department of Justice, *Colombian Narco-Terrorist Extradited to United States,* December 31, 2004, Washington DC, www.america.gov/st/washfile-english/2005/January/20050103142132A SrelliM0.8359339.html.

40. Constance M. Turnbull, *The Straits Settlements: From Indian Presidency to Crown Colony, 1824–1867* (Singapore: Oxford University Press, 1975), 109–10.

41. Eva Bertram et al., *Drug War Politics: The Price of Denial* (Berkeley: University of California Press, 1996).

42. Office of the Superintendent of India, *Report on East Indian Finances— Papers Relating to the Opium Question* (Calcutta: Office of the Superintendent of Government Printing, 1872), 10.

43. See Trocki's *Opium, Empire and the Global Political Economy: A Study of the Asian Opium Trade 1750–1950* (New York: Routledge, 1999); and his *Opium and Empire: Chinese Society in Colonial Singapore, 1800–1910* (London: Cornell University Press, 1990).

44. Sidney W. Mintz, "The Forefathers of Crack," *NACLA Reports on the Americas* 22 (March 1989): 31–32; Jo Ann Kawell, "The Addict Economies," *NACLA Report on the Americas* 22 (March 1989): 33–40.

45. Mark Rabine, "The War on Drugs," *Z-Magazine,* January 1989, www.zcommunications.org/the-war-on-drugs-rabine.

46. Alfonso L. Michelsen and Enrique Calderon, *Palabras Pendientes: Conversaciones Con Enrique Santos Calderon* (Bogotá, El Ancora Editores, 2001).

47. Rabine, "The War on Drugs," 94.

48. Hargreaves, *Snowfields*; Mortimer, *History of Coca*.

49. These imperial adventures have been documented in a number of important publications and some have been written as populist literature to avoid breaching U.S. secrecy laws. For former agents, see Rodney Stich, *Drugging America: A Trojan Horse* (California: Diablo Western Press, 1999); Rodney Stich, *Defrauding America: Encyclopedia of Secret Operations by the CIA, DEA, and Other Covert Agencies,* 3rd ed. (California: Diablo Western Press, 2001); Michael Levine and Laura Kavanau-Levine, *The Big White Lie: The CIA and the Cocaine/Crack Epidemic* (New York: Thunder's Mouth Press, 1993); Michael Levine, *Deep Cover* (New York: Delacorte Press, 1990); Kenneth C. Bucchi, *Operation Pseudo Miranda: A Veteran of the CIA Drug Wars Tells All* (Granite Bay, CA: Penmarin Books, 2000); Kenneth C. Bucchi, *C.I.A. Cocaine in America?: A Veteran of the C.I.A. Drug Wars Tells All* (New York: S.P.I. Books, 1994); Celerino Castillo III and Dave Harmon, *Powderburns: Cocaine, Contras & the Drug War* (London: Sundial, 1994); Al Martin, *The Conspirators: Secrets of an Iran Contra Insider* (Pray, MT: National Liberty Press, 2002). For other authors, see Gary Webb, *Dark Alliance: The CIA, the Contras, and the Crack Cocaine Epidemic* (New York: Seven Stories Press, 1998); Alfred W. McCoy, *The Politics of Heroin: CIA Complicity in the Global Drug Trade* (Chicago: Lawrence Hill Books, 2003); Peter D. Scott, *Drugs, Oil, and War: The United States in Afghanistan, Colombia, and Indochina* (New York: Rowman & Littlefield Publishers, 2003); Peter D. Scott and Jonathan Marshall, *Cocaine Politics: Drugs, Armies, and the CIA in Central America,* repr. (Berkeley: University of California Press, 1998); Douglas Valentine, *The Strength of the Wolf: The Secret History of America's War on Drugs* (New York: Verso, 2004); Leslie Cockburn, *Out of Control* (New York: Atlantic Monthly Press, 1987); Alexander Cockburn and Jeffrey St. Clair, *Whiteout: The CIA, Drugs and the Press* (New York: Verso, 1998); Larry Collins, *Black Eagles* (New York: HarperCollins, 1993).

50. Francisco Thoumi, *Illegal Drugs, Economy, and Society in the Andes* (Washington DC: Woodrow Wilson Center Press, 2003).

51. Robert E. Grosse, *Drugs and Money: Laundering Latin America's Cocaine Dollars* (London: Praeger, 2001), 20–22.

52. Ibid.

53. U.S. Drug Enforcement Administration (DEA), *The Drug Trade in Colombia: A Threat Assessment,* DEA Intelligence Division, March 2002, http://usregsec.sdsu.edu/docs/DEAMarch2002.pdf; Toledo et al., *War in Colombia;* William C. Gilmore and Alastair N. Brown, *Drug Trafficking and the Chemical Industry: Chemical Precursors and International Criminal Law* (Edinburgh: Edinburgh University Press, 1997).

54. Tim Golden and Steven L. Myers, "U.S. Plans Big Aid Package to Rally a Reeling Colombia," *New York Times,* September 15, 1999.

55. U.S. Foreign Broadcast Information Service (FBIS), *Joint Study Sums Up FARC, ELN Earnings*. Document No. FTS199990517001601, CIA Directorate of Science and Technology (Virginia, May 1999). The FBIS is now called the Open Source Center.

56. DEA, "The Drug Trade in Colombia."

57. Ibid.

58. Michael L. Smith et al., *Why People Grow Drugs: Narcotics and Development in the Third World* (London: Panos, 1992).

59. Adam Isacson, *The State Department's Data on Drug-Crop Cultivation*, Center for International Policy, Press Release, March 22, 2004, www.ciponline.org/colombia/040322coca.pdf; White House Office of National Drug Control Policy, *Pulse Check: Trends in Drug Abuse*, January 2004, www.whitehousedrugpolicy.gov/publications/drugfact/pulsechk/ january04/index.html; White House Office of National Drug Control Policy, *National Drug Control Strategy 2008 Annual Report*, www.whitehousedrugpolicy.gov/publications/policy/ndcs08/index.html; U.S. Depart-ment of Justice, National Drug Intelligence Center, *National Drug Threat Assessment*, August 2011, Washington DC, www.justice.gov/ ndic/pubs44/ 44849/44849p.pdf; Frances Robles, "Cocaine No Longer the Drug of Choice," *The Sacramento Bee*, September 19, 2011.

60. U.S. Department of State, *International Narcotics Control Strategy Report 2004*, Bureau for International Narcotics and Law Enforcement Affairs, www.state.gov/g/inl/rls/nrcrpt/2003/; U.S. Department of State, *International Narcotics Control Strategy Report 2008*, Bureau for International Narcotics and Law Enforcement Affairs, www.state.gov/ p/inl/rls/nrcrpt/2008/index.htm. O'Conner, Dermot. "The Political Economy of Colombia's Cocaine Industry." Papel Politico 14 (January–June 2009), 81–106.

61. Toledo et al., *War in Colombia*.

62. Elaine Silvestrini, "'Express' Tracking Colombian Cocaine," *Tampa Tribune*, July 4, 2004.

63. Ibid.

64. DEA, *The Drug Trade in Colombia*; U.S. Drug Enforcement Administration (DEA), *Changing Dynamics of Cocaine Production in the Andean Region*, Drug Intelligence Brief, June 2002, www.usdoj.gov/ dea/pubs/omte;/02033/02033p.html.

2. FROM THE GOLDEN TRIANGLE TO THE CRYSTAL TRIANGLE

1. Peter D. Scott, *Drugs, Oil, and War: The United States in Afghanistan, Colombia, and Indochina* (New York: Rowman & Littlefield Publishers, 2003).

2. Ibid.; Mao Tse-tung, "Analysis of the Classes in Chinese Society," in *Selected Works of Mao*, vol. 1 (Peking: Foreign Languages Press, 1926);

Edward Slack, *Opium, State, and Society: China's Narco-Economy and the Guomindang, 1924-1937* (Honolulu: University of Hawaii Press, 2001).

3. Penny Lernoux, *In Banks We Trust: Bankers, and Their Close Associates, the CIA, the Mafia, Drug Traders, Dictators, and the Vatican* (New York: Anchor/Doubleday, 1984); Frederic Laurent, *L'orchestre noir* (Paris: Stock, 1978); Magnus Linklater, Isabel Hilton, and Neal Ascherson, *The Nazi Legacy* (New York: Holt, Rinehart, and Winston, 1984).

4. Mao Tse-tung, "Analysis of the Classes," 3; Scott, *Drugs, Oil, and War;* Slack, *Opium, State, and Society;* Francis W. Belanger, *Drugs, the U.S., and Khun Sa* (Bangkok: Editions Duang Kamol, 1989).

5. Carl Trocki, *Opium and Empire: Chinese Society in Colonial Singapore, 1800-1910* (London: Cornell University Press, 1990). Christopher P. Spencer and Visweswaran Navaratnam, *Drug Abuse in East Asia* (Kuala Lumpur: Oxford University Press, 1981).

6. Bruce Cumings, *The Origins of the Korean War* (Princeton: Princeton University Press, 1990), 872.

7. Ibid.

8. Trocki, *Opium and Empire;* Timothy Brook and Bob T. Wakabayashi, *Opium Regimes: China, Britain, and Japan, 1839-1952* (Berkeley: University of California Press, 2000).

9. Trocki, *Opium and Empire;* Jonathan Marshall, "Opium and the Politics of Gangsterism in Nationalist China, 1927-1945," *Bulletin of Concerned Asia Scholars* (July–September 1976): 19–48.

10. Cumings, *Origins of the Korean War.*

11. Ross Y. Koen, *The China Lobby in American Politics* (New York: Macmillan, 1960).

12. Ibid., ix. These revelations led the publisher (Macmillan) to withdraw Koen's book and deny ever publishing it. The book was eventually republished by Octagon in 1974.

13. Alexander Cockburn and Jeffrey St. Clair, *Whiteout: The CIA, Drugs and the Press* (New York: Verso, 1998), 216.

14. "Drug War: Covert Money, Power and Policy: LSD," Drugwar.com, http://www.drugwar.com/lsd.shtm.

15. Elaine Shannon, *Desperados: Latin Drug Lords, US Lawmen, and the War America Can't Win* (New York: Viking Press, 1988).

16. Cockburn and St. Clair, *Whiteout;* William R. Corson, *The Armies of Ignorance: The Rise of the American Intelligence Empire* (New York: Dial Press, 1977); David Wise and Thomas B. Ross, *The Invisible Government* (New York: Random House, 1964).

17. Shannon, *Desperados.*

18. Frank C. Darling, *Thailand and the United States* (Washington, DC: Public Affairs Press, 1965).

19. Alfred W. McCoy, *The Politics of Heroin: CIA Complicity in the Global Drug Trade* (Chicago: Lawrence Hill Books, 2003).

20. The Nazi Anti-Komintern and Eastern European Ostpolitik were put together under Hitler but taken over by the CIA's Office of Policy Coordination in 1948.

21. Anthony Summers and Robbyn Swan, *The Arrogance of Power: The Secret World of Richard Nixon* (New York: Viking Press, 2000).

22. Cumings, *Origins of the Korean War;* Anna C. Chennault, *Chennault and the Flying Tigers* (New York: Eriksson, 1963); Koen, *The China Lobby;* Peter D. Scott, *Deep Politics and the Death of JFK* (Berkeley: University of California Press, 1993).

23. Douglas Valentine, *The Strength of the Wolf: The Secret History of America's War on Drugs* (New York: Verso, 2004); Lernoux, *In Banks We Trust;* Robin T. Naylor, *Hot Money and the Politics of Debt* (New York: Simon & Schuster, 1987); Scott, *Deep Politics and the Death of JFK;* Alan Block, *Masters of Paradise: Organized Crime and the Internal Revenue Service in the Bahamas* (Piscataway, NJ: Transaction Publishers, 1991).

24. U.S. Congress, Senate, Select Committee on Improper Activities in the Labor or Management Field, Hearings, 85th Cong. 2d sess. (Washington DC: U.S. Government Printing Office, 1959); Naylor, *Hot Money and the Politics of Debt;* Peter D. Scott and Jonathan Marshall, *Cocaine Politics: Drugs, Armies, and the CIA in Central America,* repr. (Berkeley: University of California Press, 1998); Scott, *Drugs, Oil and War.*

25. McCoy, *Politics of Heroin.*

26. Valentine, *Strength of the Wolf.*

27. Ibid.

28. McCoy, *Politics of Heroin.*

29. Cockburn and St. Clair, *Whiteout.*

30. Harry J. Anslinger and Will Oursler, *The Murderers* (New York: Farrar, Straus & Cudahy, 1961).

31. Cockburn and St. Clair, *Whiteout.*

32. Rodney Stich, *Defrauding America: Encyclopedia of Secret Operations by the CIA, DEA, and Other Covert Agencies,* 3rd ed. (California: Diablo Western Press, 2001).

33. Scott and Marshall, *Cocaine Politics.*

34. John K. Cooley, *Unholy Wars: Afghanistan, America, and International Terrorism* (London: Pluto, 2000); Michael Griffin, *Reaping the Whirlwind: The Taliban Movement in Afghanistan* (London: Pluto, 2001); Peter L. Bergen, *Holy War, Inc.: Inside the Secret World of Osama bin Laden* (New York: Free Press, 2001).

35. Dilip Hiro, *War without End: The Rise of Islamic Terrorism and the Global Response* (New York: Routledge, 2003); Steve Coll, *Ghost Wars: The Secret*

History of the CIA, Afghanistan, and Bin Laden, from the Soviet Invasion to September 10, 2001 (New York: Penguin Press, 2004); Michel Chossudovsky, *America's War on Terrorism* (Montreal: Global Research, 2005).

36. U.S. General Accounting Office, *Drug Control: U.S. Supported Efforts in Burma, Pakistan, and Thailand,* U.S. General Accounting Office Report (Washington DC: U.S. Government Printing Office, 1988); Lawrence Lifshultz, "Inside the Kingdom of Heroin," *The Nation,* 14 November 1988.

37. Jonathan Beaty and Sam C. Gwynne, *The Outlaw Bank: A Wild Ride into the Heart of BCCI,* repr. (Washington DC: Beard Books, 2004).

38. Coll, *Ghost Wars.*

39. U.S.Department of State, *Foreign Relations of the United States, 1961–1963,* vol. 2: *American Republics* (Washington DC: U.S. Government Printing Office, 1996), 13.

40. Ibid

41. Noam Chomsky, *Rogue States: The Rule of Force in World Affairs* (Cambridge, MA: South End Press, 2000).

42. Hank Messick, *Of Grass and Snow: The Secret Criminal Elite* (Englewood Cliffs, NJ: Prentice-Hall, 1979); Simon Strong, *Whitewash: Pablo Escobar and the Cocaine Wars* (London: Macmillan, 1995).

43. Lars Schoultz, *National Security and United States Policy toward Latin America* (Princeton: Princeton University Press, 1987); William M. LeoGrande, *Our Own Backyard: The United States in Central America, 1977–1992* (Chapel Hill: University of North Carolina Press, 1998).

44. Scott Anderson and Jon. L. Anderson, *Inside the League: The Shocking Exposé of How Terrorists, Nazis, and Latin American Death Squads Have Infiltrated the World Anti-Communist League* (New York: Mead, 1986).

45. Linklater et al., *The Nazi Legacy.*

46. Scott and Marshall, *Cocaine Politics;* Jonathan Marshall, Peter D. Scott, and Jane Hunter, *The Iran-Contra Connection* (Montreal: Black Rose Books, 1987).

47. Valentine, *Strength of the Wolf;* Henrick Kruger, *The Great Heroin Coup: Drugs, Intelligence, and International Fascism* (Boston: South End Press, 1980); John Dinges and Saul Landau, *Assassination on Embassy Row* (New York: Pantheon Books, 1980).

48. Scott and Marshall, *Cocaine Politics;* James Petras, "Bolivia: Between Colonization and Revolution," *Canadian Dimension* 38 (January–February 2004): 33–36.

49. Francois Houtart, "Nicaragua: A Revolution Forgotten," *Le Monde Diplomatique,* December 13, 2001.

50. Paul Eddy, Hugo Sabogal, and Sara Walden, *The Cocaine Wars* (London: Century, 1988); Cockburn and St. Clair, *Whiteout.*

51. Linklater et al., *The Nazi Legacy;* Erhard Dabringhaus, *Klaus Barbie: The Shocking Story of How the US Used This Nazi War Criminal as an Intelligence Agent* (Washington DC: Acropolis Books, 1984). The Nazi fugitive was Klaus Barbie. Barbie headed the Gestapo office in Lyons, France, during the Second World War. He is credited with tracking down Jean Moulin, the French Resistance leader.

52. Michael Levine and Laura Kavanau-Levine, *The Big White Lie: The CIA and the Cocaine/Crack Epidemic* (New York: Thunder's Mouth Press, 1993), 55–60.

53. Anderson and Anderson, *Inside the League;* Warren Hinckle and William Turner, *The Fish Is Red* (New York: Harper & Row, 1981).

54. Marshall et al., *The Iran-Contra Connection.*

55. Michael Levine, *Deep Cover* (New York: Delacorte Press, 1990), 87, 92

56. Clare Hargreaves, *Snowfields: The War on Cocaine in the Andes* (London: Zed Books, 1992), 42; Cockburn and St. Clair, *Whiteout;* Levine and Kavanau-Levine, *The Big White Lie.*

57. Randall, *Colombia and the United States.*

58. John D. Waghelstein, "Latin American Insurgency Status Report," *Military Review* 67 (February 1987): 42–47.

59. Rachel Ehrenfeld, *Narcoterrorism: The Kremlin Connection* (New York: Heritage Foundation, 1986); *Narcoterrorism and the Cuban Connection* (Miami: Cuban American National Foundation, 1988); and *Narcoterrorism* (New York: Basic Books, 1990).

60. Alonso Salazar and Ana M. Jaramillo, *Medellín: Las Subculturas del Narcotrafico, Coleccion Sociedad y Conflicto* (Bogotá: CINEP, 1992).

61. Ibid.

62. Stich, *Defrauding America.*

63. Ibid.

64. Ibid..

65. Rensselaer W. Lee III, *The White Labyrinth: Cocaine and Political Power* (New Brunswick, NJ: Transaction, 1998); Scott and Marshall, *Cocaine Politics.*

66. Scott, *Drugs, Oil, and War.*

67. Stich, *Defrauding America.*

68. Ibid., 389; Joseph Contreras and Fernando Garavito, *Biografía No Autorizada de Álvaro Uribe Vélez: El Señor de las Sombras* (Bogotá: Editorial Oveja Negra, 2002).

69. Kenneth C. Bucchi, *Operation Pseudo Miranda: A Veteran of the CIA Drug Wars Tells All* (Granite Bay, CA: Penmarin Books, 2000); see also Kenneth C. Bucchi, *C.I.A. Cocaine in America?: A Veteran of the C.I.A. Drug Wars Tells All* (New York: S.P.I. Books, 1994); and Al Martin, *The Conspirators: Secrets of an Iran Contra Insider* (Pray, MT: National Liberty Press, 2002).

According to Bucchi, in attendance was John Hull (a CIA asset in Costa Rica), a Peruvian drug lord named Luis Porto, and representatives from the Medellín cartel and La Corporacion organization of Bolivia. Bucchi's book tells of secret meetings with George Bush, William Casey, Medellín cartel leaders Pablo Escobar and Fabio Ochoa, Panama's Manuel Noriega, a CIA agent named Claire George, and midlevel officials from different government agencies that included the DEA, DIA, FBI, and DOD. Bucchi claims he spent three years in Operation Pseudo Miranda where the CIA negotiated with the heads of the dominant cartels. This deal would allow the cartels to operate under the condition they give up half of their cocaine exports to the CIA.

70. Bucchi, *Operation Pseudo Miranda.*
71. CNN, "The Drug War: Where Should the Battle Lines Be Drawn?", *The Point with Greta Van Susteren,* April 23, 2001.
72. Bruce Bagley, "Colombia and the War on Drugs," *Foreign Affairs* 67 (Fall 1988): 70–92.
73. "The Godfather of Cocaine," *Frontline,* produced by William Cran and Stephanie Tepper, written and directed by William Cran, aired March 25, 1997, www.pbs.org/wgbh/pages/frontline/shows/drugs/archive/godfather-cocaine.html.
74. Ibid.
75. Ibid.
76. Salazar and Jaramillo, *Medellín.*
77. Cockburn and St. Clair, *Whiteout.*
78. Ibid; Scott, *Drugs, Oil, and War;* Stich, *Defrauding America.*
79. Ibid.; Stich, *Defrauding America;* Christopher Robbins, *Air America: The True Story of the CIA's Mercenary Fliers in Covert Operations from Pre-War China to Present Day Nicaragua* (London: Corgi Books, 1988).
80. Stich, *Defrauding America.*
81. Robbins, *Air America,* 172.
82. Strong, *Whitewash,* 184.
83. Smith et al., *Why People Grow Drugs.*
84. Doug Stokes, *America's Other War: Terrorizing Colombia* (New York: Zed Books, 2005), 25.
85. Scott, *Drugs, Oil, and War.*
86. Ivan Molloy, *Rolling Back Revolution: The Emergence of Low Intensity Conflict* (London: Pluto Press, 2001).
87. Molloy, *Rolling Back Revolution;* Cockburn and St. Clair, *Whiteout.*
88. U.S. Congress, *Senate Committee on Foreign Relations, Subcommittee on Terrorism, Narcotics and International Operations Report, Drugs, Law Enforcement, and Foreign Policy* (Washington DC: U.S. Government Printing Office, 1989). This report is commonly known as the Kerry

Report, as it emerged from the subcommittee chaired by Senator John Kerry.

89. Michael Levine cited in Michael L. Montalvo, "Investigative Report: Politics and Covert Operation Policy in the Drug War," *We the People*, http://www.wethepeople.la/montal1.htm; Levine, *Deep Cover*.

90. Marshall et al., *The Iran-Contra Connection*. Their sources are from leading corporate newspapers in the United States.

91. Ibid.

92. Ibid.

93. Saul Landau, *The Dangerous Doctrine: National Security and US Foreign Policy* (Boulder, CO: Westview Press, 1988), 173.

94. James Petras and Morris Morley, *US Hegemony Under Siege: Class, Politics and Development in Latin America* (London: Verso, 1990); Guy Gugliotta and Jeff Leen, *Kings of Cocaine: An Astonishing True Story of Murder, Money and International Corruption* (New York: Simon and Schuster, 1990); Association d'Études Geopolitiques des Drogues, "Peru: The Unsaid in the Montesinos Scandal," *Geopolitical Drug Newsletter*, December 2000.

95. Shannon, *Desperados*, 528.

96. Larry Rohter, "Former Smuggler Ties Top Officials of Cuba and Nicaragua to Drug Ring," *New York Times*, 21 Nov. 1991.

97. Merrill Collett, *The Cocaine Connection: Drug Trafficking and Inter-American Relations* (New York: Foreign Policy Association Headline Series, Fall 1989); Merrill Collett, "Colombia's Drug Lords Waging War on Leftists," *Washington Post*, November 14, 1987; Lee, *The White Labyrinth*.

98. Holly Sklar, *Washington's War on Nicaragua* (Boston: South End Press, 1988).

99. U.S. Congress, Senate Committee on Foreign Relations, Subcommittee on Terrorism, *Narcotics and International Operations Report, Drugs, Law Enforcement, and Foreign Policy* (Washington DC: U.S. Government Printing Office, 1989).

100. U.S. Court of Appeals for the DC Circuit Division for the Purpose of Appointing Independent Counsel, *Final Report of the Independent Counsel for Iran/Contra Matters*, vol. 1: *Investigations and Prosecutions Lawrence E. Walsh, Independent Counsel* (Washington DC: U.S. Government Printing Office, 1993).

101. Joseph J. Trento, *The Secret History of the CIA* (New York: Forum/Crown/Random House, 2001); Peter Truell and Larry Gurwin, *False Profits: The Inside Story of BCCI, the World's Most Corrupt Financial Empire* (Boston: Houghton Mifflin, 1992); Beaty and Gwyne, *The Outlaw Bank*.

102. Lernoux, *In Banks We Trust*.

103. Truell and Gurwin, *False Profits;* Trento, *The Secret History of the CIA;* Beaty and Gwynne, *The Outlaw Bank.*

104. Cockburn and St. Clair, *Whiteout.*

105. James Petras, "Dirty Money: Foundation of US Growth and Empire," *La Jornada,* May 19, 2001.

3. A NARCO-STATE AND A NARCO-ECONOMY

1. U.S. Department of the Treasury, *Financial Crimes Enforcement Network 2000–2005 Strategic Plan* (Washington DC: U.S. Government Printing Office, 2000), 2.

2. Kris Hinterseer, *Criminal Finance: The Political Economy of Money Laundering in a Comparative Legal Context* (London: Kluwer Law International, 2002).

3. Ibid.

4. Francisco Thoumi, *Illegal Drugs, Economy, and Society in the Andes* (Washington DC: Woodrow Wilson Center Press, 2003).

5. Nazih Richani, *Systems of Violence: The Political Economy of War and Peace in Colombia* (New York: State University of New York Press, 2002).

6. UN High Commissioner for Human Rights, *Report on the Human Rights Situation in Colombia* (New York: United Nations Publications, 2001).

7. Amnesty International, *Colombia: Human Rights Developments—"Death Squads" on the Defensive?* (New York: Amnesty International Publications, 1989).

8. Richani, *Systems of Violence.*

9. Dan Russell, *Drug War: Covert Money, Power & Policy* (Camden, New York: Kalyx, 2000), http://www.drugwar.com/dwindex.shtm.

10. Ibid.

11. Grace Livingstone, *Inside Colombia: Drugs, Democracy, and War* (New Brunswick, NJ: Rutgers University Press, 2003).

12. Alejandro R. Posada. "Compras de Tierra por Narcotraficantes," in *Drogas Illicitas en Colombia, su Impacto Economico, Politico y Social,* ed. Francisco Thoumi (Bogotá: PNUD/DUE/Ariel Ciencia Politica, 1997), 280–346.

13. Human Rights Watch, "The Ties that Bind: Colombia and the Military-Paramilitary Links," February 2000, www.hrw.org/reports/2000/colombia/.

14. Doug Stokes, *America's Other War: Terrorizing Colombia* (New York: Zed Books, 2005); Peter D. Scott, *Drugs, Oil, and War: The United States in Afghanistan, Colombia, and Indochina* (New York: Rowman & Littlefield Publishers, 2003); Jeremy Bigwood, "Doing the US's Dirty Work: The Colombian Paramilitaries and Israel," *Narco News Bulletin,* April 8, 2003.

15. Human Rights Watch, "The Ties That Bind."
16. Richani, *Systems of Violence.*
17. Nazih Richani, *Systems of Violence: The Political Economy of War and Peace in Colombia* (Binghamton, NY: State University of New York Press, 2002).
18. Scott, *Drugs, Oil, and War*; Bert Ruiz, *The Colombian Civil War* (London: McFarland & Company Inc. Publishers, 2001).
19. Alfonso L. Michelsen and Enrique Calderon, *Palabras Pendientes: Conversaciones Con Enrique Santos Calderon* (Bogotá: El Ancora Editores, 2001).
20. Forrest Hylton, "An Evil Hour: Uribe's Colombia in Historical Perspective," *New Left Review* 23 (September–October 2003): 51–93.
21. Ibid.
22. Gomez was awarded the 2002 International Press Freedom Award. Upon accepting the award, the U.S. press censored this comment: "The picture of war is getting blurry—and Americans, whose taxes and whose drug consumption fuel this war, should be concerned."
23. "Entrevista con Ignacio 'Nacho' Gómez, reciente ganador del Premio Internacional de Libertad de Prensa del Comité Mundial para la Protección de los Periodistas (CPJ)," *Medios y Libertad de Expresion en las Americas,* November 25, 2002, www.libertad-prensa.org/nacho.html.
24. Ibid.; Peter D. Scott, "Colombia: Washington's Dirtiest 'War on Drugs,'" *Tikkun* 12 (May–June 1997): 27–31; Mark Bowden, *Killing Pablo* (New York: Atlantic Monthly Press, 2001); Merrill Collett, *The Cocaine Connection: Drug Trafficking and Inter-American Relations* (New York: Foreign Policy Association Headline Series, Fall 1989); Rensselaer W. Lee III, *The White Labyrinth: Cocaine and Political Power* (New Brunswick, NJ: Transaction, 1998).
25. Peter D. Scott and Jonathan Marshall, *Cocaine Politics: Drugs, Armies, and the CIA in Central America,* repr. (Berkeley: University of California Press, 1998).
26. Joseph Contreras and Fernando Garavito, *Biografía No Autorizada de Álvaro Uribe Vélez: El Señor de las Sombras* (Bogotá: Editorial Oveja Negra, 2002).
27. Forrest Hylton, *Evil Hour in Colombia* (London: Verso Books, 2006).
28. Contreras & Garavito, *Biografía No Autorizada de Álvaro Uribe Vélez.*
29. Alfredo Molano, "Peor el remedio," *El Espectador,* September 1, 2002.
30. U.S. Drug Enforcement Administration, *Report on January 17, 1998 Shipment of 10,000 Kilograms of Potassium Permanganate, December 16, 1997 Shipment of 20,000 Kilograms of Potassium Permanganate and November 17, 1997 Shipment of 20,000 Kilograms of Potassium Permanganate; Suspension of Shipments,* statement by Donnie R. Marshall, August 3, 2000, http://federalregister.gov/a/00-21482.

31. Rensselaer W. Lee III, "Perverse Effects of Andean Counternarcotics Policy," *Orbis* 46 (Summer 2002): 537–54.

32. U.S. General Accounting Office, *Drug Control: Narcotics Threat from Colombia Continues to Grow* (Washington DC: U.S. Government Printing Office, 1999), 15;

33. Ibid; Livingstone, *Inside Colombia*.

34. Michael G. Roskin, "Crime and Politics in Colombia: Considerations for US Involvement," *Parameters: US Army War College Quarterly* (Winter 2001–2002).

35. Livingstone, *Inside Colombia*.

4. THE NARCO-CARTEL SYSTEM (1980–1993)

1. Rensselaer W. Lee III, "Perverse Effects of Andean Counternarcotics Policy," *Orbis* 46 (Summer 2002): 537–54; Ted G. Carpenter, *Bad Neighbor Policy: Washington's Futile War on Drugs in Latin America* (New York: Palgrave Macmillan, 2003); Julia Buxton, *The Political Economy of Narcotics: Production, Consumption and Global Markets* (New York: Zed Books, 2006); Noam Chomsky, "An American Addiction: Drugs, Guerrillas, Counterinsurgency: U.S. Intervention in Colombia," produced by David Barsamian, Alternative Radio, May 12, 2000.

2. Alfred W. McCoy, *The Politics of Heroin: CIA Complicity in the Global Drug Trade* (Chicago: Lawrence Hill Books, 2003).

3. Rensselaer W. Lee II and Patrick Clawson, *The Andean Cocaine Industry* (New York: St. Martin's Press, 1998).

4. Ibid.; U.S. Drug Enforcement Administration (DEA), *The Drug Trade in Colombia: A Threat Assessment,* DEA Intelligence Division, March 2002, http://usregsec.sdsu.edu/docs/DEAMarch2002.pdf.

5. Michael Massing, *The Fix: Solving the Nation's Drug Problem* (New York: Simon & Schuster, 2000); Stan Zimmerman, *A History of Smuggling in Florida: Rum Runners and Cocaine Cowboys* (Charleston: History Press, 2006); Fabio Castillo, *Los Nuevos Jinetes de la Cocaina* (Bogotá: Editorial Oveja Negra, 1996).

6. Lee, "Perverse Effects"; Castillo, *Los Nuevos Jinetes de la Cocaina;* Sidney J. Zabludoff, "Colombian Narcotics Organisations as Business Enterprises," *Transnational Organised Crime* 3 (Summer 1997): 20–49.

7. Peter Reuter, "Eternal Hope: America's Quest for Narcotics Control," *Public Interest* 79 (Spring 1985): 83.

8. Anthony R. Henman, "Coca and Cocaine: Their Role in Traditional Cultures in South America," *Journal of Drug Issues* 20 (1990): 577–88.

9. Ibid.

10. Hernando G. Buendia, *Violencia, Narcotrafico y Produccion Agropecuaria en Colombia* (Bogotá: Instituto de Estudios Liberales, 1989).
11. Ibid.
12. Ibid.
13. Fabio Castillo, *Los Jinetes de la Cocaina* (Bogotá: Editorial Documentos Periodisticos, 1987).
14. Mark Bowden, *Killing Pablo* (New York: Atlantic Monthly Press, 2001); Gary Webb, *Dark Alliance: The CIA, the Contras, and the Crack Cocaine Epidemic* (New York: Seven Stories Press, 1998); Guy Gugliotta and Jeff Leen, *Kings of Cocaine: An Astonishing True Story of Murder, Money and International Corruption* (New York: Simon and Schuster, 1990); Michael Levine and Laura Kavanau-Levine, *The Big White Lie: The CIA and the Cocaine/Crack Epidemic* (New York: Thunder's Mouth Press, 1993); Michael Levine, *Deep Cover* (New York: Delacorte Press, 1990); Kenneth C. Bucchi, *Operation Pseudo Miranda: A Veteran of the CIA Drug Wars Tells All* (Granite Bay, CA: Penmarin Books, 2000); Kenneth C. Bucchi, *C.I.A. Cocaine in America?: A Veteran of the C.I.A. Drug Wars Tells All* (New York: S.P.I. Books, 1994); Celerino Castillo III and Dave Harmon, *Powderburns: Cocaine, Contras & the Drug War* (London: Sundial, 1994); Alexander Cockburn and Jeffrey St. Clair, *Whiteout: The CIA, Drugs and the Press* (New York: Verso, 1998); Simon Strong, *Whitewash: Pablo Escobar and the Cocaine Wars* (London: Macmillan, 1995); Paul Eddy, Hugo Sabogal, and Sara Walden, *The Cocaine Wars* (London: Century, 1988).
15. Strong, *Whitewash*; Alonso Salazar and Ana M. Jaramillo, *Medellín: Las Subculturas del Narcotrafico, Coleccion Sociedad y Conflicto* (Bogotá: CINEP, 1992).
16. Jenny Pearce, *Colombia: Inside the Labyrinth* (London: Latin America Bureau—Research and Action, 1990).
17. Strong, *Whitewash*; Salazar and Jaramillo, *Medellín*; Lee and Clawson, *The Andean Cocaine Industry*.
18. Peter A. Lupsha, "Transnational Narco-corruption and Narco Investment: A Focus on Mexico," *Transnational Organized Crime* (Spring 1995): 87.
19. Lee and Clawson, *The Andean Cocaine Industry*.
20. Strong, *Whitewash*, 49-50.
21. Ibid.
22. Ibid.
23. Ibid.
24. Ibid.; Pearce, *Inside the Labyrinth*.
25. Ibid.
26. Strong, *Whitewash*, 57.
27. Eddy et al., *The Cocaine Wars*; Bruce Bagley, "Colombia and the War on Drugs," *Foreign Affairs* 67 (Fall 1988): 70-92.

28. Duncan Campbell, "The Bush Dynasty and the Cuban Criminals," *The Guardian*, December 2, 2002; Hank Messick, *Of Grass and Snow: The Secret Criminal Elite* (Englewood Cliffs, NJ: Prentice-Hall, 1979); Peter D. Scott and Jonathan Marshall, *Cocaine Politics: Drugs, Armies, and the CIA in Central America*, repr. (Berkeley: University of California Press, 1998).

29. Eddy et al., *The Cocaine Wars*.

30. Bagley, "Colombia and the War on Drugs," 82.

31. Jack Anderson and Dale Van Atta, "The Kings of the Medellín Cartel," *Washington Post*, 24 August 1988.

32. From the data presented by Lee and Clawson, *The Andean Cocaine Industry;* and Mario Arango and Jorge Child, *Los Condenados de la Coca* (Medellín: Editorial J. M. Arango, 1985).

33. Shannon, *Desperados;* Rensselaer W. Lee III, *The White Labyrinth: Cocaine and Political Power* (New Brunswick, NJ: Transaction, 1998).

34. Ibid; "Estamos con la patria," *Medellín Cívico*, March 1981.

35. Lee and Clawson, *The Andean Cocaine Industry*.

36. Dario Betancourt and Martha L. Garcia, *Contrabandistas, Marimberos y Mafiosos: Historia Social de la Mafia Colombiana (1965-1992)* (Bogotá: Tercer Mundo Editores, 1994).

37. Alvaro C. Guizado and Alvaro G. Barney, *Colombia: Cuidad y Violencia* (Bogotá: Foro Nacional, 1990).

38. Lee, *The White Labyrinth*.

39. Arango and Child, *Los Condenados de la Coca*.

40. Jorge E. Orozco, *Lehder . . . El Hombre* (Bogotá: Plaza y Janes, 1987).

41. Arango and Child, *Los Condenados de la Coca*.

42. Lee and Clawson, *The Andean Cocaine Industry*.

43. "Del pueblo Colombiano," *Medellín Cívico*, March 12, 1984; "Medellín: epicentro de la mafia," *El Nacional*, January 16, 1985.

44. "En la mitad del camino," *Medellín Cívico*, March 17, 1984, 3.

45. Lee, *The White Labyrinth*, 135.

46. "Una leccion de educacion civica de Pablo Escobar a la Secretaria de Educacion," *Medellín Cívico*, March 20, 1984.

47. "Pablo es La Paz," *Medellín Cívico*, March 24, 1984, 7.

48. Lee, *The White Labyrinth*.

49. Orozco, *Lehder*, 150-51.

50. Ibid.

51. Arango and Child, *Los Condenados de la Coca*, 129-33.

52. Gabriel G. Marquez, *News of a Kidnapping* (London: Penguin, 1998).

53. Webb, *Dark Alliance*.

54. Gugliotta and Leen, *Kings of Cocaine*.

55. Campbell, "The Bush Dynasty and the Cuban Criminals"; Scott and Marshall, *Cocaine Politics;* James Mills, *The Underground Empire: Where*

Crime and Governments Embrace (New York: Doubleday, 1986).

56. Campbell, "The Bush Dynasty and the Cuban Criminals"; Scott and Marshall, *Cocaine Politics;* Rodney Stich, *Defrauding America: Encyclopedia of Secret Operations by the CIA, DEA, and Other Covert Agencies,* 3rd ed. (California: Diablo Western Press, 2001).

57. Nazih Richani, *Systems of Violence: The Political Economy of War and Peace in Colombia* (New York: State University of New York Press, 2002).

58. Francisco Thoumi, *Political Economy and Illegal Drugs in Colombia* (London: Lynne Rienner, 1995).

59. Betancourt and Garcia, *Contrabandistas, Marimberos y Mafiosos,* 191.

60. Francisco Thoumi, "Corruption and Drug Trafficking: General Considerations and References to Colombia," unpublished conference paper presented at U.S. War College Conference on Colombia, December 1998, Carlisle, Pennsylvania.

61. Scott and Marshall, *Cocaine Politics.*

62. See Luis E. Murillo, *The Noriega Mess: The Drugs, the Canal, and Why America Invaded* (London: Verso, 1995); David Harris, *Shooting the Moon: The True Story of an American Manhunt Unlike Any Other, Ever* (New York: Back Bay Books, 2002); Manuel Noriega and Peter Eisner, *America's Prisoner: The Memoirs of Manuel Noriega* (New York: Random House, 1997).

63. Noriega and Eisner, *America's Prisoner;* William Blum, *Rogue State: A Guide to the World's Only Superpower* (Monroe, ME: Common Courage, 2005).

64. Bowden, *Killing Pablo.*

65. Ibid.

66. Ibid.

67. Amnesty International, press release, "President Clinton Must Order Investigation into Allegations of U.S. Collusion with Colombian Death Squads," April 25, 2001, www.amnestyusa.org/news/2001/colombia04252001_2.html.

68. See Ana Carrigan, "War or Peace? Colombia's New President Must Choose between Washington and His Own People," *In These Times,* August 2, 2002; and Lee and Clawson, *The Andean Cocaine Industry.*

69. Bowden, *Killing Pablo.*

70. Peter D. Scott, *Drugs, Oil, and War: The United States in Afghanistan, Colombia, and Indochina* (New York: Rowman & Littlefield Publishers, 2003), 88; Scott Wilson, "Commander of Lost Causes," *Washington Post,* July 6, 2003; Bowden, *Killing Pablo.*

71. Bowden, *Killing Pablo.*

72. Mark Bowden, "Colombia: Killing Pablo—A Deadly Manhunt Guided by the US," *Philadelphia Inquirer,* November 12, 2000.

73. Ibid.
74. National Security Archive, George Washington University, "New National Police Chief Appointed, U.S. Embassy Bogotá cable," December 20, 1993, http://www.gwu.edu/~nsarchiv/NSAEBB/NSAEBB243/19931220.pdf.
75. David Van Biema, "Sweet, Sweet Surrender: A Cali Cartel Chief Proposes to Give Up under Conditions So Lenient that They May Strain US-Colombian Relations," *Time,* November 7, 1994.
76. "Jailed Drug Dons' $2.8b Comedown," *Sydney Morning Herald,* September 27, 2006; Lloyd de Vries, "Cali Cartel Drug Kingpins Plead Guilty," CBS News, September 26, 2006.
77. "Colombian drug lords to go free," *BBC World News,* November 2, 2002. According to the BBC, the Cali cartel's founders were released for good behavior and participation in a prison work-study program.
78. Linda Robinson, "The Fugitive: An Account of the Search for the Head of the Medellín Drug Cartel," *New York Times,* June 17, 2001.

5. THE POST-CARTEL SYSTEM

1. Robert E. Grosse, *Drugs and Money: Laundering Latin America's Cocaine Dollars* (London: Praeger, 2001).
2. "Los Nuevos Narcos," *Semana,* May 8, 2001.
3. Rensselaer W. Lee III, "Perverse Effects of Andean Counternarcotics Policy," *Orbis* 46 (Summer 2002): 537–54.
4. Peter D. Scott, *Drugs, Oil, and War: The United States in Afghanistan, Colombia, and Indochina* (New York: Rowman & Littlefield Publishers, 2003); Ricardo Rocha, "The Colombian Economy after 25 Years of Drug Trafficking," United Nations Drug Control Program (UNDCP) 2000, Bogotá Country Office, http://www.undcp.org/colombia/rocha.html.
5. As shown by Lee, "Perverse Effects," heroin is not new to Colombia; small-scale opium cultivation and heroin processing has existed for approximately thirty years. In recent years, a similar process has developed, paving the way for new drug markets in amphetamines such as speed, Ecstasy, and "ice." However, cocaine remains Colombia's premier illicit export.
6. Phil Williams and Carl Florez, "Transnational Criminal Organizations and Drug Trafficking," *United Bulletin on Narcotics* 46 (January 1994): 14.
7. See Phil Williams, "The Nature of Drug-Trafficking Networks," *Current History,* 97 (April 1998), 154–159. Ivelaw L. Griffith, *The Political Economy of Drugs in the Caribbean* (New York: Palgrave Macmillan, 2000); Michael C. Kenney, "Intelligence Games: Comparing the Intelligence Capabilities of Law Enforcement Agencies and Drug Trafficking Enterprises," *International Journal of Intelligence and*

Counterintelligence 16 (2003): 212–43; David Ronfeldt, *Tribes, Institutions, Markets, Networks: A Framework about Societal Evolution* (Santa Monica, CA: Rand Corporation, 1996).

8. Rodney Stich, *Defrauding America: Encyclopedia of Secret Operations by the CIA, DEA, and Other Covert Agencies*, 3rd ed. (California: Diablo Western Press, 2001); Scott, *Drugs, Oil, and War*; Grosse, *Drugs and Money*; Scott Ehlers, "Drug Trafficking and Money Laundering," *Foreign Policy in Focus*, June 1, 1998, http://www.fpif.org/reports/drug_trafficking_and_money_laundering; James Petras and Henry Veltmeyer, *Globalization Unmasked: Imperialism in the 21st Century* (London: Zed books, 2001); Paula Dwyer, "The Citi that Slept," *Business Week*, November 2, 1998.

9. Tim Reason, "The Corporate Connection: How Drug Money Is Finding Its Way to the Bottom Line," *CFO Magazine*, March 1, 2001.

10. Lowell Bergman, "U.S. Companies Tangle in Web of Drug Dollars," *New York Times*, October 10, 2000.

11. Orina Zill and Lowell Bergman, "U.S. Business and Money Laundering," *Frontline*, October 2000, www.pbs.org/wgbh/pages/frontline/shows/drugs/special/us.html.

12. Orina Zill and Lowell Bergman, "The Bell Helicopter Case," *Frontline*, October 2000, www.pbs.org/wgbh/pages/frontline/shows/drugs/special/bell.html.

13. Bergman, "U.S. Companies Tangle."

14. Ibid.

15. UN Office on Drugs and Crime, *Drugs and Development*, vol. 6, June 1994, 2, www.unodc.org/pdf/Alternative%20Development/Drugs_Development.pdf.

16. UN Office on Drugs and Crime, *Drug Therapy Instead of Criminalizing Drug Addicts*, Committee paper presented at Vienna International Model United Nations, August 4–8, 2002.

17. According to Richani, a similar arrangement occurred with emerald traffickers beforehand.

18. Richani, *Systems of Violence*; Comision de Superacion de la Violencia, "Pacificar la Paz," Instituto de Estudios Politicos Relaciones Internacionales (IEPRI), Universidad Nacional de Colombia (Bogotá: IEPRI/CINEP/Comision Andina de Juristas/CECOIN, 1992).

19. Richani, *Systems of Violence*.

20. "Los Paras Ganan La Guerra," *Revista Nota Economica*, 17 November 1997; Departamento Nacional de Planeacion, *La Paz: El Desafio para el Desarrollo* (Bogotá: TM Editores, 1998); Jemima Garcia-Godos and Knut Andreas O. Lid, "Transitional Justice and Victims' Rights before the End of a Conflict: The Unusual Case of Colombia," *Journal of Latin American Studies* 42 (2010): 487–516.

21. Richani, *Systems of Violence*.
22. Ibid.
23. Gallegos Medina, *Autodefensas, Paramilitares y Narcotrafico en Colombia Origin, Desarollo y Consolidacion el Caso Puerto Boyaca* (Bogotá: Editorial Documentos Periodisticos, 1990).
24. Rocha, "The Colombian Economy after 25 Years of Drug Trafficking."
25. Justin Podur, "How Would Drug Legalization in the United States Affect Colombia?" *Colombia Journal*, March 17, 2003, http://colombiajournal. org/how-would-drug-legalization-in-the-united-states-affect-colombia.htm
26. Elaine Silvestrini, " 'Express' Tracking Colombian Cocaine," *Tampa Tribune*, July 4, 2004.
27. U.S. Drug Enforcement Administration (DEA), *The Drug Trade in Colombia: A Threat Assessment*, DEA Intelligence Division, March 2002, http://usregsec.sdsu.edu/docs/DEAMarch2002.pdf.
28. U.S. Drug Enforcement Administration (DEA), *Changing Dynamics of Cocaine Production in the Andean Region*, Drug Intelligence Brief, June 2002, http://www.usdoj.gov/dea/pubs/omte;/02033/02033p.html.
29. Dermot O'Conner, "The political economy of Colombia's cocaine industry," *Papel Politico* 14 (January–June 2009), 81–106.
30. Paul Kaihla, "The Technology Secrets of Cocaine Inc.," *Business 2.0*, July 2002; Andy McCue, "IT Myths: Colombian drugs gang's mainframe-assisted assassinations?" Silicon.com, July 10, 2003, www.silicon.com/ technology/hardware/2003/07/10/it-myths-colombian-drugs-gangs-main-frame-assisted-assassinations-10005093/.
31. Kaihla, "The Technology Secrets."
32. Ibid.
33. Ibid.
34. Ibid.; James R. Richards, *Transnational Criminal Organizations, Cybercrime, and Money Laundering: A Handbook for Law Enforcement Officers, Auditors, and Financial Investigators* (Boca Raton, FL: CRC Press, 1998); Donato Masciandaro, *Global Financial Crime: Terrorism, Money Laundering, and Off Shore Centres* (London: Ashgate Publishing, 2004).
35. Gonzalo Guillen and Steven Salisbury, "Ex-General: DEA Agents Were Involved in Murders in Colombia," *Miami Herald*, December 10, 2003.
36. Kaihla, "The Technology Secrets."
37. Ibid.
38. Ibid.; Chris Mathers, *Crimes School: Money Laundering: True Crime Meets the World of Business and Finance* (New York: Firefly Books, 2004);
39. Mathers, *Crimes School*; Peter W. Singer, *Corporate Warriors: The Rise of the Privatized Military Industry* (Ithaca, NY: Cornell University Press, 2004).

40. Kaihla, "The Technology Secrets."
41. Ibid.; Bruce Schneier, *Secrets and Lies: Digital Security in a Networked World* (New York: Wiley, 2004).
42. Kaihla, "The Technology Secrets."
43. Ibid.; Schneier, *Secrets and Lies*; Kevin D. Mitnick and William L. Simon, *The Art of Deception: Controlling the Human Element of Security* (New York: Wiley, 2003).
44. Mireya Navarro, "Russian Submarine Drifts Into Center of a Brazen Drug Plot," *New York Times*, March 7, 1997.
45. Kaihla, "The Technology Secrets."
46. Jaime Guaraca, *Colombia y Las FARC-EP: Origen de la Lucha Guerrillera* (Tafalla, Spain: Txalaparta, 1999); James Petras, *The New Development Politics: The Age of Empire Building and New Social Movements* (London: Ashgate Publishing, 2003); Richani, *Systems of Violence*; Paul A. Beckley, "Maintaining the Violent Status Quo: The Political Economy of the Colombian Insurgency," master's thesis, U.S. Navy Postgraduate School, Monterey, CA, 2002; Thomas Marks, *Colombian Army Adaptation to FARC Insurgency* (Carlisle, PA: Strategic Studies Institute, 2002); Angel Rabasa and Peter Chalk, *Colombian Labyrinth: The Synergy of Drugs and Insurgency and its Implications for Regional Stability* (Santa Monica, CA: Rand Corporation, 2001); Dennis Rempe, *The Past as Prologue? A History of US CI Policy in Colombia, 1958–66* (Carlisle, PA: Strategic Studies Institute, 2002); Bert Ruiz, *The Colombian Civil War* (London: McFarland & Company, 2001); Charles Bergquist, Ricardo Penaranda, and Gonzalo Sanchez, *Violence in Colombia 1990–2000: Waging War and Negotiating Peace* (Wilmington: Rowman & Littlefield, 2003); Alfredo R. Suarez, *Guerreros y Politicos: Dialogo y Conflicto En Colombia, 1998–2002* (Bogotá: Intermedio Editores, 2003); Michael Radu, "The Perilous Appeasement of Guerrillas," *Orbis* 44 (Summer 2000): 363–82; David Passage, *The United States and Colombia: Untying the Gordian Knot* (Carlisle, PA: Strategic Studies Institute, 2000); Richard Downes, *Landpower and Ambiguous Warfare: The Challenge of Colombia in the 21st Century* (Carlisle, PA: Strategic Studies Institute, 1999); James J. Brittain, *Revolutionary Social Change in Colombia: The Origin and Direction of the FARC-EP* (New York: Pluto Press, 2010).
47. "Interview with Professor James Petras: Behind Colombia's Civil War," *Committees in Solidarity with Latin America & the Caribbean*, March 25, 2002, www.mail-archive.com/marxist-leninist-list@lists.econ.utah.edu/msg02521.html.
48. Radu, "The Perilous Appeasement of Guerrillas."
49. Nick Trebat, "Drugs Replace Communism as the Point of Entry for US Policy on Latin America," Council on Hemispheric Affairs, August 24, 1999, www.icdc.com/~paulwolf/colombia/hemisphr.htm.

50. Statement by James Milford, Deputy Administrator of the U.S. Drug
     Enforcement Administration, House International Relations Committee,
     Subcommittee on the Western Hemisphere, July 16, 1997, http://www.jus-
     tice.gov/dea/pubs/cngrtest/ct970716.htm.
51. Karen DeYoung, "Colombia's Non-Drug Rebellion," *Washington Post,*
     April 17, 2000.
52. Ricardo Vargas, "The Revolutionary Armed Forces of Colombia (FARC)
     and the Illicit Drug Trade," Transnational Institute, June 1999,
     www.tni.org/briefing/revolutionary-armed-forces-colombia-farc-and-illic-
     it-drug-trade.
53. Richard Davenport-Hines, *The Pursuit of Oblivion: A Global History of
     Narcotics 1500–2000* (London: Weidenfeld & Nicolson, 2004).
54. Mortimer, *History of Coca.*
55. Richani, *Systems of Violence.*
56. James Petras, "The Geopolitics of Plan Colombia," *Monthly Review* 53
     (May 2001): 30–49.
57. Revolutionary Armed Forces of Colombia—People's Army, *FARC-EP:
     Historical Outline* (Toronto: International Commission, 2000), 48.
58. Ibid.
59. Ibid.
60. Jorge Castañeda, *Utopia Unarmed: The Latin American Left after the Cold
     War* (New York: Alfred Knopf, 1993).
61. Radu, "The Perilous Appeasement of Guerrillas."
62. FARC-EP, *Historical Outline*; Guaraca, *Colombia y Las FARC-EP.*
63. Marks, *Colombian Army Adaptation to FARC Insurgency;* Passage, *United
     States and Colombia;* Downes, *Landpower and Ambiguous Warfare.*
64. See Paul Collier and Anke Hoeffler, *Greed and Grievance in Civil War*
     (Washington DC: World Bank, 2000); and Paul Collier and Anke Hoeffler,
     "Justice-Seeking and Loot-Seeking in Civil War," paper presented on Civil
     Conflicts, Crime and Violence in Developing Countries, World Bank
     Workshop, London, April 26–27, 1999.
65. Brittain, *Revolutionary Social Change in Colombia.*
66. Larry Rohter, "Colombia Adjusts Economic Figures to Include Its Drug
     Crops," *New York Times,* June 27, 1999; Roberto Steiner, "Hooked on
     Drugs: Colombian-US Relations," in *The United States and Latin
     America: The New Agenda,* ed. Victor Bulmer-Thomas and James
     Dunkerley (London: Institute of Latin American Studies, 1999), 159–76;
     Rebecca Toledo et al., eds., *War in Colombia: Made in U.S.A.* (New York:
     International Action Center, 2003).
67. Adam Isacson and Ingrid Vaicius, "International Policy Report–Plan
     Colombia's 'Ground Zero,'" Center for International Policy, March 9–12,
     2001, http://www.ciponline.org/colombia/0401putu.htm.

68. Toledo et al., *War in Colombia*.

69. Scott Wilson, "Coca Trade Booming Again in Peru: U.S.-Sponsored Eradication Plans Spark Peasant Protests," *Washington Post*, March 22, 2003.

70. Statement by Donnie R. Marshall, Administrator of the U.S. Drug Enforcement Administration, Senate Caucus on International Narcotics Control, February 28, 2001, www.justice.gov/dea/pubs/cngrtest/ct022801.htm.

71. James Petras, "The FARC Faces the Empire," *Latin American Perspectives* 27 (September 2000): 134–43; Alfredo Molano, "The Evolution of the FARC: A Guerrilla Group's Long History," *NACLA Report on the Americas* 34 (Sept–Oct 2000): 23–31.

72. Petras, *New Development Politics*.

73. Beckley, "Maintaining the Violent Status Quo."

74. FARC-EP, *Historical Outline*.

75. Richani, *Systems of Violence*.

76. Brittain, *Revolutionary Social Change in Colombia*.

77. Richani, *Systems of Violence*.

78. Michael G. Roskin, "Crime and Politics in Colombia: Considerations for US Involvement," *Parameters: US Army War College Quarterly* (Winter 2001–2002): 126–34; Golden W. Mortimer, *History of Coca: The Divine Plant of the Incas* (San Francisco: And/Or Press, 1974). The process of producing coca leaves is a proud native tradition dating back to the Inca Empire. Chewing coca leaves was found to have the effect of satisfying the appetites of manual laborers as they worked during the time of the Incas. Similarly, the leaves were found to reduce the feeling of nausea that often affects hikers at high altitudes. In the high Andean Mountains, this relief is a welcome solution to an age-old-problem. These uses of the coca plant have been known and followed by the Andean forefathers for more than five centuries.

79. Richani, *Systems of Violence*.

80. Vladimir I. Lenin, "The Dual Power," in *Lenin Collected Works*, vol. 24 (Moscow: Progress Publishers, 1917).

81. Marks, *Colombian Army Adaptation to FARC Insurgency*.

82. Ibid., 4.

73. Stephen E. Ambrose and Douglas G. Brinkley, *Rise to Globalism: American Foreign Policy since 1938*, 8th rev. ed. (London: Penguin Books, 1997); Alan P. Dobson and Steve Marsh, *US Foreign Policy since 1945* (New York: Routledge, 2001).

84. Marks, *Colombian Army Adaptation to FARC Insurgency*.

85. Garry M. Leech, *Killing Peace: Colombia's Conflict and the Failure of U.S. Intervention* (New York: Information Network of the Americas, 2002).

86. Revolutionary Armed Forces of Colombia–People's Army (FARC-EP), "The Demilitarized Zone, A Laboratory of Peace," *Resistencia International* 26 (2001).

87. Christina Lamb, "Colombian Rebels Plan for Cocaine War," *Telegraph*, September 3, 2000; "FARC Aprovechan Zona del Despeje para Lanzar Ataques," *El Mercurio*, July 27, 1999; Robert D. Novak, "Terrorism Close to Home," *Washington Post*, April 19, 1999; Ruth Morris, "UN Tries to Avert War in Colombia," *The Independent*, January 13, 2002; "Colombian Rebels to Leave Enclave as Talks Fail," *New York Times*, January 23, 2002.

88. Morris, "UN Tries to Avert War in Colombia."

89. Forrest Hylton, "Colombia's Three-Year Truce Ends: From 'Peace' to War," Countercurrents.org, April 28, 2002, www.countercurrents.org/hylton280402.htm.

90. Morris, "UN Tries to Avert War in Colombia."

91. "Colombian Rebels to Leave Enclave as Talks Fail," *New York Times*, January 23, 2002.

92. Hylton, "Colombia's Three-Year Truce Ends."

93. Adam Isacson, " 'Getting in Deeper': The United States Growing Involvement in Colombia's Conflict," Center for International Policy, February 2000, www.ciponline.org/coipr/coipr002.htm (June 15, 2006).

94. Ibid.; Jared Israel, "Washington: Parent of the Taliban and Colombian Death Squads," Emperor's Clothes.com, June 5, 2001, http://emperorsclothes.com/articles/jared/mis.htm.

95. Extreme poverty is measured as earning less than $2 a day.

96. Mario A. Murrillo, *Colombia and the United States: War, Unrest and Destabilization* (New York: Seven Stories Press, 2004).

97. The BBC survey cited in "Latin American Publics are Skeptical about US—but not about Democracy," World Public Opinion.org, March 7, 2007, www.worldpublicopinion.org/pipa/articles/brlatinamericara/328.php?nid=&id=&pnt=328&lb=brla; see also FARC-EP website at www.farcejercitodelpueblo.org/.

98. "Stopping It: How Governments Try—and Fail—to Stem the Flow of Drugs," *The Economist*, July 28, 2001.

99. Washington Office on Latin America, "Data Shows Record Low Prices of Cocaine and Heroin," November 1, 2004, www.wola.org/index.php?option=com_content&task=viewp&id=397.

100. Richani, *Systems of Violence*, 81.

101. Michael Taussig, *Law in a Lawless Land: Diary of a 'Limpieza' in Colombia* (New York: New Press, 2003).

102. Ricardo Vargas, *Drogas, Poder y Region en Colombia* (Bogotá: CINEP, 1994).

103. Taussig, *Law in a Lawless Land*.

104. Richani, *Systems of Violence.*
105. Richani, email to authors, August 12, 2005.
106. Robert Jervis, *System Effects Complexity in Political and Social Life* (Princeton: Princeton University Press, 1999).
107. Toledo et al., *War in Colombia;* Richani, *Systems of Violence.*
108. Rabasa and Chalk, *Colombian Labyrinth.*
109. Azalea Robles, "250 mil desaparecidos claman justicia, y Falsimedia confunde para seguir desapareciendo la verdad," *Rebelion,* March 22, 2011, http://www.rebelion.org/noticia.php?id=122896.
110. James Petras, "Colombia: The FARC and the Trade Unions," *Rebelion,* December 11, 2001, http://rebelion.org/petras/english/farcunions010102.htm.
111. Richani, *Systems of Violence.*

6. THE UNITED STATES AND "PLAN COLOMBIA"

1. Larry K. Storrs and Nina M. Serafino, "Andean Regional Initiative (ARI): FY 2002 Assistance for Colombia and Neighbors," *Congressional Research Service Report* (Washington DC: Library of Congress Congressional Research Service, February 14, 2002); Oliver Villar, Drew Cottle, and Angela Keys, "The Kill for Drugs Policy? Ecocide in Rural Colombia," paper presented at the 14th Ecopolitics Conference of the Ecopolitics Association of Australasia, RMIT University, Melbourne, November 27–29, 2003.

2. See Sarah Holsen, José Egas, and Laura Glynn, "Plan Colombia—Definition and Funding," www.derechos.net/cedhu/plancolombia/PLAN-COLOMBIAINGLES.html.

3. Andres A. Pastrana, *La Palabra Bajo Fuego* (Bogotá: Planeta, 2005), 48, 51.

4. Ibid.; Grace Livingstone, *Inside Colombia: Drugs, Democracy, and War* (New Brunswick, NJ: Rutgers University Press, 2003).

5. Pastrana, *La Palabra Bajo Fuego,* 203.

6. Livingstone, *Inside Colombia.*

7. Ibid.

8. Dan Gardner, "Losing the Drug War," *Ottawa Citizen,* September 6, 2000.

9. Livingstone, *Inside Colombia;* Jose Miguel Vivanco, Director of Human Rights Watch Americas Division, testimony before U.S. Senate, Subcommittee on the Western Hemisphere, April 24, 2002, http://hrw.org/english/docs/2001/07/11/colomb184.htm.

10. Al Giordano, "Bush Ups Ante on Plan Colombia," *The Lindesmith Center Drug Policy Foundation,* March 13, 2001.

11. See "U.S. Military and Police Aid," Center for International Policy, http://www.ciponline.org/colombia/aidprop.htm; see also "U.S. Aid to Colombia, All Programs, 2006–2011," Just the Facts.org, http://justf.org/Country?country=Colombia.

12. Arlene B. Tickner, "Colombia and the United States: From Counternarcotics to counterterrorism," *Current History* 102 (February 2003), 77–85.

13. 'El Gran Fracaso,' Revista Cambio.com, May 13, 2001; Jason Web, "Colombia Produces More Cocaine than Thought–Source,." Reuters, May 15, 2001.

14. Anonymous, "Colombia: Uribe Seeks Extension of Plan Colombia," *NACLA Report on the Americas* 37 (May–June 2004), 45.

15. "Quick Data: U.S. Military and Police Aid Grants by Country (Total Aid since 1996)," Just the Facts.org, http://justf.org/Country?country= Colombia

16. Rebecca Toledo et al., eds., *War in Colombia: Made in U.S.A.* (New York: International Action Center, 2003).

17. Peter Gorman, "Marines Ordered into Colombia: February 2003 Is Target Date," *The Narco News Bulletin,* October, 25, 2004; Jim Garamone, "U.S., Colombia Will Continue Pressure on Narcoterrorists," *American Forces Press,* April 12, 2005.

18. See Alfredo Schulte-Bockholt, *The Politics of Organized Crime and the Organized Crime of Politics: A Study in Criminal Power* (Lanham, MD: Lexington Books, 2006); Ada K. Izaguirre, *Private Participation in Infrastructure: Trends in Developing Countries in 1990–2001* (Washington DC: World Bank Publications, 2003).

19. Justin Podur and Manuel Rozental, "Prepare for 4 Years of the Uribe Model: Change and Continuity after Colombia's Elections," *Z-Magazine,* May 30, 2002,www.zmag.org/content/Colombia/podur_rozental-uribemodel.cfm.

20. Anonymous, "Profile: Colombia," *NACLA Report on the Americas* 36 (September–October 2002): 13.

21. Louis Kraar and Jonas Blank, "The Drug Trade," *Fortune,* June 20, 1988.

22. Garry M. Leech, "An Interview with FARC Commander Simon Trinidad," *NACLA Report on the Americas* 34 (September–October 2000): 24–25.

23. James Petras, "The FARC Faces the Empire," *Latin American Perspectives* 27 (September 2000): 134–43; Belen Boville, *The Cocaine War in Context: Drugs and Politics* (New York: Algora Publishing, 2004).

24. Ana Carrigan, "War or Peace? Colombia's New President Must Choose between Washington and His Own People," *In These Times,* August 2, 2002; UN Drug Control Program, "Global Illicit Drug Trends Survey 2002," http://www.unodc.org/pdf/report_2002-06-26_1/report_2002-06-26_1.pdf; UN Office on Drugs and Crime, "World Drug Report 2010," www.unodc.org/unodc/en/data-and-analysis/WDR-2010.html.

25. UN Drug Control Program, "Global Illicit Drugs Trends Survey 2002."
26. Daniel Trotta, "Cost of War at Least $3.7 Trillion and Counting," *Reuters*, June 29, 2011; Josh White, "Iraq War Cost Put at $1.7 Trillion," *The Age*, November 14, 2007.
27. Dermot O'Conner, "The Political Economy of Colombia's Cocaine Industry," *Papel Politico* 14 (January–June 2009), 6.
28. Anonymous, "Profile: Colombia";Livingstone, *Inside Colombia*.
29. ANIF cited in Anonymous, "Profile: Colombia."
30. Justin Podur, "How Would Drug Legalization in the United States Affect Colombia?" *Colombia Journal*, March 17, 2003, http://colombia journal.org/how-would-drug-legalization-in-the-united-states-affect-colombia.htm.
31. As analyzed by Vladimir I. Lenin, "Imperialism, the Highest Stage of Capitalism," *Lenin Selected Works*, vol. 1 (Moscow: Progress Publishers, 1917); and Robin T. Naylor, *Hot Money and the Politics of Debt* (New York: Simon & Schuster, 1987).
32. Peter Andreas and Coletta Youngers, "U.S. Drug Policy and the Andean Cocaine Industry," *World Policy Journal* 6 (Summer 1989): 529–62.
33. Alfredo Rangel Suarez, *Colombia: Guerra en el Fin de Siglo* (Bogotá: TM Editores, 1998), 189.
34. Al Gedicks, "Colombia 'Drug War' a Sham," *Abu Saleh*, September 16, 2002.
35. "Megaprojects and Neocolonialisation in Colombia," *Archive of Global Protests*, January 2001, www.nadir.org/nadir/initiativ/agp/free/colombia/ mega.htm; "Colombia-Country Profile," *Archive of Global Protests*, www.nadir.org/nadir/initiativ/agp/free/colombia/colombia.htm (12 October 2007).
36. "Colombia Monthly Report 1997," cited in *Plan Colombia & Proceso de Comunidades Negras (PCN)*, www2.renacientes.org:8080/renacientes.
37. Alejandro R. Posada. "Conflicto armado y territorio en Colombia," in *Colonizacion del Bosque Humedo Tropical*, ed. Humberto Rojas Ruiz (Bogotá: Corporacion Aracuara, 1989), 112–33.
38. Mario A. Murrillo, *Colombia and the United States: War, Unrest and Destabilization* (New York: Seven Stories Press, 2004).
39. Corporacion Colectivo de Abogados Jose Alvear Restrepo, *Terrorismo o Rebelion?* (Bogotá: Intermedio Editores, 2001).
40. Ibid.

7. NARCO-STATE TERROR

1. U.S. Naval War College, "Maoist Strategic Theory and the Chinese Civil War," Newport, Rhode Island, http://www.nwc.navy.mil/defaultf.htm.

2.   Theodore Shackley, *The Third Option: An American View of Counterinsurgency Operations* (New York: McGraw Hill, 1981); Rodney Stich, *Drugging America: A Trojan Horse* (California: Diablo Western Press, 1999); Michael McClintock, *Instruments of Statecraft* (New York: Pantheon, 1992); Alexander Cockburn and Jeffrey St. Clair, *Whiteout: The CIA, Drugs and the Press* (New York: Verso, 1998).

3.   Douglas Valentine, *The Strength of the Wolf: The Secret History of America's War on Drugs* (New York: Verso, 2004); Cockburn and St. Clair, *Whiteout.*

4.   See, for instance, Emily O. Goldman, *Information and Revolutions in Military Affairs* (New York: Routledge, 2005).

5.   Jim Garamone, "Special Operations Part of US-Colombia Plan to Reinforce Success," American Forces Press Service, April 1, 2004.

6.   Center for International Policy, "Special Operations Forces, Latin America and the Caribbean," http://www.ciponline.org/facts/sof.htm.

7.   Ibid.

8.   World Organization Against Torture, *El Terrorismo de Estado en Colombia* (Brussels: Editorial NCOS, 1992); Rebecca Toledo et al., eds., *War in Colombia: Made in U.S.A.* (New York: International Action Center, 2003); Sean Donahue, "The Life and Crimes of General Montoya Uribe," *School of the Americas Watch,* May 22, 2002, www.soaw.org/about-the-soawhinsec/colombia/2709; Revolutionary Armed Forces of Colombia, "Paramilitarismo Como Politica Contrainsurgente de Estado," Mountains of Colombia, January 1999, www.reocities.com/athens/cyprus/6597/ Farc/param.html.

9.   Toledo et al., *War in Colombia.*

10. Michael Taussig, *Law in a Lawless Land: Diary of a 'Limpieza' in Colombia* (New York: New Press, 2003).

11. Taussig, *Law in a Lawless Land*; Silvio Waisbord, *Watchdog Journalism in South America, News Accountability and Democracy* (New York: Columbia University Press, 2001).

12. School of the Americas Watch, "Notorious Graduates from Colombia," http://www.soaw.org/index.php?option=com_content&id=235.

13. Paul Wolf, "America's Dirty War in Colombia," www.icdc.com/~paulwolf/colombia/whde.htm, August 25, 1998.

14. Stan Goff, "Blurring of the Lines," in *War in Colombia: Made in U.S.A.,* ed. Toledo et al. (New York: International Action Center, 2003), 77–83.

15. Garamone, "Special Operations Part of US-Colombia Plan to Reinforce Success."

16. U.S. Department of Defense, *Dictionary of Military and Associated Terms* (Washington DC: U.S. Government Printing Office, 1987), 291.

17. Ivan Molloy, *Rolling Back Revolution: The Emergence of Low Intensity Conflict* (London: Pluto Press, 2001).

18. Ibid.
19. Tayacan, *Psychological Operations in Guerrilla Warfare the CIA's Nicaragua Manual* (New York: Vintage Books, 1985). This manual was written in English by John Kirkpatrick, a former U.S. Green Beret, and published in Spanish shortly after. The manual gives advice on political assassinations, blackmailing, mob violence, kidnappings, and blowing up buildings. It advocates the use of shock troops armed with clubs, iron rods, placards, and small firearms, to be hidden together with knives, razors, chains, clubs and bludgeons in anti-government demonstrations. Under the heading "Selective Use of Violence," instructions are given to neutralize carefully selected and planned targets such as court judges, police, or state security officials and urges the Contras to kidnap all officials or agents of the Sandinista government.
20. Doug Stokes, *America's Other War: Terrorizing Colombia* (New York: Zed Books, 2005).
21. Ibid., 147.
22. Ibid.
23. Peter D. Scott, *Drugs, Oil, and War: The United States in Afghanistan, Colombia, and Indochina* (New York: Rowman & Littlefield Publishers, 2003).
24. James J. Brittain, "War, Evil, and the End of History: Review Essay of Bernard-Henri Lévy's Book Concerning the Global Shift toward Apolitical Conflict," *Rethinking Marxism* 19 (2007): 1–3.
25. Tayacan, *Psychological Operations in Guerrilla Warfare*.
26. Taussig, *Law in a Lawless Land*.
27. Ibid.; Mauricio Archila and Mauricio Pardo, *Movimientos Sociales, Estado y Democracia en Colombia* (Bogotá: Centro de Estudios Sociales, Universidad Nacional de Colombia, 2001).
28. Waisbord, *Watchdog Journalism in South America;* Silvio Waisbord, "Grandes Gigantes: Media Concentration in Latin America," www.opendemocracy.net/media-globalmediaownership/article_64.jsp, February 27, 2002.
29. Colombia Solidarity.org, www.colombiasolidarity.org.uk/articles/bulletin-archive/42-bulletin-issue7-julyseptember-2002/223-when-democracy-is-dictatorship.
30. International Labor Rights Forum, "Colombian Unravels Government-Paramilitary Ties," March 20, 2007, www.laborrights.org/end-violence-against-trade-unions/news/10862.
31. Juan Forero, "Prosperous Colombians Flee, Many to US, to Escape War," *New York Times,* April 10, 2001.
32. Taussig, *Law in a Lawless Land,* 9.
33. James Petras, "Non-Governmental Organizations in a Conjuncture of Conflict and War Psychosis," *Rebelion,* December 4, 2001, http://rebe-

lion.org/petras/english/ngo170102.htm. This political endorsement was common practice during the Cold War as well; see for instance, Frances S. Saunders, *Who Paid the Piper: The CIA and the Cultural Cold War* (London: Granta Books, 1999).

34. Heather Cottin, "Human Rights Watch Cover Up," in *War in Colombia: Made in the U.S.A.,* ed. Toledo et al. (New York: International Action Center, 2003), 99–109.

35. Manuel Salgado Tamayo, "The Geostrategy of Plan Colombia," *CovertAction Quarterly,* 71 (Winter 2001), 37–40.

36. Human Rights Watch, "Colombia: Human Rights Watch Testifies before the Senate," Testimony of José Miguel Vivanco, New York, April 24, 2002, http://reliefweb.int/sites/reliefweb.int/files/reliefweb_pdf/node-103491.pdf.

37. "Colombia Rebels Deny Club Attack," *BBC World News,* March 11, 2003; Reuters, "Colombia Blames Rebels for Bogotá Club Bomb," February 8, 2003; Vanessa Arrington, "Colombians Protest Car Bomb Attack," Associated Press, February 9, 2003.

38. Associated Press, "Colombia Rebels Admit to Killings," March 10, 1999; Revolutionary Armed Forces of Colombia, "Communiqué," Mountains of Colombia, March 10, 1999; Agencia de Noticias Nueva Colombia, "The Wrong Pig on Trial," June 2, 2003; Reuters, "Peace Czar Says FARC Not Responsible for Necklace Bomb," May 21, 2000; Agencia de Noticias Nueva Colombia, "UN Confirms: Colombian Army Implicated in Bojaya Tragedy," May 24, 2002; Agencia de Noticias Nueva Colombia, "Top US Official Lied about Al Qaida-FARC Link," September 12, 2002; Agencia de Noticias Nueva Colombia, "President Blamed for the Killing of 10 Prisoners," May 14, 2003; Human Rights Watch, "You'll Learn Not to Cry: Child Combatants in Colombia," September 2003, www.hrw.org/reports/2003/colombia0903/. The following cases are examples of PSYOP campaigns to discredit the FARC: the killing of three American U'Wa indigenous activists in 1999; a necklace bomb in 2000; a church bombing in 2002; the alleged FARC-Al Qaeda link in 2002; a failed rescue attempt and the killing of prisoners in 2003; and the most sinister charge to date, the "drinking of blood" forced on child soldiers in 2003.

39. Karl Penhaul, "IRA Suspects Set Free in Colombia," CNN, June 16, 2004.

40. Reuters, "Colombia Blames Rebels for Bogotá Club Bomb," February 8, 2003.

41. Ibid.

42. Ibid.

43. Paul Wolf, "United States and Colombia," *Z-Magazine,* March 1999, www.thirdworldtraveler.com/US_ThirdWorld/United%20States_Colombia.html.

44. Comision de Superacion de la Violencia, "Panorama de Derechos Humanos y Derecho Humanitario," Instituto de Estudios Politicos

Relaciones Internacionales, Universidad Nacional de Colombia (Bogotá: IEPRI/CINEP/Comision Andina de Juristas/CECOIN, 2001).

45. Juan E. Mendez, *Colombia: Political Murder & Reform: The Violence Continues,* 1st ed. (New York: Human Rights Watch, 1992), 58–59.

46. Fernando C. Ospina, *Colombia, Laboratorio de Embrujos: Democracia y Terrorismo de Estado* (Madrid: Ediciones Aka, 2008); Human Rights Watch, "Colombia's Killer Networks: The Military-Paramilitary Partnership and the United States," November 1996, www.hrw.org/reports/1996/killertoc.htm; Aram Roston, "It's the Real Thing: Murder. US Firms like Coca-Cola Are Implicated in Colombia's Brutality," *The Nation,* September 3, 2001; James J. Brittain, *Revolutionary Social Change in Colombia: The Origin and Direction of the FARC-EP* (New York: Pluto Press, 2010); Garry M. Leech, *Killing Peace: Colombia's Conflict and the Failure of U.S. Intervention* (New York: Information Network of the Americas, 2002).

47. More union activists are killed in Colombia than in the rest of the world combined. The most persecuted is the largest peasant and rural workers' union, the National Unitarian Federation of Agrarian Unions (FENSUA-GRO). See James J. Brittain, "FENSUAGRO's Struggle for Social Justice," *Peace Review: Journal of Social Justice* 19 (2007): 417–26.

48. Nelson V. Larios, *FENSUAGRO-CUT-FSM: 30 Años 1976–2006 Organizacion, Lucha y Resistencia* (Bogotá: Impreso en Colombia, 2006); Ospina, *Colombia, Laboratorio de Embrujos.*

49. Cecilia Zarate-Laun, "CIA, Cocaine, and Death Squads," *Covert Action Quarterly* (Fall/Winter 1999): 16–17.

50. Douglas Farah and Laura Brooks, "Colombian Army's Third in Command Allegedly Led Two Lives; General Reportedly Served as a Key CIA Informant while Maintaining Ties to Death Squads Financed by Drug Traffickers," *Washington Post,* August 11, 1998.

51. Ibid.

52. Ibid.

53. Ibid.

54. Chris Kraul, "Colombia General Gen. Mario Montoya Resigns," *Los Angeles Times,* November 5, 2008.

55. See Donahue, "The Life and Crimes of General Montoya Uribe."

56. Karl Penhaul, "Outlaw Role Seen in Colombia," *Boston Globe,* March 28, 2001.

57. UN High Commissioner for Refugees, "2005 Global Refugee Trends: Statistical Overview of Populations of Refugees, Asylum-Seekers, Internally Displaced Persons, Stateless Persons, and Other Persons of Concern to UNHCR," June 9, 2006, http://www.unhcr.org/cgi-bin/texis/vtx/home/opendocPDFViewer.html?docid=4486ceb12&query =global trends 2005; Brittain, *Revolutionary Social Change in Colombia.*

58. Angel Rabasa and Peter Chalk, *Colombian Labyrinth: The Synergy of Drugs and Insurgency and Its Implications for Regional Stability* (Santa Monica, CA: Rand Corporation, 2001); Garry M. Leech, "Informers for a Day," *Colombia Journal*, April 7, 2003, colombiajournal.org/informers-for-a-day.htm.

59. Jeremy Bigwood, "Doing the US's Dirty Work: The Colombian Paramilitaries and Israel," *Narco News Bulletin*, April 8, 2003.

60. Taussig, *Law in a Lawless Land*.

61. Anthony W. Pereira, *Political (In)Justice: Authoritarianism and the Rule of Law in Brazil, Chile, and Argentina* (Pittsburgh: University of Pittsburgh Press, 2005); Ospina, *Laboratorio de Embrujos*.

62. Winifred Tate, "Colombia: The Right Gathers Momentum," *NACLA Report on the Americas* 35 (May–June 2002): 13–17.

63. Taussig, *Law in a Lawless Land*.

64. Sean Donahue, "Mano Firme, Corazon Pequeño: Uribe Takes Hardline in Colombia with Bush's Blessing," *Counterpunch*, August 22, 2002, www.counterpunch.org/donahue0821.html. According to Donahue, similar militias were set up by Guatemala's military dictatorship during the civil war. They were later found to have carried out assassinations, massacres, and the burning of villages, as in Vietnam.

65. Ibid.

66. Ibid.

67. Taussig, *Law in a Lawless Land*.

68. "Peace and Justice for Colombia," http://colombiasolidarity.net/. Azalea Robles, a Colombian investigative journalist, estimates there are 7,500 political prisoners in Colombia; see Robles, "250 mil desaparecidos claman justicia, y Falsimedia confunde para seguir desapareciendo la verdad," *Rebelion*, March 22, 2011, www.rebelion.org/noticia.php?id=122896.

69. Associated Press, "U.S Asks for Immunity in Colombia," August 15, 2002; Scott Wilson, "US Seeks Court Immunity for Troops in Colombia, US Trying to Protect Nationals from International Courts," *Washington Post*, August 15, 2002.

70. Ibid.; Jim Lobe, "US Punishes 35 Countries for Signing Onto Int'l Court," *Inter Press Service Agency*, July 1, 2003. Under U.S. anti-terrorism legislation signed by President Bush in 2002, U.S. military aid would be cut off to countries that ratified the treaty, except those granted a waiver by the White House. Colombia ratified the Protocol but did not sign article 98, which grants them a waiver.

71. Juan E. Corradi et al., *Fear at the Edge: State Terror and Resistance in Latin America* (Riverside: University of California Press, 1992).

72. Matthew Thompson, "The Secret War of Colombia," *Sydney Morning Herald*, August 17, 2008.

73. Jim Wyss, "Colombian Ex-Spy Chief Gets 25-Year Sentence," *Miami Herald,* September 14, 2011.

74. Gretchen Gordon and Noah Smith, "Truth behind Bars: Colombian Paramilitary Leaders in U.S. Custody," International Human Rights Clinic, University of California, Berkeley, School of Law, February 2010, www.law.berkeley.edu/files/IHRLC/Truthbehindbars.pdf

75. Ibid.

76. Ibid.

77. STRATFOR, "The Splintering of Colombia's AUC," Basic Global Intelligence Brief, October 8, 2004.

78. Center for International Policy, "New paramilitaries and violence in Cordoba,"*Plan Colombia and Beyond,* November 9, 2009, http://www.cipcol.org/?p=1196.

79. Ibid.; "Vicente Castaño habría matado a su hermano,"*El Pais,* February 1, 2007.

80. Garry M. Leech, "Colombian Army Selectively Targets Paramilitaries," *Colombia Journal,* October 4, 2004, http://colombiajournal.org/colombian-army-selectively-targets-paramilitaries.htm; Wyss, "Colombian Ex-Spy Chief Gets 25-Year Sentence."

81. Ospina, *Colombia, Laboratorio de Embrujos.*

8. THE CONSEQUENCES OF RELOCATION AND REGIONALIZATION

1. U.S. Southern Command, http://www.southcom.mil/AppsSC/index.php; Doug Stokes, *America's Other War: Terrorizing Colombia* (New York: Zed Books, 2005).

2. Ibid.

3. Peter Pace, "Advance Questions for Lieutenant General Peter Pace: Defense Reforms," U.S Senate Committee on Armed Services, 2000, http://www.senate.gov/~armed_services/statemnt/2000/000906pp.pdf.

4. Ibid.; Stokes, *America's Other War.*

5. Stokes, *America's Other War,* 123; James T. Hill, "Posture Statement," U.S. Southern Command, House Armed Services Committee, March 12, 2003.

6. Michael Levine, *The Triangle of Death* (New York: Delacorte Press, 1996), 234–40.

7. David Carey, Director of the Central Intelligence Agency Crime and Narcotics Center, "Plan Colombia's Potential Impact on the Andean Cocaine Trade: An Examination of Two Scenarios of Plan Colombia Was the Massive Aerial Spraying of the Chemical Glyphosate on Illicit Crops in Colombia," September 19, 2000; U.S. Department of State, "Fact Sheet on

Plan Colombia," March 14, 2001, www.state.gov/p/wha/rls/fs/2001/ 1042.htm. The CIA was aware of the potential global consequences several years earlier with knowledge of "trends in transnational criminal activity," the "impact of crime and corruption on political and economic stability in foreign countries," as well as the expansion of "international networks and cooperation among criminal organizations." See David Carey, testimony to House International Relations Committee on International Organized Crime, January 31, 1996, https://www.cia.gov/news-information/speeches-testimony/1996/carey_13196.html.

8.   National Security Archive, George Washington University, "U.S. Intelligence Listed Colombian President Uribe among 'Important Colombian Narco-Traffickers in 1991,'" September 23, 1991, www.gwu.edu/~nsarchiv/NSAEBB/NSAEBB131/index.htm.

9.   The following trafficking figures, important to the construction of the cocaine drug trade, rank as follows: Manuel Noriega, ex-president of Panama, number 66; Fidel Castaño, the brother of deceased AUC leader Carlos Castaño who is not on the list, number 77; Pablo Escobar, number 79; Diego Londono White, one of Escobar's first narco-bourgeoisie connections, number 86.

10. Ed Vulliamy, "US Sprays Poison in Drugs War," *Observer International*, July 2, 2000.

11. James A. Inciardi, "Crack Cocaine in Miami," in *The Epidemiology of Cocaine Use and Abuse*, ed. Susan Schober and Charles Schade (Washington, DC: U.S. Government Printing Office, 1991), 263–75; James A. Inciardi, "Beyond Cocaine: Basuco, Crack, and Other Coca Products," *Contemporary Drug Problems* (Fall 1987): 461–92; Ronald K. Siegel, "History of Cocaine Smoking," *Journal of Psychoactive Drugs* 14 (Oct-Dec 1982): 277–99. James Inciardi contends that coca paste may well have been the prototype for crack-cocaine, which caused a drug epidemic in the United States during the 1980s, precisely at the time when heroin was losing popularity.

12. Donald C. Hildebrand and Arthur H. McCain, "The Use of Various Substrates for Large-Scale Production of Fusarium oxysporum f. sp. cannabis Inoculum," 68 *Phytopathology* (July 1978): 1099–1101.

13. Dan Russell, "Agent Green: McCollum's 'Silver Bullet' in the Head," Drugwar.com, 23 February 2001, www.drugwar.com/fusarium.shtm; Rensselaer W. Lee II and Patrick Clawson, *The Andean Cocaine Industry* (New York: St. Martin's Press, 1998).

14. Martin Jelsma, "Vicious Circle: The Chemical and Biological War on Drugs," paper presented at Transnational Institute, Amsterdam, March 2001, www.xs4all.nl/~tni/archives/jelsma/viciouscircle-e.pdf.

15. Jeremy Bigwood, "The Drug War's Fungal 'Solution' in the Amazon," Conference Paper, Society for the Anthropology of Lowland South

America, Annapolis, MD, June 8, 2002, www.jeremybigwood.net/Lectures/SALSA/Annapolis2002.htm.

16. Jelsma, "Vicious Circle."

17. Ed. Vulliamy, "Going Backwards: US Prepares to Spray Genetically-Modified Herbicides on Colombians," London *Observer*, July 2, 2000.

18. Paul Rogers, Simon Whitby, and Malcolm Dando, "Biological Warfare against Crops," *Scientific American* (June 1999): 70–76.

19. Jeremy Bigwood, "Drug Warriors Push Eye-Eating Fungus," *In These Times*, June 6, 2006; authors' email correspondence with Bigwood, October 26, 2007.

20. Bigwood, "The Drug War's Fungal 'Solution' in the Amazon."

21. Victoria B. Solberg et al., "Penetration of (sup 3 H) T-2 Mycotoxin through Abraded and Intact Skin and Methods to Decontaminate (sup 3 H) T-2 Mycotoxin from Abrasions," 28 *Toxicon* (January 1990): 803–11.

22. Bigwood, "The Drug War's Fungal 'Solution' in the Amazon."

23. T. D. Allman, "Blow Back," *Rolling Stone*, May 8, 2002.

24. Jeremy Bigwood, "Toxic Drift: Monsanto and the Drug War in Colombia," *CorpWatch*, June 21, 2001, www.corpwatch.org/article.php?id=669.

25. Vargas, "The Anti-Drug Policy."

26. Augusto C. Fernandez, "Feast of Lies: The Supposed Reduction in Colombian Coca Crops in 2002," *Narco News Bulletin*, May 22, 2003; Adam Isacson, Ingrid Vaicius, "Plan Colombia's 'Ground Zero,'" Center for International Policy, March 9–12, 2001, www.ciponline.org/colombia/0401putu.htm.

27. Oliver Villar, Drew Cottle, and Angela Keys, "The Kill for Drugs Policy? Ecocide in Rural Colombia," paper presented at the 14th Ecopolitics Conference of the Ecopolitics Association of Australasia, RMIT University, Melbourne, November 27–29, 2003.

28. Ricardo Vargas, *Fumigación y Conflicto: Políticas Antidrogas y Deslegitimación del Estado en Colombia* (Bogotá: Tercer Mundo Editores, 1999).

29. Brian Tokar, "Monsanto: A Checkered History," *The Ecologist* 28 (September–October 1998): 254–60.

30. Vargas, *Fumigacion y Conflicto*.

31. Ibid.

32. Bigwood, email correspondence, October 26, 2007.

33. Associated Press, "Altered Coca Plants, a New Possible Threat in Drug War, Said to Lurk in Colombia's Jungles," September 1, 2004; Jeremy McDermott, "New Super Strain of Coca Plant Stuns Anti-Drug Officials," *The Scotsman*, August 27, 2004; "Super Coca?" Drug Policy Briefing No. 8, Transnational Institute, Amsterdam, September 2004, www.tni.org/detail_page.phtml?page=policybriefings_brief8.

34. Bigwood, email correspondence, October 27, 2007.
35. "Colombia Displaces and Ecuador Receives Refugees by Violence," *Momento 24,* 9 November 2010.
36. National Security Archive, George Washington University, "US Embassy Colombia Cable, Aerial Eradication in Guaviare, Caqueta and Putumayo," July 16, 1996, www.gwu.edu/~nsarchiv/NSAEBB/NSAEBB69/col44.pdf.
37. National Security Archive, George Washington University, "U.S. Embassy Colombia Cable, Protesting Coca Growers Continue Stand-Off," July 24, 1996, www.gwu.edu/~nsarchiv/NSAEBB/NSAEBB69/col45.pdf.
38. Ibid.
39. Mandala Project, "Deforestation in Colombia," Trade and Environment Database (TED), School of International Service, American University, http://www1.american.edu/ted/ (June 17, 2008). According to the Mandala Project, Colombia's forests are home to fifty-five thousand plant species, one-third of which are endemic. Over two thousand plant species have yet to be identified, and an even greater number have yet to be analyzed for potential curative purposes. The country also possesses 358 mammal species, 15 percent of the world's primates, and 18 percent of the world's birds.
40. Nazih Richani, *Systems of Violence: The Political Economy of War and Peace in Colombia* (New York: State University of New York Press, 2002).
41. "Olor a desierto en la Amazonia y Orinoquia," *El Espectador*, September 16, 1998.
42. Vargas, *Fumigación y Conflicto.*
43. Editorial, "De la fumigacion a la sustitución," *El Tiempo*, March 1, 2000.
44. "Ministro del Interior acusa a ecologistas de 'complot mundial,'" *EcoNoticias,* July 16, 2002.
45. Heather Cottin, "Human Rights Watch Cover-Up," in *War in Colombia: Made in the U.S.A.,* ed. Toledo et al. (New York: International Action Center, 2003), 99–109.
46. James J. Brittain, "Government, NGOs and the Paramilitary: A Colombian Contradiction," *Development* 50 (2007): 122–27.
47. Revolutionary Armed Forces of Colombia–People's Army (FARC-EP), "Colombia: Legalization of Drug Consumption, the Only Serious Alternative for the Elimination of the Narcotics Traffic," Secretariat of the Central General Staff, Plenum of the Central General Staff, Mountains of Colombia, March 29, 2000; Vargas, "The Revolutionary Armed Forces of Colombia (FARC) and the Illicit Drug Trade."
48. Villar et al., "The Kill for Drugs Policy?"
49. Coletta Youngers and Eileen Rosin, *Drugs and Democracy in Latin America: The Impact of U.S. Policy* (Boulder, CO: Lynne Rienner Publishers, 2005); Frank O. Mora, "Victims of the Balloon Effect: Drug

Trafficking and US Policy in Brazil and the Southern Cone of Latin America," *Journal of Social, Political, and Economic Studies* 21 (Summer 1996): 115–40.

50. Peter D. Scott and Jonathan Marshall, *Cocaine Politics: Drugs, Armies, and the CIA in Central America,* repr. (Berkeley: University of California Press, 1998); Michael Levine, *Deep Cover* (New York: Delacorte Press, 1990).

51. Mora, "Victims of the Balloon Effect."

52. Clare Hargreaves, *Snowfields: The War on Cocaine in the Andes* (London: Zed Books, 1992), 42, 188.

53. Frank O. Mora, "Brazil and the Southern Cone: An Annotated Bibliography," in *Drug Trafficking Research in the Americas,* ed. Bruce Bagley (Boulder, CO: Lynne Rienner Publisher, 1996), 249–97.

54. Scott MacDonald, "The Next Wave of the Latin Drug Trade," *Times of the Americas,* June 27, 1990.

55. Council on Hemispheric Affairs, "Washington Report on the Hemisphere," September 27, 1989, cited in Noam Chomsky, *Deterring Democracy* (London: South End Press, 1992), 115.

56. Jefferson Morley, "The Great American High: Contradictions of Cocaine Capitalism," *The Nation,* October 2, 1989; Derrick Z. Jackson, "Our Fraudulent War on Drugs," *Boston Globe,* September 13, 1996.

57. Council on Hemispheric Affairs, "Washington Report on the Hemisphere."

58. Brook Larmer, "US, Mexico Try to Halt Chemical Flow to Cartels," *Christian Science Monitor,* October 23, 1989.

59. Ibid.

60. Randolph Ryan, "Shifting the Drug War," *Boston Globe,* March 10, 1989.

61. Nathan Adams, "The Hunt for Andre," *Reader's Digest,* March 1973; "Heroin: Now It's the Latin Connection," *Newsweek,* January 24, 1972.

62. Frank O. Mora, "Paraguay International Drug Trafficking," in *Drug Trafficking in the Americas,* ed. Bruce Bagley and William Walker (New Brunswick, NJ: Transaction Publishers, 1994), 351–73; Alfred W. McCoy, *The Politics of Heroin: CIA Complicity in the Global Drug Trade* (Chicago: Lawrence Hill Books, 2003); Scott and Marshall, *Cocaine Politics;* Levine, *The Triangle of Death.*

63. Jose L. Simon, "Narcotrafico via Paraguay irrita a Washington," *Sendero,* January 15, 1988.

64. Robin T. Naylor, *Hot Money and the Politics of Debt* (New York: Simon & Schuster, 1987); Penny Lernoux, *In Banks We Trust: Bankers, and Their Close Associates, the CIA, the Mafia, Drug Traders, Dictators, and the Vatican* (New York: Anchor/Doubleday, 1984); Peter D. Scott, *Deep Politics and the Death of JFK* (Berkeley: University of California Press, 1993); Alan Block, *Masters of Paradise: Organized Crime and the Internal*

Revenue Service in the Bahamas (Piscataway, NJ: Transaction Publishers, 1991).

65. UN International Narcotics Control Program, "International Narcotics Control Board, 1994 Report," www.incb.org/pdf/e/ar/incb_report_1994_1.pdf.

66. Juan Forero, "Hide-and-Seek among the Coca Leaves," *New York Times*, June 9, 2004.

67. Robin Moroney, "Cocaine Keeps Getting Cheaper and Cheaper," *Wall Street Journal Blogs*, June 6, 2007, http://blogs.wsj.com/informedreader/2007/06/06/cocaine-keeps-getting-cheaper-and-cheaper/.

68. UN Office on Drugs and Crime, "World Drug Report," June, 23, 2011, www.unodc.org/documents/data-and-analysis/WDR2011/World_Drug_Report_2011_ebook.pdf.

69. Adam Isacson, "The State Department's Data on Drug-Crop Cultivation," Center for International Policy press release, March 22, 2004, www.ciponline.org/colombia/040322coca.pdf; U.S. Drug Enforcement Administration, "Illegal Drug Price and Purity Report," April 2003, www.usdoj.gov/dea/pubs/intel/02058/02058.html; White House Office of National Drug Control Policy, *Pulse Check: Trends in Drug Abuse*, January 2004, www.whitehousedrugpolicy.gov/publications/drugfact/pulsechk/january04/index.html; White House Office of National Drug Control Policy, *National Drug Control Strategy 2008 Annual Report*, http://www.whitehousedrugpolicy.gov/publications/policy/ndcs08/index. html; Matthew B. Robinson and Renee G. Scherlen, *Lies, Damned Lies, and Drug War Statistics* (Albany: State University of New York Press, 2007); Moises Naím, "The Five Wars of Globalization," *Foreign Policy*, January 1, 2003; "Cocaine Prices Have Fallen Steeply since 1980s," National Public Radio (NPR), May 15, 2007; U.S. Department of Justice, National Drug Intelligence Center, *National Drug Threat Assessment*, August 2011, Washington DC, www.justice.gov/ndic/pubs44/44849/44849p.pdf; Frances Robles, "Cocaine No Longer the Drug of Choice," *The Sacramento Bee*, September 19, 2011.

70. U.S. Department of State, Bureau for International Narcotics and Law Enforcement Affairs, *International Narcotics Control Strategy Report 2004*, www.state.gov/g/inl/rls/nrcrpt/2003/; and *International Narcotics Control Strategy Report 2008*, www.state.gov/p/inl/rls/nrcrpt/2008/index.htm.

71. "An Honest Citizen," Episode, "Map: Colombia, Cocaine and Cash: Colombia," *Wide Angle*, PBS Television Documentary Series, directed by Angus Macqueen, aired June 15, 2008, http://www.pbs.org/wnet/wideangle/episodes/an-honest-citizen/map-colombia-cocaine-and-cash/colombia/536/. "The Godfather of Cocaine," *Frontline*, produced by William Cran and Stephanie Tepper, written and directed by William Cran, aired March 25, 1997.

72. U.S. Department of State, Bureau for International Narcotics and Law Enforcement Affairs, *International Narcotics Control Strategy Report 2001,* www.state.gov/p/inl/rls/nrcrpt/2001/.

73. Council on Foreign Relations, Independent Task Force, "Andes 2020: A New Strategy for the Challenges of Colombia and the Region," April 1–June 30, 2004.

74. Hazel Feigenblatt, "US Says Coca Area Up in Bolivia and Down in Peru," Reuters, November 18, 2003; "The Americas: Spectres Stir in Peru; Drugs in the Andes," *The Economist,* February 16, 2002.

75. "Colombia Coca Cultivation Survey Results, A Question of Methods," Drug Policy Briefing No. 22, Transnational Institute, Amsterdam, June 2007, http://www.tni.org/detail_page.phtml?act_id=17020.

76. Ibid.

77. "Chiquita Admits Paying Fighters," *BBC World News,* March 14, 2007, http://news.bbc.co.uk/2/hi/americas/6452455.stm.

78. "Chiquita Sued Over Colombia Role," *BBC World News,* June 7, 2007, http://news.bbc.co.uk/2/hi/business/6732739.stm.

79. Garry M. Leech, "Slap on the Wrist for Corporate Sponsors of Terrorism," *Colombia Journal,* March 19, 2007, http://colombiajournal.org/slap-on-the-wrist-for-corporate-sponsors-of-terrorism.htm.

80. "Ecuador Hit by Colombia Conflict," *BBC World News,* July 20, 2001, http://news.bbc.co.uk/2/hi/world/monitoring/media_reports/1447666.stm.

81. Jelsma, "Vicious Circle."

82. Matthew Lee, "Albright Pleased by Bolivian Fight, Unable to Promise Aid," Agence France Presse, August 18, 2000.

83. Ricardo Rocha, "The Colombian Economy after 25 Years of Drug Trafficking," United Nations Drug Control Program (UNDCP) 2000, Bogotá Country Office, http://www.undcp.org/colombia/rocha.html.

84. Joseph Treaster, "Cocaine Manufacturing Is No Longer Just a Colombia Monopoly," *New York Times,* June 30, 1991.

85. Katherine Ellison, "Alleged Drug Ties Rattle Brazil's Already Beleaguered Government," *Miami Herald,* April 9, 1994; Julia Michaels, "Brazil's Drug War Extends to Its Congress," *Christian Science Monitor,* September 10, 1991.

86. "Narcotrafico invade pueblos amazonios," *Nuevo Herald,* April 15, 1996.

87. Alma Guillermoprieto, "Mexico's Shocking New Saints," *National Geographic,* May 2010; Laura Carlsen, "A Plan Colombia for Mexico," *Foreign Policy in Focus,* September 10, 2010, www.fpif.org/articles/a_plan_colombia_for_mexico.

88. Gregory Wilpert, "Chávez's Venezuela and 21st-Century Socialism," *Research in Political Economy* 24 (Spring 2007): 23.

89. Paul Wolf, "FARC Not a Terrorist Group," *Colombia Journal,* January 12, 2008, http://colombiajournal.org/farc-not-a-terrorist-group.htm.

90. "End Struggle, Chávez Urges FARC," *BBC News*, June 9, 2008.
91. Gabriel Marcella, *War without Borders: The Colombia-Ecuador Crisis of 2008*, (Pennsylvania: Strategic Studies Institute, 2008).
92. Humberto Marquez, "Venezuela: Chávez Says 'Invasion' Planned in Miami and Colombia," *Global Information Network*, May 13, 2004; Jhony Corto, "Fears of War between Colombia and Venezuela," *Agencia de Noticias Nueva Colombia (ANNCOL)*, April 16, 2004.
93. Andres Oppenheimer, "Uribe Being Driven a Lot Closer to Chávez," *Miami Herald*, October 4, 2007.
94. Phil Stewart, "Ecuador Wants Military Base in Miami," Reuters, October 22, 2007.
95. Oppenheimer, "Uribe Being Driven a Lot Closer to Chávez."
96. Patrick Markey, "Hope for US hostages after 5 years," Reuters, February 12, 2008.
97. Helen Murphy and Blake Schmidt, "Colombia's Spy Scandal Turns Uribe against Former Ally Santos," Bloomberg, September 15, 2011, http://www.bloomberg.com/news/2011-09-15/colombia-s-spy-scandal-turns-uribe-against-former-ally-santos.html; Center for International Policy, "Plan Colombia and Beyond," http://www.cipcol.org/; "Colombian Demonstrations Warning," Oneworld.net, January 28, 2008; "Colombia's Uribe Mired in Paramilitary Scandal," *People's Weekly World*, February 24, 2007; Garry M. Leech, "Is the Colombian Government Guilty of War Crimes?" *Colombia Journal*, July 17, 2008, http://colombiajournal.org/is-the-colombian-government-guilty-of-war-crimes.htm.
98. Azalea Robles, "250 mil desaparecidos claman justicia, y Falsimedia confunde para seguir desapareciendo la verdad," *Rebelion*, March 22, 2011, http://www.rebelion.org/noticia.php?id=122896.
99. Ibid.; Isabel Hilton, "A Dark Underbelly of Mass Graves and Electoral Fraud," *The Guardian*, March 8, 2007; James Petras, "The Revolutionary Armed Forces of Colombia–People's Army (FARC-EP): The Cost of Unilateral Humanitarian Initiatives," March 16, 2008, http://petras.lahaine.org/articulo.php?p=1728&more=1&c=1.
100. Oneworld.net, "Colombian Demonstrations Warning."
101. Forero, "Hide-and-Seek among the Coca Leaves," 2.

9. THE WAR ON DRUGS: CORPORATIZATION AND PRIVATIZATION

1. William J. Chambliss, *On the Take: From Petty Crooks to Presidents* (Bloomington: Indiana University Press, 1988); William J. Chambliss, "State-Organized Crime," *Criminology* 27 (May 1989): 183–208; Gary W. Potter and Bruce Bullington, "Drug Trafficking and the Contras: A Case of

State-Organized Crime," paper presented at annual meeting of the American Society of Criminology, Montreal, 1987. The following cases have been compiled by Potter and Bullington: First National Bank of Maryland; Palmer National Bank; Indian Springs Bank; Nugan Hand Bank; Vision Banc Savings; Hill Financial Savings; Sunshine State Bank; and Full-Service Banking.

2.   Chambliss, "State-Organized Crime," 184.
3.   Jeffrey I. Ross, *Controlling State Crime* (Piscataway, NJ: Transaction Publishers, 2000).
4.   Rodney Stich, *Drugging America: A Trojan Horse* (California: Diablo Western Press, 1999).
5.   Theodore Shackley, *The Third Option: An American View of Counterinsurgency Operations* (New York: McGraw Hill, 1981), 6.
6.   Russell Crandall, *Driven by Drugs: US Policy toward Colombia* (Boulder, CO: Lynne Rienner Publishers, 2002).
7.   U.S. Congress, Senate Committee on Foreign Relations, Subcommittee on Terrorism, *Narcotics and International Operations Report, Drugs, Law Enforcement, and Foreign Policy* (Washington DC: U.S. Government Printing Office, 1989).
8.   Heather Noss and David Spencer, "Colombia: Strategic End State, Goals and Means," Workshop Report, Center for Strategic Studies, The CNA Corporation, Arlington, 9-14,November 6, 2000..
9.   Sohan Sharma and Surinder Kumar, "The Military Backbone of Globalization," *Race and Class 3* (January–March 2003): 23–39.
10. Anonymous, "Money Laundering on the Rise," *Internal Auditor 55* (August 1998): 12.
11. Előd Takáts, "A Theory of 'Crying Wolf': The Economics of Money Laundering Enforcement," *Journal of Law, Economics, and Organization*, 27 (April 2011), 32–78; Nicholas Ryder, *Financial Crime in the 21st Century: Law and Policy* (Cheltenham: Edward Elgar, 2011); Bruce Zagaris and Scott Ehlers, "Drug Trafficking & Money Laundering," *Foreign Policy in Focus*, May 2001, www.fpif.org/briefs/vol6/v6n18launder.html.
12. Peter Dale Scott, *American War Machine: Deep Politics, the CIA Global Drug Connection, and the Road to Afghanistan* (New York: Rowman & Littlefield, 2010); Stewart Patrick, *Weak Links: Fragile States, Global Threats, and International Security* (New York: Oxford University Press, 2011); John Gibler, *To Die in Mexico: Dispatches from Inside the Drug War* (San Francisco, CA: City Lights Foundation, 2011); Raymond Gilpin, "Crime, Violence and Economic Development," United States Institute of Peace, August 2009; www.securitytransformation.org/images/even_wor_des/Raymond_Gilpin_presentation.pdf.

13. Ed Vulliamy, "How a Big US Bank Laundered Billions from Mexico's Murderous Drug Gangs," *The Observer,* April 3, 2011.

14. Catherine A. Fitts, "Narco-Dollars for Beginners (Part 2)," *Narco News Bulletin,* October 31, 2001.

15. Ibid. See also "Tapeworm Economics" at Fitts's website *The Solari Report* for an insider's perspective, http://solari.com/articles/tapeworm_economics/.

16. U.S. Department of Treasury, Comptroller of the Currency Administrator of National Banks, "Bank Secrecy Act/Anti-Money Laundering – Comptroller's Handbook," December 2000, www.occ.gov/static/news-issuances/memos-advisory-letters/2001/pub-advisory-letter-2001-7b.pdf.

17. Kalmanovitz cited in Nazih Richani, *Systems of Violence: The Political Economy of War and Peace in Colombia* (New York: State University of New York Press, 2002);

18. Robert D. Auerbach, "The Federal Reserve: Reality vs. Myth," —The Economic Policy Institute Symposium, Sponsored by Ralph Nader and the Center for the Study of Responsive Law, National Press Club, Washington D.C., January 7, 2002. Auerbach participated in a number of sessions and the symposium was aired by C-Span; however, it was largely ignored by the mainstream media.

19. Robert D. Auerbach, *Deception and Abuse at the Fed: Henry B. Gonzalez Battles Alan Greenspan's Bank* (Austin: University of Texas Press, 2008); authors' email with Auerbach, 15 December 2007.

20. Robert E. Grosse, *Drugs and Money: Laundering Latin America's Cocaine Dollars* (London: Praeger, 2001); Brett F. Woods, *The Art & Science of Money Laundering: Inside the Commerce of the International Narcotics Traffickers* (Boulder, CO: Paladin Press, 1998). The Woods book contains a list of A-Z case studies featuring countries involved in money-laundering activities, but it does not include the United States.

21. Ibid.

22. Jo-Marie Burt, "Wall Street Chief Meets with Colombian Rebels," *NACLA Report on the Americas, 33* (July–August 1999): 2–5.

23. "NYSE Chief Meets Top Colombia Rebel Leader," Reuters, June 26, 1999.

24. Ibid.

25. Secretariat of the Central General Staff, FARC-EP. Plenum of the Central General Staff, International Commission, "Colombia: Legalization of Drug Consumption. The Only Serious Alternative for the Elimination of the Narcotics Traffic," Mountains of Colombia, March, 29 2000; Revolutionary Armed Forces of Colombia—People's Army, *FARC-EP: Historical Outline* (Toronto: International Commission, 2000).

26. See "Former Bush Assistant Secretary for HUD Reveals 'Ethnic Cleansing' Connected to CIA Drug Dealing in Los Angeles," at Fitts's Dillon Read website, www.dunwalke.com/resources/events.htm.

27. Christian De Brie, "Thick as Thieves," *Le Monde Diplomatique*, May 4, 2001.

28. Ibid.

29. Ibid.

30. Irene Cabrera and Antoine Peret, "Colombia: Regulating Private Miiltary and Secuirty Companies in a 'Territorial State,' " PRIV-WAR Report – Colombia, National Report Series 19/09, University of Externado of Colombia, November 15, 2009;

31. Rolf Uesseler, *Servants of War: Private Military Corporations and the Profit of Conflict*, trans. Jefferson Chase (New York: Soft Skull Press, 2008).

32. Ibid.; Peter W. Singer, *Corporate Warriors: The Rise of the Privatized Military Industry* (Ithaca, NY: Cornell University Press, 2008); Sarah Percy, "Amid Libya Slaughter, Let's Stop Mercenaries," *USA Today*, February 25, 2011.

33. Rory Carroll, "Hillary Clinton: Mexican Drug Wars Is Colombia-style Insurgency," *The Guardian*, September 9, 2010.

34. Tania Aroyo, "Drug War: Faster and More Furious–Analysis," *Eurasia Review: News & Analysis*, September 30, 2011.

35. Karen DeYoung and Claudia J. Duque, "U.S. Aid Implicated in Abuses of Power in Colombia," *The Washington Post*, August 20, 2011; Michael Shifter, "A Decade of Plan Colombia: Time for a New Approach," *Inter-American Dialogue*, June 21, 2010, www.thedialogue.org/page.cfm?pageID=32&pubID=2407.

36. Deborah D. Avant and Renee de Nevers, "Military Contractors & the American Way of War," *Daedalus*, 140 (Summer 2011), 88–99.

37. Fernando Brancoli, "A New Security Dilemma: Plan Colombia and the Use of Private Military Companies in South America," *The London School of Economics and Political Science (LSE) Ideas*, November 16, 2010, http://blogs.lse.ac.uk/ideas/2010/11/a-new-security-dilemma-plan-colombia-and-the-use-of-private-military-companies-in-south-america/.

38. Ibid.

39. "US Reaffirms Support for Colombia's War on Drugs," *Colombia Reports*, October 7, 2011.

40. Ibid.

41. David Noto, "Is Colombia Losing Its War against Rebels and Drug Gangs?" Fox News Latino, September 26, 2011, http://latino.foxnews.com/latino/news/2011/09/26/is-colombia-is-losing-its-war-against-rebels-and-drugs-gangs/.

42. Ibid.

43. Ibid.

44. Ibid.; Valencia cited in "La nueva realidad de las FARC," *Corporación Nuevo Arco Iris*, July 17, 2011, www.nuevoarcoiris.org.co/sac/?q=node/1191.

45. Winifred Tate, "Repeating Past Mistakes: Aiding Counterinsurgency in Colombia," *NACLA Report on the Americas* 34 (September–October 2000): 16–19.

46. Jim Garamone, "Special Operations Part of US-Colombia Plan to Reinforce Success," American Forces Press Service, April 1, 2004; Center for International Policy, "US Contractors in Colombia," November 2001, http://www.ciponline.org/colombia/contractors.htm; Singer, *Corporate Warriors*.

47. Center for International Policy, "US Contractors in Colombia."

48. James J. Brittain, *Revolutionary Social Change in Colombia: The Origin and Direction of the FARC-EP* (New York: Pluto Press, 2010), 133.

49. USA-Colombia Bi-national Agreement regarding the Surrender of Persons to the International Criminal Court, September 17, 2003.

50. Jason Vauters and Michael L. Smith, "A Question of Escalation—From Counternarcotics to Counterterrorism: Analysing US Strategy in Colombia," *Small Wars and Insurgencies* 17 (June 2006), 63–196.

51. Irene Cabrera and Antoine Peret, "Colombia."

52. Ibid.

53. Esther Schrader, "US Companies Hired to Train Foreign Armies," *Los Angeles Times,* April 14, 2002.

54. Knut Royce and Nathaniel Heller, "Cheney Led Halliburton to Feast at Federal Trough," *Center for Public Integrity Report,* August 2, 2000; Kenny Bruno and Jim Valette, "Cheney & Halliburton: Go Where the Oil Is," *Multinational Monitor,* May 2001, http://multinationalmonitor.org/mm2001/01may/may01corp10.html; "USA: Government Ties Helped Cheney and Halliburton Make Millions," Bloomberg News, October 6, 2000; David Isenberg, "Combat for Sale: The New, Post-Cold War Mercenaries," *USA Today,* March 2000. According to Royce and Heller's report, Cheney won a five-year $3.8 billion payments contract for Halliburton through federal contracts and taxpayer loans. One of these loans was approved by the U.S. Export-Import Bank, which guaranteed $489 million in credits to a Russian oil company involved in drug trafficking and organized crime funds. The report suggests drug money played a role in the success achieved by Halliburton under Cheney's tenure as CEO from 1995 to 2000. During Iran-Contra, Congressmen Dick Cheney of the House Intelligence Committee was a stern supporter of Lieutenant Colonel Oliver North.

55. International Consortium of Investigative Journalists, "Making a Killing: The Business of War," Center for Public Integrity, eleven-part series, October 28, 2002, www.publicintegrity.org/bow/report.aspx?aid=147; Deborah Avant, "Private Military Companies Part of US Global Reach," *Foreign Policy in Focus,* May 2002, http://www.fpif.org/progresp/vol-

ume6/v6n17.html; Linda Robinson, "America's Secret Armies: A Swarm of Private Contractors Bedevils the US Military," *US News & World Report,* November 4, 2002; Leslie Wayne, "America's For-Profit Secret Army," *New York Times,* October 13, 2002; James Dao, "US Company to Take Over Karzai Safety," *New York Times,* September 19, 2002; David Isenberg, "There's No Business like Security Business," *Asia Times,* April 30, 2003; David Isenberg, "Security for Sale in Afghanistan," *Asia Times,* January 6, 2003; Esther Schrader, "US Companies Hired to Train Foreign Armies," *Los Angeles Times,* April 14, 2002. According to Schrader of the *Los Angeles Times,* SAIC's top five executives made between $825,000 and $1.8 million in salaries in 2001 and held more than $1.5 million worth of stock options each.

56. Bob Fitrakis, "Spook Air: How a CIA-Connected Airline Landed in Columbus," *Columbus Dispatch,* August 25, 1999.

57. U.S. Department of Transport, Docket OST-96 –1153, http://www.airline-info.com/ost-html2/347.htm.

58. Kristin S. Krause, "Good-bye Southern Air," *Traffic World* 256 (October 1998): 34.

59. Sidney Zion, "Seizing Drugs, Seizing Property," *Journal of Commerce* (July 1996): 101–2.

60. Aroyo, "Drug War: Faster and More Furious."

61. U.S. General Accounting Office, *Drug Control: The Department of State's Contract Award for Its Counternarcotics Aviation Program, U.S. General Accounting Office Report* (Washington DC: U.S. Government Printing Office, 2001).

62. Grace Livingstone, *Inside Colombia: Drugs, Democracy, and War* (New Brunswick, NJ: Rutgers University Press, 2003).

63. U.S. General Accounting Office, *U.S. Assistance to Colombia Will Take Years to Produce Results* (Washington DC: U.S. Government Printing Office, 2000); Christian Miller, "Use of Foreign Pilots Avoids Congressional Limits," *Los Angeles Times,* August 18, 2001; Dan Caldwell, and Robert E. Williams Jr., *Seeking Security in an Insecure World* (New York: Rowman & Littlefield Publishers, 2011).

64. Jeremy Bigwood, "DynCorp in Colombia: Outsourcing the Drug War," *CorpWatch Investigative Report,* May 23, 2001.

65. "US Covert Program Exposed in Colombia," *Weekly News Update on the Americas,* August 23, 1998, www.colombiasupport.net/wnu/wnu082398.html.

66. Tod Robberson, "U.S. Launches Covert Program to Aid Colombia Military, Mercenaries Hired, Sources Say," *Dallas Morning News,* August 19, 1998.

67. Bigwood, "DynCorp in Colombia."

68. Ken Guggenheim, "Drug Fight in Colombia Questioned," Associated Press, June 5, 2001, 2.

69. Jason Vest, "DynCorp's Drug Problem," *The Nation*, July 3, 2001.
70. Livingstone, *Inside Colombia*.
71. Al Martin, *The Conspirators: Secrets of an Iran Contra Insider* (Pray, MT: National Liberty Press, 2002).
72. Rebecca Smith and John R. Emshwiller, "Internal Probe of Enron Finds Wide-Ranging Abuses—Unanswered in Board Report Are Some Big Questions Regarding Legal Liability," *Wall Street Journal*, February, 2002; Neela Banerjee and Reed Abelson, "Enron's Many Strands: College Reaction; Watchdog Group Wants Investigation on Harvard Official," *New York Times*, February 1, 2002; see "The American Tapeworm," at Fitts's website, http://solari.com/learn/articles_risk.htm.
73. "World: America's Citbank Censured over Money Laundering," *BBC News*, November 9, 1999, http://news.bbc.co.uk/2/hi/americas/511951.stm
74. Allan Miller, "Wall Street Bullish on the Spoils of War; The Global Private Military Industry Is Changing How Nations Fight," *Christian Science Monitor*, August 14, 2003; Uri Dowbenko, "Part One: Dirty Tricks, Inc. The DynCorp-Government Connection," *Online Journal*, 20 March 2002, www.onlinejournal.com/archive/03-20-02_Dowbenko-Pt_1.pdf.
75. Ibid.
76. Its president, Carl Vuono, founded MPRI in 1988 along with other retired generals. Like DynCorp, MPRI executives include intelligence, military, and corporate profiles in law and business.
77. Marcel Idels, "The Political Economy of a Narco-Terror State: Colombia and Corporate Profits," *Bluegreenearth*, August 14, 2002, http://www.bluegreenearth.us/archive/article/2002/idels2.html. Uri Dowbenko, "Part Two: Dirty Tricks, Inc. DynCorp Drug Trafficking and Cover-up?" *Online Journal*, March 27, 2002, www.onlinejournal.com/archive/03-27-02_Dowbenko-Pt_2.pdf.
78. Paul De la Garza and David Adams, "Colombia: US Military Aid from the Private Sector," *St. Petersburg Times*, December 2, 2000.
79. Winifred Tate, "Repeating Past Mistakes: Aiding Counterinsurgency in Colombia," *NACLA Report on the Americas* 34 (September–October 2000): 16–19.
80. See MPRI website, http://www.mpri.com/web; Peter W. Singer, *Corporate Warriors;* "Survey: Talks of Peace, Acts of War," *The Economist*, April 21, 2001; Tate, "Repeating Past Mistakes"; Joshua Kurlantzick, "Outsourcing the Dirty Work: The Military and Its Reliance on Hired Guns," *The American Prospect*, May 2003; David Isenberg, "Combat for Sale: The New, Post-Cold War Mercenaries," *USA Today*, March 2000; Ken Silverstein, "Privatizing War: How Affairs of State are Outsourced to Corporations beyond Public Control," *The Nation*, July 28, 1997.
81. See Airscan website, http://www.airscan.com/; Duncan Campbell, "War on Error: A Spy Inc. No Stranger to Controversy," Center for Public

Integrity, June 12, 2002; "Business Intelligence and Lobbying Firms," *Intelligence Online*, No. 469, January 30, 2004, www.intelligenceonline. com/ps/AN/Arch/INT/INT_469.asp?rub=archives.

82. Bigwood, "DynCorp in Colombia"; Juan O. Tamayo, "Colombia: Private Firms Take on US Military Role in Drug War," *Miami Herald*, May 22, 2001.

83. Joshua C. Ramo, "America's Shadow Drug War," *Time*, May 7, 2001.

84. See "Clients" at Airscan website, http://web.archive.org/web/ 19980207173714/www.airscan.com/clients.htm.

85. Letter to Forest Service Associate Chief George Leonard from Assistant General Counsel Kenneth Cohen, Research and Operations Division, *Subject: Letter to Secretary from National Air Carrier Association, Inc.*, December 8, 1989,http://www.fromthewilderness.com/free/pandora/for-est_service_c130s_large.gif.

86. "Airline Does Job—Quietly Miami Company Used to Secrecy," *Miami Herald*, December 10, 1986, 2.

87. Northrop Grumman website, www.northropgrumman.com/about_us/ faq/index.html#rev.

88. Jacob Quintanilla, "The 'Invisible' U.S. War in Colombia," *Resource Center of the Americas*, June 29, 2004.

89. See Northrop Grumman website, http://www.northropgrumman.com/; Pennington Way IV, "Colombia to Receive New Radar System from US," *Defense Daily*, March 14, 2000.

90. Karen DeYoung, "Behind U.S-Peru Pact, a History of Division," *Washington Post*, April 25, 2001.

91. John McQuaid, "Fatal Mission," *Times-Picayune*, November 9, 2003; Maria Engqvist, "US Casualties on the Rise in Colombia," Agencia de Noticias Nueva Colombia, August 3, 2003; Stephen Fidler and Thomas Catan, "Private Companies on the Front Line," *Financial Times*, August 12, 2003; Rachel Van Dongen, "US's 'Private Army' Grows: In Colombia and around the World, Civilians Are Doing Work Formerly Done by the Military," *Christian Science Monitor*, September 3, 2003.

92. Department of the U.S. Air Force, "Military Construction Program," Justification Data Submitted to U.S. Congress, May 2009, http://www.cen-trodealerta.org/documentos_desclasificados/original_in_english_air_for.pdf.

93. Benjamin Dangl, "U.S. Bases in Colombia Rattle the Region," *The Progressive*, March 2010, www.progressive.org/danglmarch10.html.

CONCLUSION: U.S. NARCO-COLONIALISM AND COLOMBIA

1. Javier Farje, "Colombia: The beginning of the end for the FARC?" Latin America Bureau, November 7, 2011, http://www.lab.org.uk/index.php?

option=com_content&view=article&id=1123:colombia-the-beginning-of-the-end-for-the-farc&catid=57:focus&Itemid=39

2. Garry Leech, *The FARC: The Longest Insurgency* (New York: Zed Books, 2011).

3. "Complete Final Debate Transcript: John McCain and Barack Obama," *Los Angeles Times*, October 15, 2008, http://latimesblogs.latimes.com/washington/2008/10/debate-transcri.html.

4. Rajeev Syal, "Drug Money Saved Banks in Global Crisis, Claims UN Advisor," *The Guardian*, December 13, 2009, www.guardian.co.uk/global/2009/dec/13/drug-money-banks-saved-un-cfief-claims.

5. Javier Giraldo, *The Genocidal Democracy* (Monroe, ME: Common Courage Press, 1996).

Index

CPSIA information can be obtained at www.ICGtesting.com
Printed in the USA
BVOW020716240112

281218BV00001B/4/P